a guide to SOFTWARE PACKAGE EVALUATION & SELECTION

The R^{2}ISC Method

Nathan Hollander

T0371333

HarperCollins
Leadership

An Imprint of HarperCollins

A Guide to Software Package Evaluation & Selection

© 2000 Nathan Hollander

Published by HarperCollins Leadership, an imprint of HarperCollins Focus LLC.

Bulk discounts available. For details visit:
www.harpercollinsleadership.com/bulkquotes
Email: customercare@harpercollins.com

ISBN 978-0-8144-7337-5 [TP]

‖ Contents

Dedication

This book is dedicated to my wife Yaffa and children Ephraim and Ariella Hollander who gave me their support during the writing of this book. Also, to my parents Morris and Toby Hollander who always had faith in me.

Acknowledgments

I had a great deal of help in preparing this book and would especially like to thank Jacquie Flynn for the time, help, insight, and knowledge she has given. Without her help this book could not have been completed. I wish her and her family much joy and happiness with their new arrival, Zachary James.

I would also like to thank the following people for helping us obtain material for this book:

Phyllis Butterworth of Macola Incorporated

Steven Cohen of Executive Communication Group

Nannette Feurzeig

Jorge Lopez

Matthew Hager

Allison Haines of Gartner Group

David Kra of IBM

Sheldon Needle of CTS

Jennifer Paull

Mary Lou Savage of Gail Group

|| Introduction

This book is the culmination of fifteen years of my experience in conducting package selections. It began as a process that took three to four months and evolved into a process that can be completed in four to five weeks. Unfortunately, I have not been able to shorten the time the lawyers take to review the contracts. I have reduced the time needed to select the package to the point where it can now take less time than the final contract negotiations.

When I looked at what's important in selecting a package, I found that there are really only five important items— which we will call the R^2ISC criteria (pronounced "risk squared"). They are:

- Current Requirements: ability of the package to meet the company's current business requirements and the package's ease of use.
- Future Requirements: ability to modify the package to meet any new requirements.
- Implementability: ability to implement the package easily.
- Supportability: ability of the vendor to support both the package and the company in the future.
- Cost: total cost to implement the package and any ongoing maintenance.

This book was written to assist you in selecting a package that affects multiple departments (such as an Enterprise Resource Planning [ERP] system). However, if you are selecting a package that affects only a few departments, you can still use the R^2ISC methodology. You should merely reduce some of the formality.

The process starts with the enterprise rating each criteria. The rating depends on the criticality of the criteria to the enterprise. Each package is ranked by its ability to meet the five criteria, first at a general level then getting into finer and finer detail. Packages are eliminated at each step until only the winner remains.

The R^2ISC methodology helps reduce problems that might arise upon implementation and cause the project to fail.

I am often called in by clients and asked to tell them which is the best package for their company. I tell them that if I pick the package it will become my package and not theirs. By choosing my suggestion you may save time in the selection part of the process, but it will cost two to three times that much time in the implementation phase of the project. Choosing my suggestion can even jeopardize the entire project; when problems arise the users will say "Nate's package doesn't work," and they will not make an effort to ensure that the package is successfully implemented. This shows how important it is for a company to have its own people pick a new package.

Using this Book

The best way to use this book is to read it in its entirety before you start the project. Then you may find it helpful to refer to each chapter accordingly as you go through the process.

There are many tables in the book that are used to rate the packages. They should be used as a guide and not as a bible. They should be modified or disregarded as you feel best fits your individual package selection. The main thing is to use the R^2ISC concept.

1

R²ISC

This chapter is a high-level overview of the package selection process. The chapters that follow will discuss the details needed to determine how to analyze each package and determine how well it meets your requirements.

Companies come in all shapes, sizes, and styles; big and small, wholesale and retail, manufacturing and services provider, etc. No matter the shape or size, some processes are identical for all companies (i.e., accounts receivable) whereas others are industry specific (i.e., inventory control). The one thing your company has in common with all other companies is that you will benefit by using the "right" software package to improve your business. On the other hand, choosing the wrong software package can be a catastrophe.

Even within the same industry, companies can vary widely. For example, some manufacturers have highly automated their production. Their process begins at one end of the assembly line and the completed product comes out the other end—with no human intervention. On the other hand, there are manufacturers whose processes are completely manual and whose parts wait days between operations. A company that manufactures lift trucks may have more in common with a company that manufactures computer printers than it does with the lift truck company around the corner. Likewise, because of subtle and not so subtle differences in their processes, software that is suitable for one company may not work for another within the same industry.

Companies perform many processes, all of which work together to build a successful business. Some processes are for customer benefit, whereas others meet government requirements. Processes can include:

- Accepting a customer order
- Shipping the product to the customer

1

- Ordering the material to make the item the customer ordered
- Paying for material, etc.

Companies can perform the same process in many different ways. One example of this is accounts payable. In order to pay for an item, a company may use the traditional method of matching three pieces of information: the purchase order (quantity ordered, price, and terms), the receiving report (quantity received), and the invoice (amount owed). This is known as a three-way match. Other companies, however, feel that matching the vendor's invoice adds little additional information and only adds additional processing cost. They feel that because they know how much they owe the vendor based on the terms of the purchase order and price and the quantity that is on the receiving report that they need only match the purchase order and receiving report (two-way match). Therefore, the requirements for a process can be very different. A software package that only performs a three-way match will not work well for a company that uses a two-way match.

Selecting the wrong package can be worse than not selecting a package at all. The wrong package can lead to:

- Failing to support an important business process
- Supporting a process inaccurately or inefficiently
- Unhappy customers
- Disgruntled employees
- Loss of sales
- Poor financial performance
- Shelfware (software package that lies on the shelf because it is not being used)

Selecting a software package is like selecting a house. There are five important criteria—which we will call the R^2ISC criteria (pronounced "risk squared")—that need to be considered. They are:

Current Requirements: What do you want in the house? What type of house, neighborhood, number of rooms, etc.?

Future Requirements: How easy will it be to make changes to the house? Is it in a historic district? Is there room on the lot to expand?

Implementability: How easy will it be to move into the house? Will there be trouble getting a mortgage? Is the house in move-in condition?

Supportability: What type of maintenance will the house require (the older the house the more likely something will need to be fixed)? Is the exterior wood or aluminum siding, etc.?

Cost: Total cost of the house including purchase price, mortgage, taxes, maintenance, etc.

With regard to choosing a software package, the R^2ISC criteria can be defined as the following:

Current Requirements: Ability of the package to meet the company's current business requirements.

Future Requirements: Ability to modify the package to meet the company's new requirements as they become known.

Implementability: Ability to implement the package easily.

Supportability: Ability of the vendor to support both the package and the company in the future.

Cost: Total cost to purchase and implement the package as well as ongoing maintenance and support costs. If employees will quit or there will be more employee absenteeism, the impact should be translated into the dollar impact on the company.

Although the list may seem simple enough, because of the criteria interaction with each other it therefore becomes complicated. Your company's goal is probably to have a package that not only meets all your current and future requirements, but is cheap, easy to modify and implement, and is fully supported by the vendor. Unfortunately, this is usually an unrealistic expectation. Before you choose a software package you must determine, based on the company's vision and strategy, the relative importance of each of the R^2ISC criteria.

For example, a company may want a package that meets their future requirements and is easy to implement. But meeting future requirements often requires purchasing a package that uses the latest technology. A package that is based on the latest technology can be problematic to implement. Because the package is new and has not been successfully implemented by other companies, it will likely contain bugs. This will cause the package to be difficult to implement.

There are different technology choices a company has to pick from when selecting a new package, just as you may have a few houses to pick from when looking to buy one. When a company wants to use the latest technology and software it is known as a *leading edge* or *bleeding edge* company. Companies understand that it is hard to implement this type of technology. If they did not understand it before the project began, they understand soon after they start implementation. But they believe that the benefits of having an ultramodern package gives the company a strategic advantage over its competitors, and therefore far outweighs the drawbacks (additional effort, cost, and inconvenience).

Other companies want to be *close followers*. Namely, they want most of the bugs removed before they implement the package. Even though this removes much of the potential risk and inconvenience, these companies lose some of the advantage the leading edge company has gained.

Still other companies, *risk avoiders*, may want to drastically minimize their risk by using only proven software. This means there is no competitive advantage.

Just because a company chooses to be bleeding edge in one area does not mean it has to be in all areas. It can decide that in certain areas bleeding edge or close follower software will give it a competitive advantage whereas in areas where there is no competitive advantage proven software is a better bet.

R²ISC Worksheet

The R^2ISC worksheet will help you determine which package is right for you, and here's how you fill it in. First, allocate 100 points among the five R^2ISC criteria, based on their relative importance, with the most important receiving the highest rating. Rate the criteria relative to each other. That means that the average rating for a R^2ISC criteria is twenty. If a criteria is extremely more important than the other cri-

R²ISC Rating	Relative Importance
40	Extremely Important
35	Very Important
30	Important
25	Slightly Above-Average Importance
20	Average Importance
15	Slightly Below-Average Importance
10	Little Importance
5	Very Little Importance
0	No Importance—Do Not Use

Figure 1-1. Relative Importance of R²ISC Criteria Rating

teria then you rank the criteria forty. On the other end of the spectrum if the criteria has absolutely no importance rate it a zero (this is very unusual). Figure 1-1 describes the meaning of the criteria rating. Remember, the total of the R²ISC criteria must total 100. This ensures that you have relative ratings.

Enter this rating onto the R²ISC Worksheet (Figure 1-2) in the column marked Company's Need. The R²ISC criterion that the company cares most about is the Current Requirements. Relative to the other criteria, it considered it more important that the other criteria. It considered the Future Requirements above-average importance. Implementability was of average importance. Supportability is

R²ISC Worksheet					
R²ISC Criteria	Company's Need	Package A Raw Score	Package A Weighted Score	Package B Raw Score	Package B Weighted Score
Current Requirements	30				
Future Requirements	25				
Implementability	20				
Supportability	15				
Cost	10				
	---------	---------	---------	---------	---------
Package's Total Score	100				

Figure 1-2. R²ISC Worksheet

slightly below average importance when compared with the other criteria, whereas Cost had relatively little importance.

Later in the selection process you will determine how each of the packages you are considering stack up against each of the R^2ISC criteria. At that point you will enter each of the package's ratings onto the R^2ISC Worksheet in the package's column Raw Score. Then you will multiply the package's Raw Score by the Company's Need to determine the package's Weighted Score. Adding the package's weighted scores for the five criteria determines the package's total score. This will allow you to determine which package most closely meets your needs. Follow these steps to fill out the R^2ISC Worksheet:

1. Company's Need: Allocate 100 points among the five R^2ISC criteria (based on their relative importance to the enterprise).
2. Package's Raw Score: Rate the package's ability to meet the R^2ISC criteria. (This will be described in Chapter 5.)
3. Package's Weighted Score: Multiply the company's need by the package's Raw Score.
4. Package's Total Score: Total the package's Weighted Scores for each of the five R^2ISC categories.

The package's scores are updated throughout the selection process, and much like a game whose object is to score the most points, the winning package is the one that has the highest Total Score. Once the worksheets have been completed, they become the documentation for why the winning package was selected.

R^2ISC Graph

For a visual picture of the information on the R^2ISC Worksheet, graph the appropriate scores on the R^2ISC Graph (Figure 1-3). You can see the company R^2ISC criteria rating (solid line) and each of the package's R^2ISC criteria rating (broken lines). When a package line extends beyond the company line, then the package's criteria is higher than the packages. For example, for Implementability,

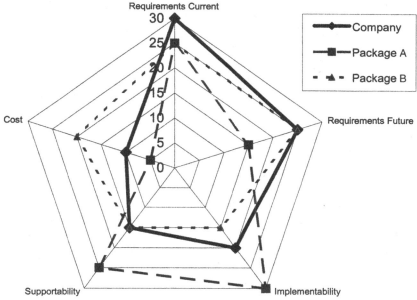

Figure 1-3. R^2ISC Graph

Package A extends two lines more than the company rating (10 points) and for Future Requirements the package extends two lines more than the package rating (10 points). The package that comes closest to the company plot is the package that most closely meets the company's needs.

Developing R^2ISC Criteria

The R^2ISC criteria form is the standard against which *each package* will be measured. Therefore, it is essential to define the criteria clearly. Using a poorly defined standard is like shooting an arrow while blindfolded and hoping it will hit the bull's-eye (Figure 1-4). Not only is it unlikely to hit the bull's-eye, it probably would never come close. Even if a package meets all of the criteria and hits the bull's-eye, no one would know because the original target was not clearly defined.

In most cases, there is no one perfect package. However there is usually at least one package that will hit the target somewhere and is

Figure 1-4. Choosing a Software Package

a viable solution. The important prerequisite is that you know the package's features and limitations before you sign the contract.

Now that you have an overview of the R²ISC methodology, the next three chapters will go into the detailed analysis of the R²ISC methodology. Chapter 2 discusses the first R—Current Requirements. Chapter 3 discusses the second R—Future Requirements. Chapter 4 discusses ISC—Implementability, Supportability, and Cost.

2

Current Requirements

This chapter describes the first R in the R²ISC methodology, i.e., Current Requirements. It describes how you can develop your current requirements and prioritize them based on your need. In Chapter 5 you will ask the vendors how they rate against your current requirements. In Chapter 6 we will analyze the vendors' responses and rate each vendor. In Chapter 7 we will ask the vendors to show you how they meet your current requirements

Current Requirements

To determine if the package meets your current requirements and hits your target, you need to know exactly *what* you need the package to do and you must be able to articulate it. This may sound obvious but you would be surprised at how many companies have problems determining what they need. One company thought that its requirements for a new package were the thirty requirements that their current package did not perform. When asked about the thousand or so other requirements that their current package performed, they said, "every package does what our current package does." They failed to realize that the system they were using had been modified over the last ten years to meet their specific needs. They then added, "Anyway, we do not have the time to go through a full selection process, we have to start to implement in order to meet our deadline for having the package up and running." To make a long story short, because they did not have a good foundation, two years later, way past their deadline, they were still trying to implement the package. They were about to abandon the project because the package could not meet certain critical requirements and modifying the package would have been very expensive. Because of the package's limitations, the users' morale was low; they had been told the package would meet all their needs yet it could not. If they had spent an additional month or two performing a good package selection phase they would have saved a year or more on the implementation. More importantly, they would have had a successful implementation instead of shelfware (a package that sits on the shelf instead of being used). Using the R^2ISC criteria you will know how close the package comes to meeting your target.

When you develop the current requirements you should include all requirements that you know you will need, even if you do not need them now but will need them in the future. In order to be able to determine the requirements you will need in the future more accurately, make sure that management has given you their vision and strategy for the future of the company. One company that was in the process of selecting an Enterprise Resource Planning (ERP) package was going to "right size" its operation by shedding certain divisions and buying another company. But management did not want their employees to know their plan so they did not tell the employees who were selecting the new package. The package they selected was an overkill for the remaining divisions but more importantly it did not meet some requirements of the company they bought. Therefore, if management is planning major changes that will impact the area(s) the new package will cover, they should either inform the selection team or postpone the selection process until the changes are announced and their impact on the requirements are understood.

There are companies that go beyond describing "what" the package should do to describe "how" the package should work. One company gave me the requirements that they had developed. From looking at their requirements it became evident that they were trying to duplicate their current system on a client server environment. For example, they described how each function key should be used. (i.e., Function Key 12 = help, Function Key 6 = back to previous screen, etc., yet it should be of little concern as to which key is designated "help" or "back to previous screen").

Make sure your list of current requirements includes all requirements you know will be needed, including those you'll need in the future. Future requirements deals with the requirements that you do not know and the package's ability to adapt.

There are current requirements that are critical to the business and others that are important to the business. There are other current requirements that would be nice to have and others that might be used if the package had the functionality.

Process Redesign

When developing your requirements, understand that companies usually gain very little from a new system if they keep processes the same. If the only reason you are changing to a new system is to be able to perform an inefficient process more efficiently, the only thing you will save is some computing time, which is often a small cost savings. Even if the new system moves the company off a mainframe computer and eliminates the associated expenses, many companies have found after the fact that the cost did not justify the expense of new system. But by redesigning the process, the new system often becomes easy to justify.

The question arises as to whether you should redesign your process before you select the package or after it is selected and use the package to drive the new process? My feeling is that the strategic nature of the process determines when it should be redesigned. If the way the process is performed gives you a strategic advantage, then redesign the process before selecting the package because you want the package to be able to perform the process in a specific manner. If there is no strategic advantage or other compelling reason, let the package drive the process redesign.

Involving Users in Requirement Development

Users should be involved in developing the detailed business' current requirements. Holding a workshop is the best way to pool the knowledge of users from multiple departments and locations, allowing them to brainstorm together and make a complete requirements list. When beginning the workshop, users may have preconceived notions about requirements they need to perform their job, and they may conflict with other users' preconceptions. By holding a workshop, users can see why their colleagues' requirements are different from their own. To help reach a consensus of what is best for the business, have a facilitator lead the workshop. If a disagreement arises within the workshop that cannot easily be resolved, a small group should research the requirement in dispute and report back to the entire group. The added benefit of a workshop is that users from different organizations come to appreciate the work of their colleagues and better understand why and how a package is selected. See Chapter 10 for a complete discussion on workshops.

It is important to include users in the development of the current requirements, because getting the users to "buy-in" to the process and the selected package will make the implementation easier. But bear in mind that users know what they are doing but they often do not understand why they are doing it. For example, for the last five years purchasing agents have been sending the blue copies of purchase orders to Joe in the Internal Audit Department. It all began five years ago when Joe was performing an audit on the accounting department. He had asked to receive a copy of all purchase orders for one month. Unfortunately no one stopped sending Joe copies of the

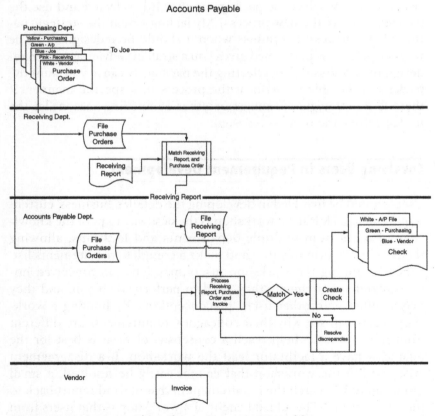

Figure 2-1. Process Flow Chart—Accounts Payable

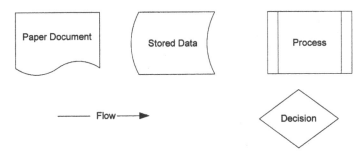

Figure 2-2. Process Shape Description

purchase orders and now everyone has forgotten why they were sending him copies; they just assume he needs them. Now when Joe receives purchase orders, all he does is trash them. The added step of sending Joe the blue copies is no longer necessary, but no one knows this because no one has stepped back and observed the overall process. A good way to see the big picture is to follow the process using a Process Flow Chart (Figure 2-1). Figure 2-2 defines each shape in the process flow diagram.

Customer and Vendor Involvement

If the new package affects your most important customers or your most important vendors, consider involving them in the development of the package's requirements. They will give you other insights on what is important and how they see other companies perform the process. It can also be a good marketing tool by showing your customers that you care about them.

Developing Current Requirements

A good way to start compiling a list of current requirements is by reading vendors' literature that list features of the software designed for your industry and the process(es) that you are automating. As you are reading the material, create a list of the features you require. Also, list any features that come to mind even when they are not in the vendors' literature. In addition, there are books and software available

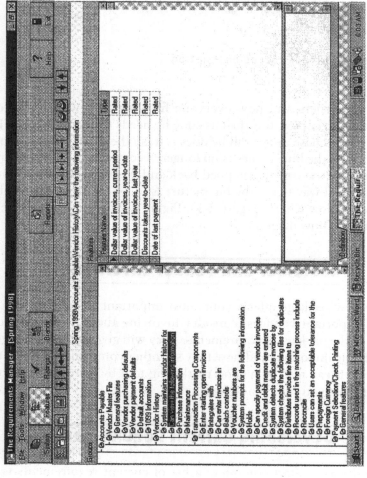

Figure 2-3. Sample Software Requirements Screen. Reprinted with permission of CTS

that list the common requirements for many types of industry and processes and packages. Figure 2-3 is a sample of a software tool for developing requirements from CTS (www.ctsguides.com). These books and software are good aids for developing an initial requirements list.

If the package is to cover multiple business areas (i.e., accounts payable, accounts receivable, payroll, etc.) then organize the requirements by business area.

Format of Current Requirements

The best way to define current requirements is in a bulleted list. Each requirement should be described in one or two brief but detailed sentences. The requirement should be verifiable so that everyone will know if the package meets the requirement, making it easier to compare the package to the requirement. For example:

- Ability to automatically perform a three-way match (purchase order, receiving report, and invoice) for paying an invoice.
- Ability to automatically perform a two-way match (purchase order and receiving report) for paying an invoice.

Types of Current Requirements

There are two types of current requirements—business area and general. The business area requirements are those unique to a business area (i.e., ability to place an invoice on hold). The general requirements are those that are needed by most business areas within your company. Their importance may differ from department to department. Examples of general requirements groupings include:

- Security
- Report writer
- Navigation, i.e., the way you move between screens.

Business Area Requirements

If the package is to cover multiple business areas (i.e., accounts payable, accounts receivable, payroll, etc.), a particular package may meet the requirements of certain business areas better than those of other business areas. To ensure that the package selected best meets your company's overall current requirement, determine which business areas are most important. This is done by rating each business area in its importance to the company. Follow these easy steps to complete the Business Area Summary Worksheet (Figure 2-4).

1. Rate the company need as high (H), medium (M), or low (L).
2. Convert the H, M, L to a numerical value (see code chart, Figure 2-5).

For example, management of the company shown in Figure 2-4 determined that order management was the most important business process of the new package. They therefore rated it a High. General accounting, accounts payable, and payroll were of average importance and therefore rated a Medium. Management would like the package to perform the accounts receivable and human resources function but it was of little importance because it could be done manually. The company found that rating of the business areas had to be

Business Area Summary Worksheet					
Business Area	Company Need	Package A Percentage Fit	Package A Weighted Percentage Fit	Package B Percentage Fit	Package B Weighted Percentage Fit
General Accounting	7				
Accounts Payable	7				
Accounts Receivable	3				
Payroll	7				
Order Management	10				
Human Resources	3				
	---------	---------	---------	---------	---------
TOTAL	37				
Maximum Value (Total Company Need x 100%)					
Percentage Fit Current Requirements					

Figure 2-4. Business Area Summary Worksheet

Business Area Functional Code Sheet		
Code	Need	Rating
H	High (Must Have)	10
M	Medium (Should Have)	7
L	Low (Like to Have)	3
X	Not Needed	0

Figure 2-5. Business Area Functional Code Sheet

done by management because when the business areas tried rating the areas each one felt that its area was a High.

Best of Breed

When a package needs to cover multiple business areas, there is the possibility of choosing different packages, or modules from different business areas, and then integrating them (make them work together). This is known as *best of breed.* It can lead to a solution that most closely meets the current requirements. This complex method is much more expensive, and there is considerable risk involved in completing the integration successfully. Deciding if best of breed is the right solution for your company can be determined in the same way you analyze any other single vendor packages, giving it its own R^2ISC rating. Keep in mind that to consider a best of breed solution, your R^2ISC ratings should be very high for both Current Requirements and Future Requirements and very low for Implementability, Cost, and Supportability.

Application Requirements

To determine the current requirements for a process you should create a flow chart. This will greatly reduce the number of overlooked requirements. Consider for example the accounts payable process described in Figure 2-1. The first step is to define the objective of the process, which, in the case of accounts payable is to pay the vendors on time and take the allowable discounts. The next step is decomposing the process into the steps needed to accomplish the end results. When there are paper documents, show where each copy goes. In our example, there are four copies of the purchase order, one copy going to purchasing, accounts payable (A/P), one to receiving, and one to the vendor. For the accounts payable process we are only interested in what happens to the receiving and accounts payable copies of the purchase order. For each box on the Process Flow Chart develop the requirements associated with the process.

By following the grouping for each business area, the required functionality and the associated data can be identified. If mathematical calculations are used, they should be clearly specified. For example, ability of the system to calculate the labor efficiency variance using the formula Actual Labor Cost divided by Frozen Standard Labor Cost. This sounds obvious to a cost accountant. Yet one major package did not use the frozen standard cost and for those companies that assumed it did found at the end of the year that they had major financial discrepancies. So, remember, do not assume the package is performing the calculation correctly.

For example, when the average company develops the current requirements for an accounts payable system, the requirements list looks like those in Figure 2-6. The first column is a number that lets

Current Requirements Worksheet						
Ref. No.	Requirement	Company Need	Package A Rating	Package A Cost To Modify	Module	Package A Weighted Rating
123	Capability to enter the invoice.	H				
124	Ability to automatically perform a three-way match—purchase order, receiving report, & invoice.	L				
125	Ability to automatically perform a two-way match—purchase order & receiving report.	M				
126	Ability to place an invoice on hold.	M				
127	Ability to create a debit memo.	M				
128	Capability to cut checks to vendors.	M				
129	Capability to automatically cut checks to vendors based on due date.	L				
130	Ability to calculate amount owed a vendor based on the price on the purchase order and the quantity received.	L				
250	Ability to produce list of all invoices due for payment in a user-defined date range.	H				
	Total Business Area (Accounts Payable)					

Figure 2-6. Current Requirements Worksheet

you identify the specific requirement. The second column describes the requirement. The third column is the company need. The fourth column is the vendor's rating. The fifth column is the cost of modifying the package if it did not meet current requirements. The sixth column is for the module. The seventh column is for the weighted vendor rating.

Prioritizing

Once you have identified the current requirements you are ready to prioritize. Requirements are a wish list—some are needed to run the business whereas others are nice to have. Prioritizing the current requirements helps set the target in determining which vendors should be finalists. You need to determine your need for each of the current requirements by ranking them as follows:

- H   High (Must have in order to run business)
- M   Medium (Should have to run the business)
- L   Low (Like to have but not needed to run the business)
- X   Not needed

The requirement and its need should be entered onto the Company Need column on the Current Requirements Worksheet (Figure 2-6). Once this has been completed, the package's current requirements can be evaluated.

Data

The way a package stores and uses its data is very important. A missing process can often be easily be developed as long as the package collects and stores the required data. There are those who select a package by developing a data model for the company and compare it to the packages data model. (A data model is the description of the organization of a database; it includes an entity relationship diagram [describes the relationships between different pieces of data].) There is another school of thought that says that the only reason for capturing and storing data is to be able to perform a business function. If

Field	Req. Size	Req. Alpha Numeric	Req. Decimal
Accounts Payable Check Amount	10	N	2
Part Number	10	A/N	–
Cost	10	A	4
Department	6	N	–

Figure 2-7. Data Analysis Worksheet

there is no business requirement that uses the data, then there is no need to collect the data. I recommend the second approach: analyze the functionality. If there is a problem with the data it will appear in the functionality or in the performance of the package. The performance will show up when you check the system's performance later on in the process.

Performing a partial data analysis is a good double check to ensure that you have identified all of your company's current requirements. Determine the data elements that you require but do not develop their relationships, cross-referencing all data with your current requirements

The first step in the partial analysis is then to analyze your data and to identify the minimum size, alpha/numeric structure, and decimal place for each piece of data. If you require certain data to have minimum size (i.e., part number, 10 positions; unit price, 10 positions, four to the right of the decimal point) or contain both letters (alpha) and numbers (numeric) (i.e., part number uses both numbers and letters) they should be included in the system requirements. These requirements should be entered in the Data Analysis Worksheet (Figure 2-7).

The next step is to determine if there is a requirement that uses the field, for example, part number used in the purchase order, inventory control, etc. If you have a field called Prescription Number and do not have a function that uses a prescription number, then you missed a requirement or you do not need a field for Prescription Number.

3

Future Requirements

Understanding the Package's Development Environment and Architecture[1]

The second of the R²ISC criteria is Future Requirements. This is the ability of the package to meet your future requirements. Remember, if you know a requirement exists, even if you will need it in the future, it is a Current Requirement. So, how do you analyze the ability of the package to meet your Future Requirements if you do not know them? The answer is you cannot. What you can analyze is how easily a package can be made to meet your changing requirements, which is based on the technology the package uses. Therefore, this chapter is a primer for computer technology. You need to understand how the technology package you are considering impacts on the R²ISC criteria. If you are not a computer professional, you may need to have one have perform the evaluation for this criterion.

The only constant in the business world today is constant change. The ability of the package you select now to meet the changes in your requirements next year or four or five years from now depends on how easily the package can accommodate the changing business conditions, which in part depends on the computer technology the package uses.

The technical architecture is similar to the design for a house. The architect can design the house in a way that lets you make additions and changes to the house easily or it can be designed so that additions and changes are difficult. If the architect designs the house to be able to accommodate central air conditioning, it will be easy to install it later. On the other hand, if the architect did not consider central air conditioning it can become complicated, forcing you to lose

21

closet space and adding considerable cost. Also, if you tell the architect you may want to add another floor later, it adds a small amount to the cost of the initial construction but simplifies the expansion when you decide to add the additional floor and reduces its cost.

Architectural Components

The available architectural components are continuously changing. One-day users will be able to completely modify a system without any technical expertise. Although we have come a long way from programs being written in machine language's bits and bytes that computers understand, there is still a long way to go until software comes packaged in pieces a company can easily assemble into a customized system. The pieces from multiple vendors would need to fit together easily without the need for a skilled computer professional. Unfortunately, today, if pieces for systems are bought from different vendors it is very complicated to integrate them into one cohesive system, even for a seasoned IT professional.

Several vendors have made an important step toward improved integration. They have joined together to form the Open Applications Group (OAG) in order to set standards for an open application integration architecture. *Open application integration* is defined as the ability of applications from different sources (different vendors or custom-made sources) to work together. This includes exchanging information and process.[2]

The development environment and architecture of the package also play a part in the other four R^2ISC criteria:

Current Requirements: The architecture impacts the performance of the package as well as its ease of use.

Implementability: If the pieces of the architecture are not easily integrated, there can be trouble implementing the package. This is especially true if it is the first time that the specific architecture is being used together.

Supportability: The ability to support the package and its components is directly impacted by the architecture. When a problem arises, the vendor of one piece of the architecture often blames the problem on another vendor, making resolution cumbersome.

Cost: The total cost of implementing and maintaining the package is affected by the architecture. The cost of the software can vary by computer and the size of the computer and the cost of the peripherals are impacted by the architecture.

The rest of this chapter discusses the technical parts of the package. When buying a house you need to know a little about the technical part of the house (heating system, plumbing, electrical, etc.) before you buy. But if you are not a technical person, you may need an expert to inspect them. In the same way, you may need a computer expert's help in inspecting the technical architecture of a package.

Development Environment

If the type of package you are purchasing is not the type that you will be modifying (i.e., word processor, electronic spreadsheet, etc.) then the development environment is of little concern. What you care about is whether the architecture fits with your architecture plan and whether the package vendor's future direction is in sync with your future direction.

The development environment includes:

- Computer-aided systems engineering (CASE) tool
- Programming language

CASE Tools

One piece of the development environment is the computer-aided software engineering (CASE) tool that the vendor uses to develop and build the package. It allows for the easy modification of the package. It works in the same way that computer-aided design/computer-aided manufacturing (CAD/CAM) systems are used to design and produce mechanical parts so that it easily modifies the design and produces the revised part.

CASE tools come in two major categories, conveniently called Upper CASE and Lower CASE.

Upper CASE—The Upper CASE is where the package is designed. The business rules (rule that define the way the business is run, i.e., a customer may have many accounts but only one credit limit) are defined, as is the data. This is like the renderings (pictures) that the architect draws (manually or by computer) so that you can see exactly what the house will look like once it is built. Yet, the builder cannot build the house from the renderings even if they are computer generated. The builder needs the detailed blueprints.

Lower CASE—The Lower CASE takes the designs developed in the Upper CASE tool and automatically transforms them into programs and databases that can be used by the computer. The Lower CASE tool is designed to produce program(s) that run on specific computers using specific operating system(s) and relational database(s). The program that the Lower CASE produces is similar to the blueprints that the architect gives the builder so he can build the house. If the architect produced the renderings on the computer, you want the computer to generate the blueprints so you would not have to pay the architect for a lot of the same work twice.

The use of CASE tools not only shortens the development process for the vendor it also allows the vendor to upgrade the software more easily. But, more importantly, it is one of the most important tools currently available that allows you to easily modify the package to meet your current requirements (that the base package does not meet) and change across time to meet your future requirements.

Many vendors rewrote their packages using CASE tools so that they can produce programs that will run on the UNIX operating system. This allows the vendor to easily produce programs to run on other operating systems and databases without having to modify the design in the Upper CASE tool. If the vendor wants to produce programs that run on other operating systems and/or databases, then all the software vendor has to do is tell the Lower CASE tool to produce the code for the new operating system and database. If the Lower CASE tool does not have the new operating system or database included, then the Lower CASE vendor has to build that functionality into the Lower CASE. For example, when UNIX was becoming a popular operating system, most packages were written for other operating systems but not written using a Lower CASE tool. Therefore, the programs had to be rewritten. Programs written with Lower CASE needed a new code generator module for the Lower CASE tool. This is similar to the architect who puts blueprints in a CAD system so that the blueprints can be reused. For example, if the blueprints were for a house in California and the architect wants to use the same blueprints for a house in France, the only change needed is to convert all the measurements into metric units. The architect only has to click on a button on the screen and the blueprint is automatically in metric units.

If you are receiving the CASE tool and the design files with the package, you can modify the package. The package's CASE tool will probably become the standard CASE tool that you will use to develop your other computer programs. Therefore, it becomes even more important that a good CASE is used.

As part of your analysis of the package, you should conduct the same type of R^2ISC analysis on the CASE tools as you perform on the package, to assess how well it meets your company requirements. In particular, this analysis should focus on how easy the CASE tool allows modification of the programs to meet the changing business requirements, and produces programs that will run efficiently without modification. The package vendor may not have developed the CASE tool, therefore the CASE tool vendor should undergo the same type of background check as the package vendor.

It can be very problematic if the CASE tool vendor goes out of business or has financial troubles. If the software vendor is big enough to buy the CASE tool vendor, then you need to know the relationships between the CASE tool vendor and the package vendor in case the CASE tool vendor runs into financial problems. If the software vendor will buy the CASE tool vendor, there is little concern about the CASE tool vendor's financial stability.

When you purchase the package it is essential that design files and repositories (the information about the package, including the data and their interdependencies, inputs, outputs, processes, etc.) that the CASE tool uses to produce programs be included. If the repositories are not included with the package, you will have a hard time modifying the programs, defeating your purpose of having the vendor use the tool in the first place.

Programming Language

All programs are written in a programming language either directly or indirectly through Lower CASE tools. Today most programs are written in a third-generation language (3GL) a high-level programming language such as BASIC, COBOL, Java, C, etc. These languages have their own grammar (syntax, vocabulary, semantics, and usage rules) that can be understood by a programmer and Lower CASE tools. Some programming languages, although English-like, are hard to understand whereas others are relatively easy.

If the package is written in a program language, it is important that its code is in a structured format that is easy to understand and easy to enhance. This makes it easier for programmers who need to make changes.

Although a third-generation language program can be modified, it is a time-consuming job. If the program was not well-structured or was poorly written, known as *spaghetti code*, it will be difficult to upgrade. This is similar to an architect or builder marking up a blueprint so many times that you do not know which measurements and notes are still valid.

Architecture

The type of package you select will be dictated by your concern with the technical architecture. If you select a major enterprise system such as an ERP system, then its architecture will dictate the architecture of your company. Therefore, the architecture of the system will dictate the architecture of your system. Therefore, you can require that the package have a specific architecture to fit your requirements, or you can accept the package's architecture. If you accept the package's architecture, you should perform a careful analysis to be sure it meets your requirements.

On the other hand if you are selecting a minor package such as a word processing system, even if it is enterprise-wide and costing a quarter of a million dollars, it must run on the architecture you are using. You probably will not change or modify your architecture for this type of package. In this case you need to ensure that the package runs efficiently on the architecture that you require. You need to be knowledgeable about the vendor's future direction and the response time of the system and will want to be sure the vendor is heading in the same direction as you. For example, if you are using UNIX and the vendor's current system runs on UNIX but the vendor's future direction is to move to Windows, you may have a problem in the future. The vendor may no longer support or enhance the UNIX version of the package. This can be problematic if there are enhancements that you require; a recent example of this is Y2K compliance.

Response Time

A package that meets all your needs does very little good if the users have to wait ten seconds, twenty seconds, or worse, a minute until the system responds to your request. A security protection company was replacing their mainframe system with a package that ran on an AS/400 computer. One year into the project, just two months before they were supposed to go into production, they realized that the response time would be forty-five seconds or more, which was unacceptable. The alternative they came up with was to put each of their regions on a different computer. This brought the response time to acceptable levels but it meant that it was not easy to see a complete view of a customer that had sites in multiple regions. When looking up a customer you had to know in which region(s) they were located. At least they were able to salvage the system in which they had invested millions of dollars, but other companies have not been as lucky.

Response time is a critical factor in the success of the project, therefore, when you rate its need later in this chapter make sure it is rated very high.

Components of the Architecture

The architecture is made up of many components. They include:

- Relaton database management system
- Operating system
- Hardware
- Communications
- Level of configureability

Even if there is only one component in the architecture that is inappropriate for your needs, it can make the entire system cumbersome to modify.

Many factors could lead to a future change in the requirements for your software package. One relatively common change relates to the size and organization of the company. Scalability or the ability to run the software on larger or smaller computers becomes very critical when the company is growing, shrinking, restructuring, or adding new locations.

The technical architecture is what determines the scalability of a particular system or package. Some architectures allow for easy portability from one hardware manufacture to another including running the same software on anything from a small personal computer all the way up to a super computer. On the other hand, certain architectures only allow for moving the software from one model of a specific manufacturer's series computer to another model of the same computer series by the same manufacturer. For example, software that runs on an IBM AS400 (with its proprietary operating system) often does not run on other manufacturer's hardware, but conversely, software that runs on the IBM RS6000 will often be available for other manufacturer's UNIX-based computers.

Relational Database Management System

If the package uses a database, it should be a relational database management system (RDBMS). The RDBMS is made up of a relational database, which is a repository of information. The information is connected in a series of relationships so that they reflect a small portion of the real world. The RDBMS includes the tools needed to build and maintain the relationships. This reduces the number of times the same information needs to be in the database.

Another major benefit of using an RDBMS is that it makes custom reporting relatively easy. The RDBMS also has the ability to go into the system and find the data you are looking for. This comes in handy for new users, because minimal training is required. They can easily use a report writer to access data from the system without knowing where the data is stored; all that the user needs to know is the name of the data.

Unlike the CASE tool, you may have a choice of RDBMS with the package you select because vendors support multiple RDBMSs. However, the choice of RDBMS can be limited by the hardware you will be using. For example, if you are using an AS400 you have to use the AS400 RDBMS or DB2. Oracle and Sybase will not run on an AS400.

You should determine the RDBMS that you would like to use. The vendor should also be asked which of the RDBMSs they recommend you use and the reason for their recommendation. They should also include information on the RDBMS vendor.

Operating Systems

The operating system is the master control program that runs the computer. The operating system (i.e., NT, UNIX, OS400, VMS, VM, etc.) not only affects the response time of the package (how long it takes the control to return to you once you hit the Enter key), it also affects its ability to meet your future requirements. Some operating systems allow you to run the package on different hardware (i.e., Microsoft Windows), whereas others tie you to a specific manufacturer or specific product line for a manufacturer (i.e., Apple Macintosh). The operating system is the interface between the hardware (computer, storage devices, printers, etc.) and the computer programs. It impacts:

- Performance
- Capacity
- Quality
- Security
- Scalability
- Reliability
- Availability
- Serviceability
- Operations management
- Problem management
- Disaster recovery
- Network management.

The operating system that the package uses can determine the hardware that is required. Many operating systems (i.e., OS400, AIX, MVS, etc.) are tied to a specific manufacture's hardware product line (i.e., IBM's AS400, RS6000, 360, etc.), whereas other operating systems (Windows and NT) allow you to use hardware from many vendors (i.e., Dell, Compaq, IBM PCs, Hewlett Packard [HP] PCs, etc.). The breadth of the manufacturer's hardware product line (i.e., for IBM, the product lines range from PCs to midrange AS400 and RS6000 to mainframe) will determine the scalability of the package. Also, if the hardware manufacturer decides to make the product line obsolete or goes out of business (remember the Pick operating system or the Prime computer? If you don't, you are not alone and there are those of you who wish to forget your decision to buy them) there may not be any support available for the hardware. This could make the entire package obsolete.

Open Systems—Open systems refers to the interoperability of software hardware and databases. This is accomplished by the operating system for the most part. The benefit of open systems is the ability of an operating system to run on multiple manufacturers' hardware (i.e., Microsoft Windows). This will then allow a program written for that operating system to run on any computer. UNIX is intended to be such an operating system. One benefit of an open system is that it allows the package to be scalable (e.g., run on a PC from one vendor, a minicomputer from another vendor, and a mainframe computer from a third vendor). So, if you are a small company, you can buy a package that will grow with you when you become a multibillion dollar company.

UNIX—Today UNIX is the generic name for a specific type of operating system that many vendors sell (i.e., IBM sells AIX, Sun sells Solaris, HP sells UX, etc.). Each vendor's brand of UNIX must pass specific tests to ensure that it is compliant to the UNIX standard. The UNIX-branded operating systems, in theory, allow the same application source code to be recompiled to run on more than one manufacturer's hardware platform. This would allow software to move more easily from one type of computer to another (from a PC to a minicomputer to a mainframe) without costly reprogramming.

Object-oriented Technology

In the future, systems will be built on object-oriented (OO) technology. OO programs comprise reusable modules, known as objects, to build programs. This reduces development time for applications because you can reuse these software modules in new applications with only minor changes.

Each object is self-contained including both the data and process logic required to perform a specific task, a property known as encapsulation. For example, an object will calculate the discount for a specific promotion using calculations that are stored in the object. This allows you to change a program by just changing the object.

OO also has a property called inheritance, whereby one object takes on, or inherits, all the logic and data of another object, which allows the addition of new incremental properties. Because this allows you to reuse existing objects, you help control costs and development time. This allows for easily creating a hierarchy of objects. When you change something in a higher level object, it automatically flows down to the to the lower level objects. For example, you may have a group of promotions all having a different discount percentage. All of the specific promotion discount objects can use a high-level object to define the basic calculation. If you then want to change the way you calculate the discount, for example from the entire order to only specific items, you can change the high-level object and all the lower level objects will also change.

Today most systems are not written using OO programming. When software is written using OO technology, vendors can sell objects. This will allow you to pick the objects that best meet your needs that will not need expensive systems integration. You will be able to purchase objects from different vendors that easily fit together.

Making Your Selection

In Chapter 2 you assigned a rating to the Current Requirements R^2ISC criteria. At this point in the process you should fill in the requirements for the Future Requirements Worksheet (Figure 3-1). This includes both the brand name of selected components and a rating of importance to the component. Use the Rating Code Sheet (Figure 3-2) to rate each of the components. For example, on the

Future Requirements Worksheet

Future Requirement	Company Need	Package A Rating	Package A Weighted Rating	Package B Rating	Package B Weighted Rating
Upper CASE Tool—Rational Rose	1	8	8	0	0
Lower CASE Tool—Rational Rose	1	10	10	10	10
Programming Language—Java C++	5	0	0	0	0
RDBMS–Oracle	10	8	80	8	80
Operating System–UNIX	5	10	50	10	50
Hardware—HP 9000 RS 6000	5	10	50	8	0
Middleware—If Required by Package	1	0	0	0	0
Object Oriented–Yes	5	10	50	10	50
Level of Configureability–High	10	0	0	0	0
Future Direction	10	8	80	5	50
Response Time	10	10	100	10	100
	--------	--------	--------	--------	--------
TOTAL	63		428		340
Highest Possible Score Future Requirements	10		630		630
Weighted Average–Future Requirements			68%		54%

Figure 3-1. Future Requirements Worksheet

Need	Rating
High (Must Have)	10
Medium (Should Have)	5
Low (Like to Have)	1
Not needed	0

Figure 3-2. Rating Code Sheet

Future Requirements Worksheet (Figure 3-1), the Upper CASE tool that the company would like is "Rational Rose." It is placed on the Future Requirements Worksheet next to the words Upper CASE. The need for an Upper CASE tool is low, therefore, on the Rating Code Sheet (Figure 3-2); the rating is a one that is placed in the Company Rating column of the Future Requirements Worksheet.

Evaluating the Vendors

Later in the process, after the vendors respond to the RFP, you will need to rate each of the vendors against the items on the Future Requirements Worksheet.

Notes

[1] Based on material supplied by David Kra and Jorge Lopez.
[2] *Software Magazine*, May 1995, page 12.

4

Implementability, Supportability, and Cost

Now that we have analyzed the R^2 criteria, we need to understand what makes up the ISC of the R^2ISC— implementability, supportability, and cost. This chapter describes how you rate your ISC criteria. In Chapter 5 we will ask the vendors how they rate in each of the ISC criteria. In Chapter 6 we will analyze the vendors' responses and give each vendor a rating for each of the ISC criteria. In Chapter 8 we will be independently verifying the responses and, where needed, adjusting them.

Implementability

The best package does you no good unless it is used. To reap the system's rewards you must use it!

Every package runs the inherent risk of not being successful upon implementation, thus, the existence of shelfware (a package that sits on the shelf and is not used). Imagine spending more than 100 million dollars and 30 months implementing a package, that the whole company relies on, to find out that during your busiest season the package does not work. The package allows you to take orders from your customers and make your product but has problems shipping the product to your desperate customers. This is exactly what happened to Hershey Food Corp. during the back-to-school and Halloween season. The impact[1]:

- 12 percent decline in sales
- 19 percent decline in profits
- 29 percent increase in inventory cost.

Could you afford this type of results from your new package?

You need to define the degree of risk you are comfortable with, as well as your desire to be a technology leader, a close follower, or part of the pack. In certain industries, a company must be a technology leader in order to survive, whereas in other industries being a technology leader can give the company a competitive advantage. The ability of a company to take the risk of being a technology leader depends on the company's ability to handle a software implementation that might have bumps in the road. The risk can be reduced if you are willing to use a consultant who has successfully implemented the package.

The way you rate the implementability criteria for a project depends on where you are and where you want to be on the technology curve. If you want to use technology as a strategic weapon to give you a competitive advantage, then you need to take more risks with the implementability of the package. Blockbuster Video decided to use technology as a strategic weapon when they developed a custom computer system that allowed them to track which videos were being rented and which were just sitting on the shelf taking up valuable space. The system allowed each store to decide which videos should be sold or shipped to other stores. This allowed Blockbuster to have their shelves stocked with the videos that their customers wanted. The system also used scanners to speed up the check-out and check-in process. Developing this type of program was a lot more risky than using the packages that were available that only calculated how much a customer owed. But it allowed Blockbuster to gain a competitive advantage in its industry and become the leading video chain in the world.

Interestingly, just because you decide to use technology as a strategic weapon does not mean you must do so for all your applications. In some areas of your company where it will give you a distinct advantage over your competitors you may be willing to accept a package that is harder to implement. However, in other areas, where there is no strategic advantage, there is no reason to choose a package that could be risky to implement. For example, for most companies there is no strategic advantage in general accounting, therefore you would chose an accounting package that will be relatively risk-free to implement.

Implementability Components

Implementability is made up of the following components:

- Vendor background
- Software maturity
- Technology maturity
- Modifications
- Third party
- Implementation assistance
- Quality
- Documentation
- Training

These components are listed on the Implementability Worksheet (Figure 4-1). The first column of the worksheet lists the requirements. The second column is for the Company Need rating, where you enter your need for the component. How you determine the rating to be placed in the Company Need Rating column is described below. The rest of the columns are used later in the process to determine the vendors' ratings and at that point is used to update the R^2ISC Worksheet with the vendor's score.

1. Vendor Responsiveness

The vendor's background can affect the implementability of the package. If you have a problem installing the package and the vendor does not get back to you or gives you the wrong information it can be very discouraging and puts up a road block to the successful implementation.

Your company needs for vendor responsiveness as it relates to implementability are:

Accept average responsiveness. Rating = 5

Require highly responsive vendor. Rating = 10

Enter your rating into the Company Need column of the

Implementability Worksheet					
Requirement	Company Need	Package A Rating	Package A Weighted Rating	Package B Rating	Package A Weighted Rating
1. Vendor Responsiveness	10	9	90	9	90
2. Vendor Background	7	6	42	7	49
3. Software Maturity	3	8	24	8	24
4. Technology Maturity	7	7	49	7	49
5. Modifications	10	6	60	7	70
6. Third Party	10	10	100	0	0
7. Implementation Assistance	10	9	90	9	90
8. Quality	7	8	56	6	42
9. Documentation	7	8	56	8	56
10. Training	7	8	56	3	21
	78		**623**		**491**
Total	**10**		**780**		**780**
Maximum Package Weighted Rating			**79%**		**63%**
Vendor Implementability Rating					

Figure 4-1. Implementability Worksheet

Implementability Worksheet (Figure 4-1). You will not be asking the vendor about their responsiveness, because no vendor will tell you they are not responsive. You will be verifying their responsiveness with their customers.

2. Vendor Background

The vendor's background can play a part in the implementability of the package. The items in the vendor's background that you should look at are:

Type of Customers—if the vendor has customers similar to you (industry, size, and has similar process) there is a better chance that the package will fit your company. The vendor will know your industry terminology and idiosyncrasies.

Number of Years in Business—the longer the company is in business the likelier the company's process will be able to better service you.

Size of Organization—if you are a large company with many locations that will be implementing the package then you will need a vendor who can support all those locations.

You can use the following to rate your need for the vendor's reliability:

Your company needs for vendor reliability are:

Vendor background of no importance. Rating = 0

Vendor background of average importance. Rating = 5

Vendor background of great importance. Rating = 10

Enter your rating into the Company Need column of the Implementability Worksheet (Figure 4-1).

3 and 4. Software and Technology Maturity

You may find a software package that matches your business requirements perfectly but is difficult to implement. There are many reasons why a package may be difficult to implement, including how much change to your business process is needed, the culture of the company to accept change, the quality and knowledge of the personnel, and the maturity of the software and technology. The package may never have been implemented at a company before, or the software has been changed to run on different computers. The software may have only been beta-tested (the first time that a company is using the package) at only a few locations. If this is the case, you will probably find bugs during your implementation, and there may be a poor response time of the vendor fixing the problems, because the vendor may be overwhelmed with problems being reported by other companies. Any of these problems can slow the implementation process and cause users to complain that the software does not work.

If the platform and the software are both new, chances are very good there will be problems during implementation. Bill Gates built a new home that incorporated the latest technology. The house was millions of dollars over budget and years behind schedule because they could not get some of the state-of-the-art devices to work.

In the 1970s a new electrical wiring made of aluminum for houses was touted as superior and cheaper than the copper wiring that had been used until then. Unfortunately, years later, houses built with aluminum wiring started to catch fire. Many of the owners of houses built with aluminum wiring decided to have it removed and replaced with copper wiring. The economic advantage that aluminum was supposed to have had turned out to be a economic disaster and even a safety hazard.

In the early 1990s, the UNIX operating system was starting to gain acceptance for use in business. The early pioneers found that many of the benefits they were receiving (portability, being able to run on many computers) was outweighed by the lack of many add-on programs (utilities) such as security, backup and recovery, etc. The add-on programs that were able to be easily purchased for other operating systems were not available for UNIX. Companies did not realize the problems until they purchased the package and started the implementation and had to build their utilities at additional cost whereas others decided to switch to a package that had a more mature operating system. As more and more companies started using UNIX, the utilities became available. Therefore, be cautious whenever you use new technology.

You need to rate your willingness to take a risk with both the package and the software it uses. You can use the following ratings:

Company Need for Software Maturity

Willing to accept a new package. Rating = 2

Want a package with average maturity. Rating = 6

Need a very mature package. Rating = 10

Company Need for Technology Maturity

Willing to accept new technology. Rating = 2

Want technology with average maturity. Rating = 6

Need a very mature technology. Rating = 10

Enter your rating into the Company Need column of the Implementability Worksheet (Figure 4-1).

5. Modifications

The more modification the package requires to meet your company's current requirements, the greater the risk that there will be problems during implementation. One company modified its package so much that they dramatically decreased the volume of transactions the package could handle. The end result? The package could no longer support the company's transaction volumes. The $17 million the company had spent on the project was wasted and the software became shelfware.

There are different types of modifications. Some modifications can be accomplished by adding additional programs before and or after the package. This is known as front-end or back-end modifications. These are usually easy to implement. Although other modifications require changes to the package program (known as changes to the code), these changes are more complicated because a change in one part of the program can affect other parts of the program. Sometimes the problems are obvious and other times they can be subtle and the effects unnoticed for weeks or months. You will be able to tell how complicated the modifications are by their cost.

You can use the following to rate your willingness to take the risk associated with modifications:

Company Need for Modifications

Accept heavy modifications. Rating = 0

Willing to accept some changes to the code. Rating = 3

Willing to accept many front-end and back-end modifications. Rating = 6

Willing to accept some front-end and back-end modifications. Rating = 8

Want no modifications to the package. Rating = 10

Enter your rating into the Company Need column of the Implementability Worksheet (Figure 4-1).

6. Third Party

Some software vendors only develop software and will not assist you in implementing the package or make modifications. This depends on the vendor's business model. This model can change from time to time. In some cases, the third party can be bigger than the package vendor such as the "Big 5" accounting firms or the large computer consulting firms (i.e., Computer Sciences Corporation).

If implementation or modifications are required and they are done by a third party, you need to analyze the third party as part of the implementability rating.

You can use the following to rate the use of third parties:

Company Need for Third Party

Implement and modifications to be done with no outside assistance. Rating = 0

Third party of average importance. Rating = 5

Third party very important. Rating = 10

Enter your rating into the Company Need column of the Implementability Worksheet (Figure 4-1).

7. Implementation Assistance

If you do not need the vendor to assist you in implementing the package, then rate this component a zero and proceed to the next component (quality).

If you will require the vendor's assistance in implementation of the package, then you need to determine if you want the vendor to implement the package or do you not care if a third party assists you in implementing the package.

You can use the following to rate your need for vendor support:

Company Need for Vendor Support

Implement ourselves (no outside assistance). Rating = 0

Accept vendor with below average support. Rating = 2

Accept vendor with average support. Rating = 5

Accept vendor with above average support. Rating = 7

Require vendor with excellent support. Rating = 10

Enter your rating into the Company Need column of the Implementability Worksheet (Figure 4-1).

8. Quality

The quality of the software that the vendor delivers has a large influence on the implementability of the package. If the package is full of bugs, it becomes harder to implement and could possibly fail. Users may get discouraged if they come across many bugs when trying to implement their new package. Once the bugs are fixed it becomes hard to convince the users that the package is working.

There is an international standard for quality known as ISO 9000. Vendors that are ISO 9000 certified have passed a rigorous audit by an independent certified auditor. (ISO 9000 certifies the software development process, not the software.) You should almost never accept a package with poor quality. You probably would be better off without the package because of the problem poor quality causes.

You can use the following to rate your need for the vendors' quality:

Company Need for Quality

Accept average quality. Rating = 5

Require very high quality. Rating = 9

Require ISO 9000 certification. Rating = 10

Enter your rating into the Company Need column of the Implementability Worksheet (Figure 4-1).

9. Documentation

Documentation spends most of its time just taking up shelf space. But when it is needed it can be invaluable. Packages come with different types of documentation (installation, user, system administrator, etc.). Having the manuals is not the only important thing; they must be understandable and well-organized. One of my pet peeves are package manuals that do not have indexes. It is frustrating to have a problem with a package and spend hours trying to find where it is explained in the manual.

Rate your need for documentation on a scale from 1 to 10, with 1 meaning you have little need for documentation and 10 meaning documentation is very important to you. Enter your rating into the Company Need column of the Implementability Worksheet (Figure 4-1).

9. Training

One of the often overlooked but imperative steps for a successful implementation is the training of users and data processing personnel. Even if there are generic third-party courses available, the vendor should supply specific package-related training. The training can take many different forms including:

- Train-the-Trainer—Training employees to become trainers, who will then teach the other users—course taught by vendor personnel.
- Computer-based training (CBT).
- Audio and/or video courses.
- Texts and workbooks.

The above training methods will have different values depending on the type of software, number of users, and training strategy of your company. You should rate your requirements for each of the types of training on the Training Worksheet (Figure 4-2). You should rate your need for the training type from 0 to 10 based on your need for that type of training, with 0 being you have no need for that type of training and 10 meaning you must have this type of training.

You also need to determine an overall need for training. Rate your training need from 0 to 10 based on your overall need for training, with 0 being you have no need for that type of training and 10 meaning training is very important. Enter your rating into the Company Need column of the Implementability Worksheet (Figure 4-1).

Supportability

The package may be implemented and you may be happy with it, but if there is a problem you will want the vendor around to help you fix it. There were companies who successfully implemented a package in

Training Worksheet				
Training	Company Need	Vendor A	Vendor B	Vendor C
Completeness of training plan.	10	10		
Courses meet enterprise's educational need.	10	8		
Size of classes.	10	10		
Vendor will customize courses for enterprise.	10	0		
Course is hands-on.	10	10		
Computer-based training (CBT) available.	10	10		
Audio training courses available.	0	—		
Video courses available.	0	—		
Workbooks available.	10	10		
	---------	---------	---------	---------
TOTAL	70	58		
Maximum Rating		70	70	70
Training Rating		83		

Figure 4-2. Training Worksheet

1998 only to find out that the package was not Y2K compliant. When they tried to contact the vendor, they were out of luck because the vendor was out of business. In the end they had to replace software that was working fine because it would not take them into the next millennium.

Another reason for selecting a package over a custom-designed solution is that the vendor will continuously enhance the software at a much lower cost to you than custom development. One company paid IBM to develop a customized management resource planning system (MRP) and then they gave IBM permission and even encouraged them to sell the software as a package. This was because they understood that it would cost them less if the support and enhancements to the package would be allocated over a hundred or more companies than if they had to pay for all the development costs of future improvements.

You must analyze many factors to determine the vendor's capability to support the software in the future. Supportability is made up of the following components:

- Vendor responsiveness
- Quality
- Development methodology
- Modifications
- Financial stability
- Warranty
- User Groups
- Support functions

The Supportability Worksheet

The Supportability Worksheet (Figure 4-3) lists the factors that make up the implementability of the package. Enter the numbers you de-

Supportability Summary Worksheet					
	Company Need	Package A Rating	Package A Weighted Rating	Package B Rating	Package B Weighted Rating
1. Vendor Responsiveness	10	9	90	9	90
2. Quality	10	8	80	6	60
3. Development Methodology	10	10	100	0	0
4. Modifications Support	7	6	42	9	63
5. Technology	7	8	56	9	63
6. Financial Stability	10	8	80	8	80
7. Warranty	7	9	63	9	63
8. Users Groups	7	10	70	0	0
9. Support Functions	10	7	70	7	70
	---------	---------	---------	---------	---------
TOTAL	78		651		489
Maximum Value Implementability	10		780		780
Weighted Average- Implementability			83%		63%

Figure 4-3. Supportability Summary Worksheet

termined as your need in the column of the Implementability Worksheet labeled Company Need Rating. This is used later to determine the vendor's rates and at that point, is used to update the R^2ISC Worksheet with the vendor's score.

1. Vendor Responsiveness

The responsiveness of the vendor is important in supportability just as it was in implementability. What good is it if the vendor makes wonderful promises and never fulfills them? For example, the vendor promises great enhancements in the next release but in the past its new releases have never matched its promises or are two years late.

You can use the following to rate your need for the vendors' responsiveness:

Accept average responsiveness. Rating = 5

Require highly responsiveness vendor. Rating = 10

2. Quality

The vendor's quality is an important component of the vendor's support. It becomes frustrating to have a vendor promise that it will support the package with enhancement and Help Lines only to find that the information you receive is wrong. The quality of the support is as important as having the support. Here, as in the implementability section, we will look at the vendor's quality systems.

You can use the following to rate your need for the vendor's reliability:

Accept average quality. Rating = 5

Require high vendor quality. Rating = 10

3. Development Methodology

If the package you are purchasing is not the type of package that you will not be modifying then rate this a zero and proceed to the next component (modifications).

The methodology used to develop the package can simplify some modifications. If the package was built using OO technology you might be able to modify the package by simply changing an object. A CASE tool could also simplify the modification process. If you have a specific development methodology, you should have specified it in the future requirements section. In the supportability criteria section you also need to rate the development methodology. Here you rate the tool based on how flexible it needs to be in allowing you to modify the package.

You can use the following to rate your need for development methodology:

Company Need for Development Methodology

Development methodology of no importance. Rating = 0

Development methodology of medium importance. Rating = 5

Development methodology must allow for easy modifications to the package. Rating = 10

4. Modifications

If the package you are purchasing is the type of package that you will not be modifying then rate this a zero and proceed to the next component (financial stability).

If the package needs modifications to meet your requirements, will the vendor support the modifications? Some vendors will not. This means that whenever the package is upgraded you will have to be reapply the modifications (the modifications have to be added to the new release). If the functionality of a modification is included in the upgrade then that modification need not be reapplied. Some vendors will reapply the modifications for a fee. The ideal situation is to have the vendor incorporate the modifications into their standard package so the new release will incorporate the functionality of your modifications and they will not have to be reapplied.

You can use the following to rate your need for the vendors' to support the modifications that are made:

Your Company Need for Modifications Support

Package is not the type to be modified. Rating = 0

You will reapply modifications to all new releases. Rating = 1

Third party will reapply modifications to all new releases. Rating = 6

Vendor will reapply modifications to all new releases. Rating = 8

Vendor will incorporate modifications into next release of the package. Rating = 10

5. Financial Stability

In order to ensure that the vendor will be around in the future, analyzing its financial strength becomes a criterion in the selection process. If the vendor is in very poor financial condition it may go bankrupt. Although bankruptcy is an extreme, if the vendor does not have enough money to hire enough personnel there could be problems with the Help Line, how often the package is updated (new release), or the quality of the personnel.

You can use the following to rate your need for the vendor's financial stability:

Vendor's financial condition is of no importance. Rating = 0

Vendor must have a minimum of an average financial condition. Rating = 5

Vendor must have excellent financial stability. Rating = 10

6. Warranty

The vendor should warranty that it will correct any defects (bugs) that you discover in the software without charge. How long of a warranty do you want the vendors to give? Will you require 90 days, 6 months, 1 year, 2 years? (Many vendors offer a free warranty for a given period and then continue the warranty as long as you continue paying the annual maintenance fee.)

On the Supportability Summary Worksheet (see Figure 4-3) enter the duration you want the vendor to warranty the package (90 days, six months, one year, or as long as annual maintenance is paid).

Then rate the importance of the vendor's warranty between 1 and 10. One indicating you have very little interest in the warranty and 10 meaning it is very important for the vendor to meet your warranty requirements. Then enter your rating into the Company Rating column onto the Supportability Summary Worksheet (see Figure 4-3).

7. Users Group

Many packages have users groups where the users can get together and share experiences. You can learn how other companies implement a requirement that the package did not support. Users groups also serve as a form where you can let the vendor know the types of enhancements you require.

Vendors with many users often have local users groups and a national users group. The local users groups usually meet monthly and the national group meets yearly. Other vendors may only have a national users group.

You can use the following to rate your need for users groups:

Users groups of no importance. Rating = 0

Users groups are a preference. Rating = 5

National users group is required. Rating = 8

Local and national users groups are required. Rating = 10

8. Support Functions

How the vendor reacts when you call with a problem can be very important. Vendors have support lines to assist customers with problems. When you call, what happens?

- An engineer who can resolve the problem answers the call.
- A clerk answers the call and notes your problem and then gives it to an engineer who then calls you back.
- An answering machine answers and you hope someone calls you back.
- Anything in between.

What type of response is acceptable for your package?

The coverage time (including weekend and holidays) of the Help Line is important. This becomes more important if the Help

Desk is in a different time zone. Some have guaranteed response times, others have guaranteed resolution time, and there is a big difference between the two.

When a problem arises it can sometimes be difficult to determine if the problem is caused by the package, hardware, operating system, etc. You often find that the package vendor points the finger at the hardware vendor, who says it's the operating system vendor, who says it's the package vendor. It can take days to just to determine who is responsible and then only minutes to resolve the problem. Therefore, it would be preferable to have the package vendor support the hardware and all the technologies used by the package.

Can the vendor dial into your computer to diagnose the problems remotely? This way they may not have to send a technician or consultant to your facilities. This can be both a time and money saver.

The number of people that the vendor has in its support function influences the support you will be able to receive. All other things being equal, the larger the ratio of support persons to the customer the better the support.

You can use the following to rate your need for the vendors' support:

Vendor support not important. Rating 5 2

Vendor must have guaranteed response time of one hour. Rating = 6

Vendor must have engineer on Help Desk and available during your work hours. Rating = 8

Vendor must guarantee a resolution time on all products sold. Rating = 10

Cost

Although many companies feel that the cost of the package is a large part of the total project cost, you must also consider the ongoing costs. Generally, the cost of the package is 15 percent to 25 percent of the project's total cost. The package cost is divided into two categories: one-time cost and annual operating expenses cost. One-time costs are those associated with selecting and implementing the package. Ongoing or recurring costs are the annual operating expenses that you incur by running the software.

Cost Summary Worksheet					
	Company Need	Package A Rating	Package A Weighted Rating	Package B Rating	Package B Weighted Rating
One-Time	7	6	42	0	0
Annual Operating Expenses	10	5	50	4	40
	---------	---------	---------	---------	---------
TOTAL	17		92		40
Maximum Value—Cost	10		170		170
Fit Cost	---------		54%		24%

Figure 4-4. Cost Summary Worksheet

The first step in developing your cost criteria is to allocate 100 points between the one-time cost and ongoing costs. For example, if you are as concerned about the up-front cost (cost of acquiring the package and its installation) as you are about the ongoing costs then allocate the 100 points equally to each of the two cost categories (50 to up-front cost and 50 to ongoing costs). If you are more concerned about the one-time cost, then rate it higher. This can be if you need to conserve cash now but will not have the same financial constraints in the future.

Once you have rated each cost requirement enter it onto the Cost Summary Worksheet (Figure 4-4).

The next step is to rate the components that make up the two cost criteria.

One-Time Cost

Each of the one-time cost components should be rated based on their importance to you. If the specific cost is of great concern, rate it a 10, if it is of average concern rate it a 5, if it is of no concern rate it a 0. A cost can be of no concern because you do not plan to purchase the item. The up-front costs are as follows:

- Software—Purchase price including all discounts.
- Hardware—Cost of any additional hardware required to run and maintain (test environment, etc.) the software.

- Modifications—To the package to meet your requirements.
- Installation—Of software onto the hardware including configuring the package and the installation of the hardware.
- Conversion—Of the data from your old system to the new package including cost of manually entering the data.
- Training—Of the users and the system personnel.
- Additional products—Any that are needed in order to run the package (i.e., operating system, and tools such as the CASE tool and fourth-generation language).

Annual Operating Expenses

Each of the annual operating expenses should be rated based on their importance to you. If the cost is of great concern rate it a 10, if it is of average concern rate it a 5, and if it is of no concern rate it a 0. A cost can be of no concern because you do not plan to purchase the item from the vendor.

The annual operating expenses are as follows:

- Annual maintenance base package
- Annual maintenance must have modifications
- Maintenance all modifications
- Maintenance hardware
- Maintenance other

Once you have rated each cost requirement, enter it onto the Cost Worksheet (Figure 4-5).

We Have the Target

We now know exactly what we want in the package, we have the target we are aiming at. This does not mean that we will get a package that hits the bull's-eye (matches all our requirements exactly).

Cost Worksheet				
	Cost Package A	Cost Package B	Cost Package C	Cost Package D
One-Time Cost				
Software	195,500	250,000	190,000	80,000
Modifications All	82,000	166,000	99,000	295,000
Modifications Must have Only	25,500	86,500	42,000	120,000
Implementation	50,000	3,000	15,000	3,000
Hardware	130,000	155,000	145,000	165,000
Installation	0	2,500	12,000	
Site Preparation	0	1,000	3,500	
Training	46,500	120,000	35,000	10,000
Documentation	0	2,000	800	1,200
Additional Products	0		0	15,000
TOTAL—One-Time Cost	**447,500**	**620,000**	**443,300**	**394,200**
Budget	450,000	450,000	450,000	450,000
Variance from Budget	2,500	-170,000	6,700	55,800
Percentage Variance from Budget	1%	-38%	1%	12%
Rating—One-Time Cost	**6**	**0**	**6**	**10**
Annual Operating Expenses				
Annual Maintenance Base Package	30,000	37,500	31,000	16,000
Annual Maintenance Must Have Modifications	3,700	7,000	2,400	26,000
Maintenance All Modifications	12,300	24,900	14,850	60,000
Maintenance Hardware	39,000	32,000	15,000	33,000
Maintenance Other Products	0			3,000
Total-Annual Operating Expense	**72,700**	**76,500**	**48,400**	**78,000**
Budget	70,000	70,001	70,002	70,003
Variance from Budget	-2,700	-6,499	21,602	-7,997
Percentage Variance from Budget	-4%	-9%	31%	-11%
Rating—Annual Operating Expenses	**5**	**4**	**10**	**2**
Support Services Cost				
Consulting	150/hr	200/hr	175/hr	200/hr
Programming	100/hr	125/hr	100/hr	125/hr
Telephone support	Part of annual	125/hr	Part of annual	100/hr
Rating Support Services	**10**	**6**	**9**	**6**

Figure 4-5. Cost Worksheet

53

However, we should get a package that is on the target, in other words meets approximately 80 percent of our requirements.

In the next chapter, we will start to rate the process of determining how close the packages come to our bull's-eye.

Notes

[1] *COMPUTERWORLD,* November 1, 1999, Volume 23, No. 44.

5

Narrowing the Field

In the previous chapters, you identified your requirements. In this chapter and the next you will narrow the candidate packages to between two and four finalists. Never have only one finalist because it does not allow for a comparison and limits your ability to ensure that the one package is really the correct choice. It is also not a good idea to have five or more packages; that can become very confusing. The finalists should be the packages that most closely meet your requirements.

Determining Available Packages

First, you need to identify the available packages. A list of packages for a business can be obtained from *Data Pro* (www.gartnerweb. com/public/static/datapro/main.html), *Data Sources*, which is part of the Computer Select, available as a CD-ROM or online at http:// www.computerselect.com. Figure 5-1 shows the Computer Select Software Search Screen that allows you to search for software packages for your application category (i.e., manufacturing software, accounting software, etc.). You can narrow your search by product subcategory (i.e., product category is Manufacturing Software and the subcategory is Manufacturing Integrated—MRPII), the hardware that the package runs on, and the cost of the package. You can also find lists of packages in industry magazines, on the Internet, and at conferences. Hardware and database vendors also compile lists of software packages that use or are compatible with their products.

Determining the Finalist

There are *must have* requirements that are unique to your industry or your company. These requirements are known as *key distinguishers*.

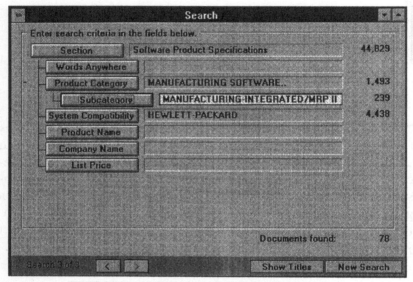

Figure 5-1. Computer Select Software Search Screen. (Computer Select is a Trademark of the Gail Group.) Reprinted with permission of the Gail Group

To determine your key distinguisher, review your must have requirements and ask yourself is this requirement unique to my company or industry, if yes it is a key distinguisher. Examples of key distinguishers for a manufacturing software package are:

- Lot tractability—The ability to identify the raw material and the equipment used to make each lot of products. Also the ability to identify the customers that purchased each lot. This function is critical for pharmaceutical and food manufacturers and is mandated by the Food and Drug Administration (FDA). The FDA requires pharmaceutical and food manufacturers to be able to recall a product if there was a problem with the raw materials (contamination, botulism, etc.). Therefore they must be able to keep track of the lot number(s) of the raw material that went into each lot of finished products. If you are required by the FDA to have lot tractability, it should be one of your key distinguishers. To build this tractability into a package that was not designed to perform this functionality is very complex and you should therefore eliminate packages that do not have the functionality.

- Multi-currency—Companies that have multiple plants or divisions in different countries (or the company sells and or purchases items in different currencies). Then the financial applications need to be able to handle the currency conversions.

A key distinguisher can also be the operating system. If there are packages that do not meet your key distinguisher, eliminate them immediately.

Many companies find it hard to determine which functions are really key distinguishers. Either they feel nothing is unique or everything is unique. Think of the way other companies work. If most other companies need the requirement then it is not a key distinguisher. If you came up with a list of fifty key distinguishers, most of them are probably not key distinguishers. Review the list and narrow the list to ten or less packages.

There are four methods that can determine how to narrow the field of vendors by comparing your key distinguishers and other requirements to the packages. They include:

- Telephone survey
- Request for information (RFI)
- Software tool
- Request for proposal (RFP)

You use one or a combination of these methods to assess which packages meet your key distinguishers and will continue in the process.

Telephone Survey

A telephone survey is a useful way to quickly obtain a limited amount of information about the software package. The survey entails calling vendors to ask if their package meets your key distinguishers. Conduct the survey using a written script containing all your questions (key distinguishers) and any additional items you would like to cover. This script should include:

- Questions that are very specific
- An indication if you want the vendor to send you information about the package
- Room to place additional vendor comments

An example of a good question is: "Does the software fully meet the FDA requirements for lot tractability." An example of a bad question is: "Can you perform lot tractability with the package?" With the last question, the software does not have to comply with FDA requirements or the software may only trace raw materials and not the equipment used in the manufacturing process.

Keep in mind that a telephone survey has both advantages and disadvantages.

Advantages of a telephone survey:

- Works quickly
- Offers a uniform response format—easy to compare responses

Disadvantages of a telephone survey:

- Compares only a few of your requirements to the software capabilities, because it would take too long for a phone call to compare all your requirements
- Offers limited information
- Depends on vendor's judgment

See Figure 5-2 for a sample Telephone Survey Script.

Request for Information

A request for information (RFI) is a formal written request to the vendors to supply you with information about how their package is rel-

Telephone Survey Script		
Vendor _____ Phone No. _____		
Contact _____ Interviewer _____		
Date _____		
Reference No.	Script	Vendor Response
1	Does your software have the functionality to meet the "full FDA requirements for lot tractability"?	
2	Does software have multi-currency general ledger?	
3	Does the package run on NT operating system?	
4	How many years has the package been released for sale?	
15	What is the cost of your software (Note: try to get as much information about cost as they are willing to divulge)?	
16	Please send us information on your package including a list of references.	
17	Thank you for your time	
Vendor comments:		

Figure 5-2. Telephone Survey Script

evant to you. The RFI allows you to obtain a better understanding of the package than a telephone survey, but does not provide a comparison between your requirements and their package's capabilities. The more information you supply the vendor, the better they can tailor their responses.

In the RFI you should give some background about your company and what you want to accomplish, then ask the vendor to supply a list of all the package's functionality, specifically mention your key distinguishers, and they should also include a list of their references. Vendors usually respond to an RFI with *boilerplate* literature that covers the highlights of the package. It probably will not list all the package's functionality.

When you receive the vendor's response to the RFI, review the materials to determine if they mention their ability to meet your key distinguishers. If the material did not contain a reference to your key distinguishers then you need to verify with the vendor that they meet the key distinguishers. For those vendors that meet your key distinguishers, review the rest of the literature to determine how closely the vendor comes to meeting the rest of the requirements. Put away the reference list that the vendor supplied for use later in the process when you will be reviewing the vendor's background.

Advantages of an RFI:

■ Obtains more information than telephone survey

Disadvantages of a RFI:

■ Does not compare your requirements to the software's capabilities
■ Provides a non-uniform responses format—hard to compare responses because the information is at different levels of detail and may expound on different areas of the package
■ Depends on vendor's judgment
■ Time consuming to analyze

Software Tool

These are software packages that compare your requirements to available software packages. The software tool has a list of predefined requirements and the ability of a package to meet those requirements. You rate each requirement based on your need. The tool then gives you the rating on the ability of the package to meet your requirements and the cost for each of the packages in its database. The software tool may not have some specific requirements that are truly unique to your company.

If a missing requirement is one of your key distinguishers, then contact the six vendors that the software tool rated the highest, to determine if they meet the missing key distinguishers. If the software tool contains your key distinguishers, check with the four vendors that the software tool rated the highest to ensure that they meet your key distinguishers. If a package does not, it should be eliminated from consideration and the next highest vendor then considered.

This tool should be used merely to narrow the field to six finalists. Figure 5-3 is a sample software select screen and Figure 5-4 is a

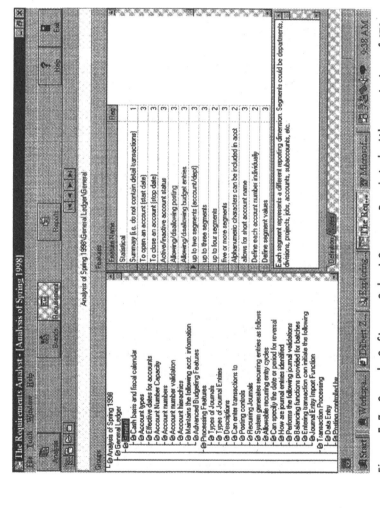

Figure 5-3. Sample Software Select Screen. Reprinted with permission of CTS

% Requirements Met By Module

12/16/1999

Analysis of Spring 19

Accounts Payable

		High	Medium	Low
AW	ACCPAC FOR WINDOWS	88.33	85.71	95.00
BW	BUSINESS WORKS FOR WINDOWS 12.0	46.67	90.00	60.00
CYIV	CYMA IV 1.3	71.67	71.43	80.00
ENC	IMPACT ENCORE	53.33	71.43	60.00
GPA	GREAT PLAINS ACCOUNTING 9.0	68.33	53.57	51.67
GPD	GREAT PLAINS DYNAMICS 4.0	75.00	75.00	75.00
MAC	MACOLA PROGRESSION 7.0	66.67	82.14	90.00
MAS	MAS90 for DOS	66.67	64.29	76.67
MASW	MAS90 FOR WINDOWS	66.67	85.71	76.67
NAV	NAVISION FINANCIALS 1.2	71.67	96.43	90.00
OS	OPEN SYSTEMS 5.2	76.67	57.14	70.00
PLAT	PLATINUM FOR WINDOWS	58.33	42.86	73.33
PLUS	ACCPAC PLUS FOR DOS	66.67	28.57	55.00
RVA	REALWORLD VISUAL ACCOUNTING 4.1	66.67	71.43	73.33
RW	REALWORLD 7.2	66.67	53.57	58.33
SBT	SBT PROFESSIONAL VERS. 5.0	78.33	85.71	66.67
SOL3	SOLOMON III BTRIEVE	51.67	85.71	58.33
SOL4	SOLOMON IV FOR WINDOWS 2.06	60.00	71.43	70.00
SW	SOUTHWARE ACCOUNTING SYSTEM	66.67	85.71	60.00
TRAV	TRAVERSE ACCOUNTING	76.67	57.14	73.33
VAM	VISUAL ACCOUNTMATE	66.67	71.43	71.67

Figure 5-4. Sample Package Fit Report. Reprinted with permission of CTS

sample package fit report, both from *The Guide to Accounting Software for Microcomputers and Requirements Analyst*™[1] software program by CTS (www.ctsguides.com).

Advantages of a software tool:

- works quickly
- provides an objective view
- compares your requirements to the software's capabilities
- allows for easy analysis

Disadvantages of a software tool:

- may be missing packages
- may not contain all your requirements
- most expensive

Request for Proposal

The request for proposal (RFP) asks the vendors to compare your requirements to their package's capabilities. The benefit of using an RFP is that the vendors are the experts on their packages. Bear in mind that the vendors may have a "different" understanding of what is being requested than you intended. The scripted demonstration, which you will conduct later in the process, allows you to determine how well the package really meets your needs.

Advantages of an RFP:

- compares your requirements to the software's capabilities
- allows for an easy analysis
- analyzes all your requirements

Disadvantages of an RFP:

- time
- not objective

■ vendors will not respond if the cost of the package is low, because there is not enough profit for them to spend days preparing their response

I recommend using the RFP for any package costing $5,000 or more even if you used any of the above methods to narrow down the field of vendors. The RFP will get you a lot of information about the package and the vendor that will be useful in later steps of the selection process.

Content of an RFP

The requirements that were developed in the previous chapters are the basis for the RFP. In addition to the requirements, the RFP should contain:

- Table of contents
- Company overview
- Project overview
- Proposal submission and timing
- Terms and conditions of proposal
- Format of response
- Proposal evaluation process
- Telephone hot line
- Glossary of terms
- Bidders conference
- Current requirements
- Future requirements
- Implementability
- Supportability
- Cost
- Implementation plan

■ Sample contracts

■ Certification of representation

Table of Contents

A table of contents allows for easily navigating the RFP. It should list each section and subsection of the RFP with its page number.

Company Overview

Include a general description of your company so the vendor can understand the need for the package. It should include the following information about your company is:

■ Products

■ Business process to be automated

■ Targeted market

■ Sales volume

■ Financial report (if company is a publicly traded corporation)

■ Number of employees

■ Other information that will allow the vendor to understand the company and its system's needs.

This will help the vendors to better understand your requirements and therefore better respond to the RFP. A vendor may realize that its package cannot meet the company's requirements and decide not to respond.

Project Overview

The project overview gives the vendor an overview of the project, the reason(s) the project is being undertaken, and the expected results. It includes:

■ Reason the project was undertaken

■ Problems the new system should address

■ Boundaries of the new system

■ Objectives for implementing the new system

- Interfaces to other systems
- Location(s) at which the system will be installed
- Key success factors
- Computer environment
- Funding is available—if approved.

Proposal Submission and Timing

Besides the due date of the response, the vendors need to know the following dates:

- RFP sent
- Bidders' conference—where the vendors assemble at your location to ask questions and review your operations
- Notification of nonresponse—vendor tells you that it will not respond to the RFP (do not feel they have a good fit to your requirements)
- Response submission due date
- Notification to finalists
- Demonstration
- Notification to winner
- Start of implementation
- Completion of implementation.

This list allows the vendor to prepare its resources for responding to the RFP and then for the demonstration and the implementation. It also lets the vendor know that you are serious about buying and are not merely window shopping.

Give the vendors at least two weeks to respond to the RFP. If there is a bidders' conference, responses to the RFP should be due at least one week after the conference. If the vendors are being asked to rush their responses, send the RFP by a next day delivery service. This proves that you understand the tight schedule they are being asked to undertake.

Terms and Conditions of Proposal

Include any conditions or terms to which the vendors will be bound by responding and in their final contract. For example:

- "Vendors will respond to the RFP at their own cost."
- "Response to the RFP will be included as part of the contract."

Often the vendor's contract will be limited to the statements in the final contract. Therefore, the vendors feel they can stretch the truth because it will not be legally binding. By including their response to the RFP in the contract, all statements become binding on the vendor.

Format of Response

To be able to analyze responses efficiently, provide all vendors with one standard RFP. This will also make for a fair and easy comparison. Where appropriate, have the vendors enter their responses directly onto the RFP or a computer electronic spreadsheet. Using a spreadsheet allows you to copy and paste the vendors' responses into the analysis worksheets without having to re-key the information. It also avoids data entry mistakes. If you are using an electronic spreadsheet use Microsoft Excel because it is the most popular spreadsheet program and most vendors use.

Proposal Evaluation Process

To help the vendors better formulate their responses to the RFP, they need to understand the evaluation process. Included in the Proposal Evaluation Process section the processes you will use to choose the winning vendor and the names and titles of the persons who will review the proposals. Also included in this section are the timing of the review process and the basis for choosing the finalists.

Telephone Hot Line

Keeping the playing field even between vendors is very important. One good way to do this is to set up a hot line. A specific phone number with voice mail where the vendors can call and leave any question they may have about the RFP. The next day the question and its answer are available to all vendors. A web site with the proper security can also be used for this purpose.

Glossary of Terms

In order to help the vendors better understand the RFP, include a definition of company-specific terms. Although you understand the terms you use, sometimes outsiders are not familiar with the terminology or can confuse its meaning. A term that often causes confusion is *purchase order*. Is a purchase order the document that your company receives from its customer, or is it the document the company sends to its vendors? Even within your company, the term purchase order often means different things to different people, so how is the vendor to know the meaning? The glossary prevents the vendors from mistaking the meaning of terms within the RFP.

Bidders' Conference

A bidders' conference allows the vendors to ask questions and tour the facilities. You should have a bidders' conference if the requirements are complex or if the package will cost more than $100,000. The location, time, and number of persons a vendor can send to the conference should be included in the RFP.

The conference provides the ability for all the vendors to hear each other's questions. And, if a question cannot be answered at the bidders' conference, then obtain the answer and make it available to all the vendors.

The bidders' conference and hot line are not mutually exclusive and should be used together to allow the vendors access to all the questions and responses.

Current Requirements

This section conveys to the vendors your current requirements. If the package is to cover multiple business areas then organize the requirements by business area and then those requirements that encompass all the business areas (i.e., security, report writer, etc.). The format is a table with the following six columns (see Figure 5-5, Current Requirements Worksheet):

1. **Reference number**—Unique identifier for each requirement. This allows for easy referral of a requirement.

2. **Requirement**—Defines the requirement.

3. **Company Need**—Defines how important the requirement is to the company. Below is an example of a rating system:

Current Requirements Worksheet					
Ref. No.	Requirement	Company Need	Package Rating	Cost To Modify	Module
123	Ability to enter the invoice.	H			
124	Ability to automatically perform a three-way match- purchase order, receiving report and invoice.	L			
125	Ability to automatically perform a two-way match- purchase order & receiving report.	M			
126	Ability to place an invoice on hold.	M			
127	Ability to create a debit memo.	M			
128	Ability to cut checks to vendors.	M			
129	Ability to automatically cut checks to vendors based on due date.	L			
130	Ability to calculate amount owed to a vendor based on the price on the purchase order and the quantity received.	L			
250	Ability to produce list of all invoices due for payment in a user-defined date range. Total Business Area (Accounts Payable) Maximum Business Area Value Percentage Fit Business Area (Accounts Payable)	M			

Figure 5-5. Current Requirements Worksheet

H	High (Must have to run business)
M	Medium (Should have to run business)
L	Low (Like to have, but not required in running the business)
X	Not needed (shows that you determined the requirement was not required and was not overlooked)

4. **Package Rating**—The vendors indicate how closely their package meets the company's current requirements. The following rating system can be used:

4 = package meets requirement

3 = the requirement can be met with 8 hours or less of modification

2 = the requirement can be met with 9 to 40 hours of modification

1 = the requirement can be met with 41 to 160 hours of modification

0 = the requirement can be met with more than 160 hours of modification.

5. **Cost to Modify**—The vendor indicates the cost of modifying the package to meet the current requirements. The costs of modifications are made independent of each other. In a later section of the RFP, ask the vendors to group the modifications that if done together would be cheaper than performing them individually.

6. **Module**—If the vendor sells the package in pieces, the vendor should list the modules that you need to meet your requirements. The list of modules should be matched against the modules listed in the pricing section of the RFP. This section is also used to ensure that all required modules are included in the final contract.

The requirements and the company needs were developed in Chapter 2 (see Figure 2-6, p. 18).

Data Analysis—There are times when software appears to meet a particular current requirement but because of the format of the data in the system the requirement is not met. We are all familiar with the "Y2K" problem. The software appeared to have all the functionality required but because the year was in two-digit numeric format, the computer thought the year 2000 was the year 1900 instead, and we all know the problems that it caused. If you must have your prices in the tenth or hundredth of a cent and the package only allows you to enter prices in whole cents, the package will not work for you.

Because of the way the system uses the data (price) it's as if it missed major functionality.

A good way to avoid problems arising from having the data in the right format is to check with the vendors to determine if the package will accommodate your data in the right size and in the right format. There are three basic types of data formats—numeric (numbers, i.e., 123), alpha (letters, i.e., abc), and alpha/numeric (letters and/or numbers, i.e., 1a2b3c). If the field is numeric you need to determine if you need a decimal point and if you do how many characters you need after the decimal point. For example, many companies sell items in whole units (i.e., one dress, 144 telephones, etc). But there are other companies that that sell items needing a decimal point (i.e., 13.75 feet of fabric) Figure 5-6, Data Analysis Worksheet, is an example of a worksheet that should be used.

This should be the same as requirements you developed in Chapter 2 (see Figure 2-7, p. 20).

Response Time—A system is of limited use if the users have to wait every time they hit the enter key. Ask the vendors to guarantee the system response time (the time it takes for the computer to respond when you hit the enter key independent of the screen or function) with either the hardware specified in the RFP or the recommended hardware. The maximum response time for a screen should be between one and five seconds; an average response time for a screen should be no more than one or two seconds. Many systems have batch processing that often takes place at night. The system must be

Data Analysis Worksheet						
Data	Req. Size	Req. Type	Req. Decimal	Package A Size	Package A Type	Package A Decimal
Accounts Payable Check Amount	10	N	2	8	N	2
Part Number	10	N		16	A/N	
Unit Cost	10	N	4	12	N	3
Department Number	6	N		8	N	

Figure 5-6. Data Analysis Worksheet

Data Volumes		
Data	Current Volume	Annual Growth
Part Number	100,000	5,000
Customer	3,000	400
Department	15	2
General Ledger Account Numbers	450	15

Figure 5-7. Data Volumes

able to perform all the nightly processes (including backup) and be ready to work the next morning. In order for the vendors to determine the response times, they need to know your company's data volumes and transaction volumes. The volumes should indicate the current volume and the anticipated growth over the next three to five years. Data volume is the number of items the system must maintain (i.e., number of parts, customers, employees, etc.) Figure 5-7 shows a Data Volumes table.

Transaction volumes are the number of items the system needs to process. The vendors require details about the transactions in order to calculate the processing times. For example, the vendor needs to know the number of customer orders. But, since much of the processing for the customer order depends on the number of lines on an order, tell the vendors both the number of orders and the average number of lines per order.

Tell the vendor your peak monthly transaction volumes. This will allow the vendor to determine the size of the hardware required. As part of the response to the RFP and later in the contract, the vendors must certify the package will meet the required response times. The guaranteed response time required is for as long as the your company uses the package. Therefore, supply the vendors with the estimated annual growth rate for both the data and transactions volumes. Figure 5-8 is an example of a Transaction Volumes Worksheet.

More than one company has found that when it was about to go live with its new system, the software and hardware would not support the volumes of data and transactions. A method of ensuring that the package will meet the required response times will be described in Chapter 8, p. 194.

Transaction Volumes Worksheet			
Transactions	Average	Maximum	Annual Growth
Orders Per Month	10,000	100,000	15%
Lines Per Order	3	6	−5%
Invoices	12,000	130,000	14%
Lines Per Invoice	4	5	0%

Figure 5-8. Transaction Volumes Worksheet

A good vendor who determines that its package cannot meet the response time will not respond to the RFP. Nonreputable vendors will answer anything in order to win the contract.

Future Requirements

Some current requirements will change from the time the package is selected until it's implemented. Some requirements will no longer be needed whereas others will become necessary. This process will continue over time.

Technology—The package's ability to keep pace with the changes in the business depends on the technology used to build it. Ask the vendors the names of the products used in building the package as well as the platforms the package can operate on. In some instances the vendors allow for multiple products; for example, the package may be able to use either Oracle or Sybase relational databases. Indicate any technology performances (i.e., hardware, operating system, database, programming language, etc.) in the RFP using the Technology Worksheet (see Figure 5-9). Express the company's preference on the Technology Worksheet as follows:

M   Must use specific vendor's technology

P   Prefer specific vendor's technology but, willing to use another vendor's technology

N   No preference to the vendor's technology.

Ask the vendors to indicate all the technologies that the package

Technology Worksheet					
Technology	Company Technology Vendor Preference	Company Preference	Package A Technology	Package A Year Released	Package B Technology
Upper CASE tool		N			
Lower CASE tool		N			
Programming Language(s)	JAVA	P			
Relational Database(s)	Oracle	P			
	Sybase	P			
Operating Systems	UNIX	M			
Hardware	HP 3000, RS600	P			
Object-Oriented	N	N			

Figure 5-9. Technology Worksheet

supports that are of interest to you. This is based on the Future Requirements Worksheet developed in Chapter 3 (Figure 3-1, p. 32).

Hardware—The vendors specify the hardware requirements for their packages, including the specific model (size) of the computer and all peripherals (i.e., model number required to properly support your company). If you will be running other programs on the hardware simultaneously with the vendor's program, identify them so the vendor can determine the system's response time.

If the packages run on multiple platforms and technologies, the vendor should recommend all the platforms and technologies that will give you the optimum response time. You can then compare the response time and cost of your preferable hardware to the vendor's optimum recommended hardware. You can then decide which hardware to choose. The specific model and cost are developed later in Chapter 6.

Implementability

This section of the RFP helps you determine how easily the package can be implemented. It will also allow you to identify specific risks associated with implementing each of the packages. Implementability is made up of the following components:

- Vendor responsiveness
- Vendor background
- Software maturity
- Technology maturity
- Modifications
- Third party
- Implementation assistance
- Quality
- Documentation
- Training

Below we review each of these components and describe how we will incorporate it into the RFP. (These were rated in Chapter 4 [Figure 4-1, p. 37].)

1. Vendor Responsiveness

Vendor responsiveness is not part of the RFP because every vendor will claim to be responsive. They will all have the verbiage to sound fantastic. So, do not bother putting this into the RFP.

2. Vendor Background

The vendor should provide background information about the company. This information should include an understanding of the vendor, its current and future direction, and its stability. Ask the vendors to detail their qualifications for supporting your company both now and in the future. The type of information the vendors should supply in this section includes:

- Client list
- Clients in same industry as your company
- Plans for the future
- White papers produced
- Years in business

- Number of local users groups and their location
- Year national users group (where users from all over the country gather to share advice, discuss war stories, tell the vendor what the users want in future releases) founded
- Number of attendees at last year's national users group meeting
- Contact name and phone number for local and National users groups
- Strategic direction
- Number of employees
- Resume of team members that will support the package installation at your company

3. Software Maturity

The vendor should supply a history of the package that will allow you to determine the software's maturity, this should include the following:

- Date of the first release of each module
- Date of subsequent releases
- List of major enhancements in each release
- Number of installations
- Number of companies using the current version of each module.

Some vendors claim a large number of implementations, but the details show that they are counting the number of modules installed not the number of installations. The difference is that one company may buy the general ledger, accounts payable, accounts receivable, order entry, and payroll modules. The vendor may claim five implementations instead of one implementation making it appear that the package is much more mature than it really is. This is especially important if there are few implementations of a module because it would not have been tested completely and you are more likely to find bugs.

This section should also include the name of the company that wrote each module. If a third party developed a module, the vendor should indicate their rights to the module. If the module was developed in a proprietary technology, the vendor should specify their rights to that technology.

In some cases the vendor selling the software does not own part or all of the software but has the rights to resell it. This was the case when Computer Associates purchased Ask Corporation. A problem arose when the software owner refused to give Computer Associates any updates to their package or the tool used to write the software.

Because many companies modify their packages, it is important to acquire the source code for the programs. The source code is the way computer programs are written by programers (they can be understood by other programers) or executed by the computer. Many vendors are reluctant to provide the source code to a client. This can become a problem if the software vendor goes out of business or is remiss about making software changes. If you do not receive the source code, a copy should be placed in escrow. The vendor should include its policy on source codes as part of the response to the RFP.

4. Technology Maturity

You will have the information you need to determine the technology maturity from the year the technology was released on the Technology Worksheet (Figure 5-9) from the Future Requirements section of the RFP.

5. Modifications

You will have the information you need to determine the modifications from the Current Requirements Worksheets (Figure 5-5) from the Current Requirements section of the RFP.

6. Third Party

If you do not require implementation assistance, skip to item 8 (quality). If you require implementation assistance you need to determine if the vendor will be assisting you or will it be one of their third-party approved consultants.

Ask the vendor to supply the same information about the third party they supplied in the vendor background section and the financial stability section described in the Supportability section.

7. Implementation Assistance

If you did not require the vendor or one of its third parties to implement the package, skip this component and continue to the quality component.

In this portion of the RFP ask the vendor if they will assist you with the implementation. If they will not assist you, ask them to supply the name of the party that they feel should assist you and if they are certified as one of their implementation consultants.

The quality of personnel that the vendor has will assist you in implementation. To determine their quality, ask for representative resumes of persons that will be assigned to your implementation and the specific resume of the person who will be leading the implementation.

The vendors should also supply sample resumes of their Help Desk personnel. If you will be using them to assist you in implementing the package, ask for resumes of the consultants, and their duties on the project (project manager, implementor, etc.) that will be assigned to them. The vendor may refuse to give you the names of the persons who will be assigned to you because they are not sure when you will be starting the implementation and they do not want to hold people on the payroll who are not billable. Therefore, they may supply you with the resumes of the type and number of persons that will be assigned to implement the package. Also the vendor should indicate if the implementation personnel will be assigned full-time or part-time. It should also be noted if these persons are permanent employees or subcontractors

The vendor should indicate the number of personnel in their implementation and their development department and also if they use personnel from the development department to implement the package. If they do, be careful because future updates to the package will be late. This is because the vendor will pull developers off the update project when they are needed for implementation.

8. Quality

The quality of the software is extremely important to the success of implementation. Review the manor in which the vendor ensures the quality of its products. If the vendor is ISO 9000 (International Standards Organization standard for quality) certified, it means that an independent auditing body has certified that the vendor's quality program is working and conforms to international standards. If the vendor is not ISO 9000 certified, request a copy of their quality procedures in response to the RFP.

ISO is the international organization setting standards used by many countries. The 9000 series is the standard for quality. ISO 9000 is the general quality standard and ISO 9003 is the quality standard specifically developed for software. Just because a vendor is not ISO 9000 certified does not mean its quality is poor; it means that no outside auditor verified the quality.

If the vendor is ISO 9000 certified ask them to include a copy of the certification with the response to the RFP.

9. Documentation

The documentation a vendor supplies is crucial to successfully implementing a package. If the documentation shows a lack of professionalism, the vendor's professionalism in other areas is in doubt. Ask the vendors to provide samples of the following types of documentation:

Users' guide—Instructions for teaching new users how to use the system and answers to questions for expert users

Technical guide—Explains to the IT staff who may need to make changes to the programs

Operations guide—Explains to the IT staff how to run the software.

Review a sample of each type of documentation to ensure they are usable. Even if you are not a documentation expert when you start comparing three or four vendors' documentation you will easily be able to tell their quality.

10. Training

In this section the vendors should detail the training they offer; some training may be bundled with software, others may need to be purchased separately. Many companies want to bring the knowledge of the package in-house. To accommodate this, many vendors offer Train-the-trainer programs in which a few of your employees are taught to become instructors. They in turn teach the program to your other employees. If you have large number of employees who need to be trained, Train-the-trainer is more economical than having the vendor train all your employees. The vendor should provide a list of courses offered and their schedules.

In addition to standard classroom instruction, vendors may offer materials to guide employees through self-paced training including:

- Computer-based training (CBT)
- VCR courses
- Audio tape courses
- Workbook training

These allow for new users to learn the system on site and at their own speed. It is also easier to train more employees because no travel is required and scheduling is less of an issue. They are also useful as refresher courses. On the other hand, classroom training allows the student to have their questions answered immediately and courses can easily be modified based on the students need. Ask the vendors to indicate the typical training plan as part of their response to the RFP.

Supportability

This section of the RFP deals with the vendor's ability to support the package in the future. Supportability is made up of the following components:

- Vendor responsiveness
- Quality

- Development methodology
- Modifications
- Financial stability
- Warranty
- Users groups
- Support functions

You have rated these in Chapter 4 (Figure 4-3, p. 45).

1. Vendor Responsiveness—We do not need to ask the vendor about its responsiveness in this section of the RFP. As in the Implementability section, if you ask the vendor how reliable they are they will tell you that they are very reliable so it is of no use to incorporate this into the RFP.

2. Quality—We do not need to ask the vendor about its quality in this section of the RFP. We will use the same response from the Implementability section to determine a rate for the vendor quality in this section.

3. Development Methodology—We do not need to ask the vendor about its development methodology in this section of the RFP. We will use the response from the Future Requirements section to determine the rate for the vendor Development Methodology in this section.

4. Modifications Support—If the package you are purchasing is not the type of package that you will not be modifying then skip this section and proceed to the next component (Modifications).

We do not need to ask the vendor about modifications in this section of the RFP. We will use the response from the Future Requirements section to determine the rate for the vendor modifications in this section.

5. Financial Stability—The vendor selected must be able to support your company and the package in the coming years. If the vendor does not have the financial ability to stay in business, it will not be able to support your company. It is wise to analyze the vendor's financial strength before making a final decision.

One client I was working for was ready to sign a contract for a large software package. While performing a complete financial check, I found that their first choice vendor owed the Internal Revenue Service (IRS) close to half a million dollars. Needless to say they did not sign the contract. Within two weeks the vendor filed for bankruptcy. Chapter 8 will go into detail of how to check for liens and other possible problems.

Ask the vendors to include an audited financial statement in their response to the RFP. If the vendor is a publicly traded company, they will have no problem supplying the information. On the other hand, if the vendor is privately owned they may not want to reveal financial information. If the vendor will not supply its financial information, it is advisable to perform additional background checks.

If the vendor is owned by another corporation, obtain the parent company's audited financial statement. If the parent company has financial problems, they may affect the vendor.

The vendors should supply two financial references including their lending bank.

They should also include information about any:

- IRS liens against the vendor
- IRS liens against the vendor's parent company
- Past due notes or loans
- Judgments against the vendor
- Litigation against the vendor
- Litigation against the vendor parent

6. Warranty—The vendor should warranty that it will correct any defects (bugs) that you discover in the software without charge. Will bugs in the software corrected for other users also be corrected for you? If the vendor finds bugs will it notify you? Will the vendor supply the improved version of the applications and if so, at what charge? What criteria will be used to determine full acceptance of the system (one month of full operation, acceptance test, etc.)? The vendor should define these items in its response to the RFP.

We also need to ask the vendor what types of modifications, if any, to the package will void the warranty.

7. Users Groups—We do not need to ask the vendor about its user groups in this section of the RFP. We will use the response from the Future Requirements section to determine the rate for the vendor user group in this section.

8. Support Functions—In this section of the RFP we ask the vendor the type of response we will receive when you call with a problem. Do they have guaranteed response times, or a guaranteed resolution time? Do they resolve problems with the hardware as well as the package? We also ask about the times that coverage of the Help Desk is available (including weekends and holidays).

Does the vendor have the capability to dial-in to your computer to be able to diagnose problems remotely? We also want to know how many people they have in their support functions.

9. Support Functions—In this section of the RFP you ask the vendor the types of support they offer and if they have a guaranteed response time. Also ask the hours of coverage for the Help Desk and the number of personnel in the support function. The vendor should also be asked if they have the capability to dial-in our computer to help diagnose problems.

Cost

The cost of a package is comprised of many pieces. To better understand the difference in cost between packages, provide the vendors with a Cost Worksheet for their reply. The Cost Worksheet should be a fill-in-the-blanks format. Divide the worksheet into three cost categories:

One-time Costs—Costs for purchasing and implementing the package and necessary hardware.

Annual Operating Expenses—Costs that will reoccur each year.

Additional Support Services—Costs for services that the vendor can supply, on an as-needed basis.

You have already rated the first to cost categories in Chapter 4 (Figure 4-4, p. 51).

One-Time Cost—The one-time cost includes:

- Software—Cost of acquiring each module required to meet the functionality identified in the current requirements section of the RFP. Break down the cost by module and include all applicable discounts. Cross check the list of modules with the list of the requirements. See Figure 5-10 for a sample Software Modules Cost Worksheet.

- Modifications—The cost of modifying the software to meet the requirements identified in the current requirements section. [In this section, the vendor details the cost by module in three ways:]

  1. Making each modification individually (see Figure 5-5).

  2. Making only Company Needs of M (must have) by module (see Figure 5-10).

  3. Making Company Needs of M (must have), and S (should have) by module (see Figure 5-10).

Having the cost broken down this way will allow for a better comparison of the cost and budgets for modifications. You will also be able to use this information to determine if all the modifications are cost justified. You may decide not to make all the modifications, but only the modifications to meet your "must have" requirements, or the "must have" and the "should have" requirements.

- Hardware—Cost of the hardware the vendor will supply. The vendor could break down the cost by piece of equipment and include all applicable discounts. See Figure 5-11 for a sample Hardware Cost Worksheet.

- Site Preparation Cost—Cost of preparing the physical site to receive the hardware. This can include air conditioning, additional electrical outlets, etc. Many vendors will not respond but it does not hurt to ask. You may get a good price.

Software Modules Cost Worksheet

Software Modules	Software List Price	Software Discounted Price	Modifications Must Have	Modifications All	Yearly Maintenance Base Package	Yearly Maintenance Modifications Must and Should Have	Yearly Maintenance Modifications All
Module 1							
Module 2							
Total							
Implementation			—	—	—	—	—
Grand Total Software							

Figure 5-10. Software Modules Cost Worksheet

Hardware Cost Worksheet							
Software	Description	Quantity	List Price	Discounted Price	Total Discounted Price	Yearly Maintenance (Unit price)	Total Maintenance
CPU							
Model							
Memory							
Storage							
Size							
Back-Up Device							
Type							
Terminals							
Model							
Printers							
Model 1							
Model 2							
System Software							
Uninterrupted Power Supply							
Shipping							
Subtotal							
Site Preparation							
Installation							
Grand Total							

Figure 5-11. Hardware Cost Worksheet

■ Documentation—Lists the documentation included at no charge. It should also list the list price and applicable discounts for additional copies of documentation. The vendor should indicate the number of copies of each manual supplied at no cost. Also indicate if you may reproduce the manuals at no cost. If they cannot be reproduced, the vendor should indicate the cost for each manual. The types of manuals that are usually available from vendors include:

Implementation guide

User documentation

Technical documentation

Operations documentation

Other

See Figure 5-12 for a sample Documentation Cost Worksheet.

■ Training—Identified by type of training required. Training should enable the proper installation and operation of the software. The training can be performed either on- or off-

Documentation Cost Worksheet					
	My Be Reproduced at No Charge	Quantity Supplied And No Charge	Unit Cost	Discounted Cost	Recommended Additional Quantity
Implementation					
User					
Technical					
User					
System					
Operations					
Other					
Grand Total					

Figure 5-12. Documentation Cost Worksheet

Training Cost Worksheet

Training Course	List Price/Student	Discount Price/Student	List Price for Private Class	Discount Price for Private Class	Number of Students for Private Class	Recommended Number of Students
Course 1						
Course 2						

Figure 5-13. Training Cost Worksheet

site. The vendor should identify any out of pocket expenses such as travel and meal allowances. Also list in this section all relevant courses with their list price and any discounts that apply. (See Figure 5-13 for a sample Training Cost Worksheet.)

■ Additional Required Products—Includes any product that are required to run the package including; the operating system, databases, CASE tool Fourth Generation Language, etc.

■ See Figure 5-14 for a sample Additional Products Cost Worksheet.

■ Installation—Includes all costs associated with installing the package, additional software and hardware. The cost should include any out-of-pocket expenses (travel, meals, etc.).

■ Annual Operating Expenses—The vendor's estimate of the total annual operating costs for the system. This includes software and hardware maintenance and any additional training required for expected software upgrades. It should also include the following items:

■ Maintenance of the base package (see Figure 5-10)

■ Maintenance for modifications (usually a percentage of the cost of the modifications the vendor is likely to do for the initial installation) (see Figure 5-10)

Additional Products Cost Worksheet						
Product	Description	Required/ Suggested	List Price	Discounted Price	Quantity	Yearly Maintenance
Product 1						
Product 2						
Grand Total Software						

Figure 5-14. Additional Products Cost Worksheet

- Support supplied by the vendor. This includes telephone support, online support, etc.
- Maintenance for hardware (if it is part of the RFP) See Figure 5-10.
- Maintenance on additional products supplied by vendor (operating systems, database, fourth-generation language, etc.) See Figure 5-14.

Additional Support Services—Although these are not part of the cost rating, you may be interested in knowing the vendors rates for services it offers. For each service, the vendor should indicate the cost for the following:

    Consulting

    Programming

    Telephone support (this may be free or included in the maintenance fee)

    Other

The vendor should indicate the hourly rates and estimated total expenses for these services. (See Figure 5-15 for a sample Additional Support Services Cost Worksheet.)

Additional Support Services Cost Worksheet			
	Standard Rate	Discounted Rate	Anticipated Need
Consulting			
Programming			
Telephone Support			
Other			

Figure 5-15. Additional Support Services Cost Worksheet

Implementation Plan

Ask the vendor to supply an implementation plan. This will let you see the level of sophistication and you can also take pieces from different vendors' plans to develop your own plan.

Sample Contracts

Ask the vendor to submit a copy of their contract. This will let you start planning your negotiation strategy as soon as you have selected the winning package.

Certification of Representation

The last thing you want is to analyze the vendor's response and then find out that the person who responded was not authorized to do so. Therefore ask that a Certification of Representation be included with the responses. This certifies that the person responding is authorized to do so by the company.

Confidentiality

If the requirements or other material included in the RFP contain confidential information, obtain an agreement of confidentiality from the vendors before sending them the RFP. Including an Agreement of Confidentiality in the RFP has questionable legal value because it was unsolicited and the vendor did not agree to it before they received the RFP.

A letter should accompany the agreement of confidentiality telling the vendors that they were selected to participate in the RFP process. If they wish to receive the RFP, they should sign and return the letter of confidentiality. Vendors are used to signing Letters of Confidentiality and may even ask you to sign one.

The Agreement of Confidentiality should specify that all materials be kept confidential and shown only to those employees required for the response. Those employees viewing the RFP should sign confidentiality agreements with the vendor.

Once you send the RFP to the vendors, you wait for their responses. The next chapter will detail what you do once you get back the responses to the RFP.

While You Are Waiting

Once you develop the RFP and have mailed it to the vendors you will have to wait until the vendors send you their responses. You will analyze the responses in the next chapter. But while you are waiting you can develop the scripts that you will need for the scripted demonstration, which is described in Chapter 7.

Notes

[1] Trademark of CTS.

6

Analyzing the Vendors' Responses to the Request for Proposal

I n the previous chapters you narrowed the field of vendors to ten
or less. In this chapter you will narrow the field to between two
and four of those that potentially have a package that can meet
your requirements. To start this chapter you should receive the responses to the RFP that you created and sent to the vendors in the
previous chapter. You will analyze each of the vendors' response to
the RFP to determine their R^2ISC scores. This process is similar to
browsing through the house listings with a realtor. The goal is to
weed through the numerous listings and find just the few houses with
good potential to visit. The more houses (vendors) you eliminate up
front the less work you'll have to do. Just make sure you have two or
three houses (vendors) to compare.

The ratings that are used in this chapter are meant as examples
and should not be taken as gospel. If there is a reason for using a different rating then by all means do so.

Method of Analyzing Responses

Once you receive the vendors' response to the RFP begin the analysis. Divide the responses into sections (i.e., current requirements,
cost, etc.) and make a person or team responsible for analyzing and
rating the same section of all the responses.

After all the responses are analyzed and rated, hold a workshop
to review the information gathered. Each person or team should give
a short presentation about the portion of the response they rated and
the reason for their ratings. If you have only three or four responses

use this analysis to determine if the vendor deserves additional consideration.

Below describes how you should analyze each of the five R^2ISC criteria. Remember that during the analysis if you rated any requirement a 0 you do not have to rate the vendor on that requirement.

Current Requirements

Analyze the package's current requirements by analyzing the Current Requirements (CR) Worksheet (Figure 5-5, p. 69) portion of the vendors' responses to the RFP. Figure 6-1, Current Requirements Worksheet—Package A, is a portion of vendor A's completed worksheet that we will use for examples in this section and later in this chapter when we review cost.

The first step is to transpose each vendor's responses from the Package Rating column of the Current Requirements Worksheet to the Package's Rating column for that package on the Current Requirements Analysis Worksheet (Figure 6-2). The vendor's ratings can then be easily compared to your business requirements as well as to those of the other vendors. Before we start the analysis we need to check if there are any problems with the vendors' responses. Problems arise when the data the package uses is not the right format or length that we need.

Field Sizes and Type

Analyzing the vendors' responses by reviewing each field for both size and type. If the package does not meet your field size and type requirement then there are business requirements that will not be met. For example, gasoline is priced at the gas station to the tenth of a penny ($1.359). If the package cannot handle tenths of a penny then there are many business requirements that will not be met. Therefore, you will need to go back to the business requirement that uses the price and change the rating.

You developed your data requirements in Figure 5-6, p. 71. For each field enter your size requirement into the Req. Size column in the Data Analysis Worksheet (see Figure 6-3). Enter your type needs—alpha, numeric, or alpha-numeric—in the Req. Type column

Current Requirements Worksheet—Package A

Ref. No.	Requirement	Company Need	Package A Rating	Package A Cost To Modify	Module
123	Capability to enter the invoice.	H	4		
124	Ability to automatically perform a three-way match—purchase order, receiving report, and invoice.	L	4		
125	Ability to automatically perform a two-way match—purchase order & receiving report.	M	3	5,000	
126	Ability to place an invoice on hold.	M	2	2,000	
127	Ability to create a debit memo.	M	4		
128	Capability to cut checks to vendors.	M	4		
129	Capability to automatically cut checks to vendors based on due date.	L	4		
130	Ability to calculate amount owed a vendor based on the price on the purchase order and the quantity received.	L	4		
250	Ability to produce list of all invoices due for payment in a user-defined date range.	H	4		
	Total Business Area (Accounts Payable)		480	$75,000	

Figure 6-1. Current Requirements Worksheet—Package A

Current Requirements Analysis Worksheet

Ref. No.	Requirement	Company Need	Company Rating	Package Rating Package A	Package Rating Package B	Package Rating Package C	Weighted Rating Package A	Weighted Rating Package B	Weighted Rating Package C
123	Capability to enter the invoice.	H	10	4	4	4	40	40	40
124	Ability to automatically perform a three-way match—purchase order, receiving report, and invoice.	L	3	4	3	3	12	9	9
125	Ability to automatically perform a two-way match—purchase order and receiving report.	M	7	3	3	0	21	21	0
126	Ability to place an invoice on hold.	M	7	2	2	4	14	14	28
127	Ability to create a debit memo.	M	7	4	4	4	28	28	28
128	Capability to cut checks to vendors.	M	7	4	4	4	28	28	28
129	Capability to automatically cut checks to vendors based on due date.	L	3	4	3	4	12	9	12
130	Ability to calculate amount owed a vendor based on the price on the purchase order and the quantity received.	L	3	4	4	2	12	12	6

Figure 6-2. Current Requirements Analysis Worksheet

Current Requirements Analysis Worksheet

				Package Rating			Weighted Rating		
Requirement		Company							
Ref. No.	Requirement	Need	Rating	Package A	Package B	Package C	Package A	Package B	Package C
250	Ability to produce list of all invoices due for payment in a user-defined date range.	H	10	4	4	3	40	40	30
	Total Business Area (Accounts Payable)	128	1,250	930	1,062	1,120	3,750	4,200	4,750
	Maximum Business Area Value						5,000	5,000	5,000
	Percentage Fit Business Area (Accounts Payable)		—				75%	84%	95%

Figure 6-2. Current Requirements Analysis Worksheet (*continued*)

Data Analysis Worksheet						
Data	Req. Size	Req. Type	Req. Decimal	Package A Size	Package A Type	Package A Decimal
Accounts Payable Check Amount	10	N	2	8	N	2
Part Number	10	N		16	A/N	
Unit Cost	10	N	4	12	N	3
Department Number	6	N		8	N	

Figure 6-3. Data Analysis Worksheet

and enter the Required Decimal places if any in the next column. Then transfer each vendor's response into the worksheet. Then compare your company's data needs against what each vendor can provide. When looking at the size requirements you need a vendor to provide a field size equal to or greater than your requirement. For the field type, you need the vendor to provide a field type that can accept your data. Remember that an alpha-numeric field can accommodate letters, numbers, or both. For example:

> **Part Number**—The company need is for a 10-digit numeric field (numbers). Package A will accept 16 alpha-numeric (letters and or numbers).The package field size (16) is larger than the company's requirement (10) therefore the package and the alpha-numeric field type will be able to accommodate part numbers. So enter a Y for yes in the Part Number for package A on the Data Analysis Summary Worksheet (Figure 6-4).

> **Accounts Payable (AP) Check Amount**—The company need is for a 10-digit number, two of which are after a decimal point (i.e., need to be able to write a check in the amount of $99,999,999.99). Package A will accept an 8-digit number, two of which are after the decimal point (i.e., $999,999.99). Package A will not be able to write a check of one million dollars and over as the company required. So N (No) is placed in the row for Accounts Payable Check Amount for package A on the Data Analysis Summary Worksheet

Data Analysis Summary Worksheet

DATA	Requirements Impacted	Meets Requirement Package A	Requirements Rating Updated	Meets Requirement Package B	Requirements Rating Updated	Meets Requirement Package C	Requirements Rating Updated
Accounts Payable Check Amount	129	N					
Part Number		Y					
Cost		Y					
Department		Y					

Figure 6-4. Data Analysis Summary Worksheet

(Figure 6-4). In the second column of the worksheet put all the current requirements that are impacted by the field. In the case of the Accounts Payable Check Amount requirement 128 (Capability To Cut Checks To Vendors) you will need to modify the program or in this case use a work-a-round (entering an invoice over one million dollars as multiple invoices each under a million dollars). Because Package A cannot accommodate the required amount, reduce the score of a vendor for requirement 128 based on the time it would take to modify the field to add the decimal place to the data field.

Interestingly vendor A rated requirement 128 a four (or meets requirement); you will need to go back to vendor A and find out how long it would take to change the field size. If the vendor says more than forty hours then the rating is changed from a four to a three.

Department Number—The company need is for a six-digit numeric field. Because Package A will accept an eight-digit number, Package A gets you a Yes for the Department Number field. Because the package can accommodate the part number, there is no problem with the functional requirements that use the Part Number data field.

Calculating Business Area Fit

The vendors' ratings treat all your requirements equally. So the first step of this analysis is to assign a numeric rating to your requirements based on your need ratings. "Must haves" should have the most weight with less weight to the "should haves" and even less to the "like to have."

Assign a weight to each requirement by converting the company need rating—M, S, L, or X in the Company Need column—to a numeric value, which is placed in the Company Rating column. Use the Company Need Valuation Table for Current Requirements (Figure 6-5) to perform the conversion. Then, to calculate the weighted ratings of the requirements for a package, multiply your company's rating by the Vendor Rating. Enter the results in the Package's Weighted Rating column.

Company Need Valuation Table for Current Requirements		
Company Need	Company Need Definition	Company Need Value
H	High (Must have in order to run business.)	10
M	Medium (Should have to run the business.)	7
L	Low (Like to have but not needed to run the business.)	3
X	Not needed.	0

Figure 6-5. Company Need Valuation Table for Current Requirements

For example, for requirement 124 (see Figure 6-2), the Company Need is L (like to have but not needed to run the business). Based on the Company Need Conversion Table L = 3. So, to calculate the weighted rating for package A:

$$\frac{\text{Weighted rating}}{\text{Package A}^{\text{Req124}}} = \frac{\text{Company Rating}^{\text{Req124}} \times \text{Package A}}{\text{Rating}^{\text{Req124}}}$$

$$= 3 \times 4$$

$$= 12$$

After calculating a package's weighted rating for each requirement, you can determine how well the package fits each of your company's business areas or the percentage fit of the package. The first step is to calculate the maximum value a package can achieve for each business area.

To do this, sum the company rating for Business Area and multiply by 4 (maximum possible weighted rating for each requirement.) Using Figure 6-2 as an example the calculation would look like this:

$$\text{Maximum Value}^{\text{AP}} = \text{The sum of the Company Ratings} \times 4$$

$$= (10 + 3 + 7 + 7 + 7 + 7 + 3 + 3$$
$$+ \ldots\ldots + 10)$$

$$= 1,250 \times 4$$

$$= 5,000$$

Enter the sum of the Company Ratings, in this case 1,250, in the Company Rating column in the row labeled "Total Business Area." Enter the Maximum Value for the Business Area 5,000 in the Weighted Rating column in the row marked "Maximum Business Area Value."

Then divide the Package's Total Weighted Rating for the business area by the Maximum Value to arrive at the Package's Percentage Business Area fit. Returning to the Requirements Worksheet for the Accounts Payable Department.

Using Figure 6-7 as an Example the calculation would look like this:

$$\text{Percentage Fit}^{PkgA} = \text{Total Weighted Rating}^{PkgA} / \text{Maximum Value}$$
$$= 3{,}750/5{,}000$$
$$= 75\%$$

Business Area Fit

Once you have calculated the package's Percentage Fit Business Area for each Business Area, you can determine how well each package meets your current requirements. You had already entered your need for each business area on The Business Area Summary Worksheet (see Figure 2-4, p. 16). Now, enter the Percentage Fit by business area for each package to the worksheet. This can be seen in Figure 6-6, The Business Area Summary Worksheet—Vendors A, B, and C, which contains the results for vendors A, B, and C. Then multiply the Package Percentage Fit by the Company Rating to calculate the Package's Weighted Percentage Fit. For Package A for the Accounts Payable Business Area the calculation looks like this:

$$\frac{\text{Package A Weighted}}{\text{Percentage Fit}^{AP}} = \frac{\text{Company Need}^{AP}}{\times \text{Percentage Fit}^{AP}}$$
$$= 5 \times 75\%$$
$$= 375\%$$

Enter this fit in the Weighted Percentage Fit column for Package A.

Business Area Summary Worksheet – Vendors A, B, and C

Business Area	Company Need	Package A Percentage Fit	Package A Weighted Percentage Fit	Package B Percentage Fit	Package B Weighted Percentage Fit
General Accounting	7	85%	595%	86%	602%
Accounts Payable	7	75%	525%	84%	588%
Accounts Receivable	3	93%	279%	88%	264%
Payroll	7	95%	665%	85%	595%
Order Management	10	92%	920%	83%	830%
Human Resources	3	65%	195%	95%	285%
TOTAL	37	505%	3,179%	521%	3,164%
Maximum Value (Total Company Need × 100%)			3,700%		3,700%
Percentage Fit Current Requirements			86%		86%

Figure 6-6. Business Area Summary Worksheet – Vendors A, B, and C

Calculating Current Requirements Fit

After calculating the package's weighted rating for each business area you can determine how well the package fits your Current Requirements. The first step is to total all columns and place the result into the row marked total. The second step is to calculate the maximum value a package can achieve.

To do this, sum the Company Rating column and place the results in the total line. Then multiply the Company Rating by 100% (The maximum total rating for each Business Area) Value. Using Figure 6-6 as an example the calculation would look like this:

$$\text{Maximum Value}^{CR} = \text{The sum of the Company Ratings} \times 100\%$$
$$= (7 + 7 + 3 + 7 + 10 + 3)$$
$$= 37 \times 100\%$$
$$= 3,700\%$$

Enter the maximum value, in this case 3,700 percent, into the row marked Maximum Value (Total Company Need × 100%) into each of the Package Weighted Percentage Fit columns.

Then divide the Package's Total Weighted Rating for the business area by the Maximum Value to arrive at the Package's Percentage fit. Using Figure 6-6 as an example the calculation looks like this:

$$\text{Total Percentage Fit}^{Pkg\ A} = \text{Total Weighted Fit}^{Pkg\ A} / \text{Maximum Value}$$
$$= 3,179/2,700\%$$
$$= 86\%$$

Then enter the Current Requirements Percentage Fit for each package from the Business Area Summary Worksheet (Figure 6-6) onto the R²ISC Worksheet (Figure 6-7). We will continue adding the package's Percentage Fit for the other R2ISC criteria as we proceed through this chapter.

Future Requirements

The response to RFP allows you to determine if the pieces of the Future Requirements (FR) are the ones that you want. But the re-

R²ISC Worksheet					
High-Level Requirements	Company's Need	Package A Percentage Fit	Package A Weighted Percentage Fit	Package B Percentage Fit	Package B Weighted Percentage Fit
Current Requirements	30	86%	26%	85%	26%
Future Requirements	25	68%	17%	54%	14%
Implementability	20	73%	15%	64%	13%
Supportability	15	78%	12%	67%	10%
Cost	10	38%	4%	24%	2%
	—	—	—	—	—
R²ISC Rating			74%		64%

Figure 6-7. R²ISC Worksheet

sponses will not tell you how well they are used, that you will have to analyzing the computer code. Use the Future Requirements Worksheet (Figure 6-8).

> **CASE Tools**—Use the schedule below to rate both the Upper and Lower CASE tools.
>
> package is written in the Upper CASE tools that you want to use. Rating Upper CASE tool = 10
>
> package is written in the Lower CASE tools that you want to use. Rating Lower CASE tool = 10
>
> package is written in the Upper CASE tools that you want to use, but Lower CASE tool is not the one you want to use. Upper and Lower CASE tools that pass information between them. Rating Lower CASE tool = 8
>
> package is written in the Upper CASE tools that you want to use, but Lower CASE tool not the one you want to use. Upper and Lower CASE tools does not pass information between them. Rating Lower CASE tool = 0
>
> package is written in the Lower CASE tools that you want to use, but Upper CASE tool not the one you want to use. Upper and Lower CASE tools pass information between them. Rating Upper CASE tool = 8
>
> package is written in the Lower CASE tools that you want to use, but Upper CASE tool not the one you want to use. Upper

Future Requirements Worksheet

Future Requirement	Company Need	Package A Rating	Package A Weighted Rating	Package B Rating	Package B Weighted Rating
Upper CASE Tool - Rational Rose	1	8	8	6	6
Lower CASE Tool - Rational Rose	1	10	10	10	10
Programming Language - Java C++	5	0	0	0	0
RDBMS - Oracle	10	8	80	8	80
Operating System - UNIX	5	10	50	10	50
Hardware - HP 6000 RS 6000	5	10	50	8	40
Middleware	1	0	0	0	0
Object Oriented	5	10	50	10	50
Level of Configurability	10	0	0	0	0
Future Prediction	10	8	80	5	50
Response Time	10	10	100	10	100
TOTAL	63		428		340, 236
Highest Maximum Value Score Future Requirements	10		630		630, 420
Percentage Fit - Future Requirements			68%		54%

Figure 6-8. Future Requirements Worksheet

and Lower CASE tool that does not pass information between them. Rating Upper CASE tool = 0

package is written in a combination of Upper and Lower CASE tools that pass information between them are not the CASE tools you would like to use. Rating for Upper and Lower CASE tools = 6

package is written in a combination of Upper and Lower CASE tools that are not connected. Rating for Upper and Lower CASE tools = 3

package does not use an Upper or Lower CASE tool. Rating for Upper and Lower CASE tools = 0

The rating should be entered into the Package Rating column of the Future Requirements Summary Worksheet (Figure 6-8).

Programming language—The implementability of the package depends on the package's code, in the structured format that is easy to understand. It would be nice to ask the vendor in the RFP if their code is structured and easy to understand. I have not found a vendor who thinks that their code is unstructured and hard to understand. Therefore, there is no benefit from asking the question. If your preferred programming language is used, rate the package a 10. If package does not use your preferred programming language, then rate packages based on your aversion to the operating system (0 for your most averse). Enter the ratings into its programming language Rating column of the Future Requirements Summary Worksheet (Figure 6-8).

RDBMS—Use the schedule below to determine the rating for the RDBMS:

package is written in a relational database that you would like to use. Rating = 10

package is not written in the relational database that you want to use but it is one of the major relational databases. Rating = 6

package is not written in the relational database that you want to use and is not one of the major relational databases. Rating = 3

package is not written in a relational database. Rating = 0

The rating should be entered into the Package's Rating column of the Future Requirements Summary Worksheet (Figure 6-8).

Operating System—Depending on the package's hardware there may be a choice of operating systems. If you have a preference, and the package uses that operating system to rate the package a 10. If the package does not use your preferred operating system, then rate packages based on your aversion to the operating system from 0 to 10 (0 for your most averse). The rating should be entered into the Package Rating column of the Future Requirements Summary Worksheet (Figure 6-8).

Hardware—If you have a preference regarding hardware vendor, that preference becomes its rating. (Rate from 0 to 10, 10 being the best score possible.) If you have no preference, all packages should be given a five. If there is a package that runs on a hardware platform that you definitely do not want to use, immediately eliminate that package. The rating should be entered into the Package Rating column of the Future Requirements Summary Worksheet (Figure 6-8).

Object-Oriented (OO)—If the package is OO, then rate the package a 10; if it is not, rate the package a 0. The rating should be entered into the Package Rating column of the Future Requirements Summary Worksheet (Figure 6-8).

Level of Configurability—This cannot be determined from the response to the RFP; this will have to be analyzed by reviewing the package. Until you perform this analysis enter a 0 for Level of Configurability for all the packages in the Future Requirements Summary Worksheet (Figure 6-8).

Future Direction—Based on the vendor's vision and future direction statements in the RFP rate the fit between your future direction and the vendor's future direction. If the vendor's future direction matches yours then the rating is a 10. If the vendor is going in a completely different direction then the rating is zero. If it is somewhere in-between then rate it accordingly on the Future Requirements Summary Worksheet (Figure 6-8).

Response Time—Based on the vendor's guaranteed response time in the RFP, rate the vendor. If it is an acceptable response time then rate it a 10 if the response time is unacceptable rate it a 0. Enter the rating on the Future Requirements Summary Worksheet (Figure 6-8). If the response time is unacceptable eliminate the vendor from consideration.

Calculating Future Requirements Fit

Now that you have rated all the packages, you need to determine each of the packages' Future Requirements rating by comparing the packages weighted score to the maximum value the package can obtain. To calculate the maximum value, using the sample data shown in the Future Requirements Summary Worksheet (Figure 6-8), total the Company Ratings column, and enter the results on the Total line. Then in the next row, enter the highest rating possible. In this case that would be 10. Multiply the two numbers and place the result into the Maximum Value—Future Requirements line for each column Package Weighted Rating. For example, the total Company rating in Figure 6-8 is 63, and the maximum value a package can achieve for a Future Requirement is 10. When the two numbers are multiplied the result is 630, which is entered in Maximum Value—Future Requirements line for each of the packages.

$$\text{Maximum Value}^{FR} = \text{The sum of the Company Ratings} \times 10$$
$$= (1 + 1 + 5 + 10 + 5 + 5 + 1 + 5 + 10) + 10 + 10$$
$$= 63 \times 10$$
$$= 630$$

Enter the maximum value, in this case 630 into the row marked Maximum Value (Total Company Rating × 10) into each of the package's Weighted Percentage Fit columns.

To calculate each package's Weighted Average, you need to divide the Total Weighted Rating for that package by the Maximum Value—Future Requirements. Enter the result on the Percentage Fit Future Requirements. For example, the Future Requirement score for Package A is:

$$\text{Total Percentage Fit}^{PkgA} = \text{Total Weighted Fit}^{PkgA} / \text{Maximum Value}$$
$$= 428/630$$
$$= 68\%$$

Then enter the Future Requirements Percentage Fit for each package from the Future Requirements Worksheet (Figure 6-8) onto the R^2ISC Analysis Matrix (Figure 6-7). We will continue adding the packages Percentage Fit for the other R^2ISC criteria as we proceed through this chapter.

Implementability

The Implementability (I) portion of the RFP must be carefully analyzed. You have already rated the implementability components in Implementability Worksheet Figure 4-1, p. 37. Implementability is made up of the following components:

- Vendor responsiveness
- Vendor background
- Software maturity
- Technology maturity
- Modifications
- Third party
- Implementation assistance
- Quality
- Documentation
- Training

Once the four finalists are selected, their Implementability will be further evaluated, but at this time the pieces are analyzed as follows:

1. Vendor Responsiveness

Because we did not ask the vendors to rate themselves on responsiveness because we can not rely on their responses, we will rate each vendor a 5. Then transfer the vendor responsiveness rating to the Implementability Worksheet (Figure 6-9).

2. Vendor Background

Use a Vendor Background Matrix (Figure 6-10) to help determine the vendor's background score. As you rate the vendor back-

Implementability Worksheet					
Requirement	Company Need	Package A Rating	Package A Weighted Rating	Package B Rating	Package B Weighted Rating
1. Vendor Responsiveness	10	5	50	5	50
2. Vendor Background	7	7	49	7	49
3. Software Maturity	3	8	24	8	24
4. Technology Maturity	7	7	49	7	49
5. Modifications	10	6	60	7	70
6. Third Party	10	10	100	10	100
7. Implementation Assistance	10	8	80	8	80
8. Quality	7	8	56	6	42
9. Documentation	7	8	56	2	14
10. Training	7	6	42	3	21
Total	78		566		499
Maximum Package Weighted Rating	10		780		780
Vendor Implementability Rating			73%		64%

Figure 6-9. Implementability Worksheet

Vendor Background Matrix				
Background		Vendor A	Vendor B	Vendor C
Number of Years in Business		8		
Size of Organization		4		
Type of Customers		10		
Total		22		
Vendor Background Rating (Total Divided by 3)		7		

Figure 6-10. Vendor Background Matrix

ground components enter them onto the Vendor Background Matrix. Rate each of the components of the vendor background as follows:

- Number of years in business. Rate the packages as follows:

  ten or more years = 10

  five to ten years = 8

  three to five years = 5

  one to three years = 2

  less than a year = 0

- Size of organization—number of employees including number of consultants available to assist with the implementation. Rate the packages as follows:

  more than 2,500 employees = 10

  1,000 to 2,499 employees = 8

  500 to 999 employees = 6

  100 to 499 employees = 4

  50 to 99 employees = 2

  under 49 employees = 0

- Type of customers. Rate the packages as follows:

  same type and size customers = 10

  same type and different size customers = 8

  different type and same size customers = 6

  different type and different size customers = 2

Once you have completed rating the vendor background components and they are all entered onto the Vendor Background Matrix sum all five components and place the packages total on the Total line. Determine the Vendor Background rating by calculating the average Vendor Background score. In other words divide the total by three (round to nearest whole number). Then enter the average onto the Vendor Background Rating line. Then transfer the Vendor Background rating to the Implementability Worksheet (Figure 6-9).

3. Software Maturity

Use a Software Maturity Matrix (Figure 6-11) to help determine the vendor's Software Maturity score. As you rate the software maturity components enter them onto the Software Maturity Matrix. Rate each of the components of the software maturity as follows:

- Year the original package was released. Rate the packages as follows:

  five or more years = 10

  three to five years = 7

  one to three years = 5

  less than a year = 1

- Year the package was released on platform the enterprise will be using. Rate the packages as follows:

  more than two years = 10

  one to two years = 6

  less than a year = 3

- Year current version was released. Rate the packages as follows:

  two years = 10

Software Maturity Matrix			
Software	Vendor A	Vendor B	Vendor C
Year the original package was released.	5	10	5
Year the package was released on platform.	10	10	6
Year current version was released.	10	10	8
Number of installations.	10	6	6
Number of installations for the modules.	6	6	3
Total	41	42	28
Software Maturity Rating (Total Divided by 5)	8	8	6

Figure 6-11. Software Maturity Matrix

one to two years = 8

less than a year = 3

- Number of installations for package. Rate the packages as follows:

  more than 50 = 10

  between 30 and 50 =8

  between 20 and 30 = 6

  between 10 and 20 =3

  10 or less = 0

- Number of installations for each of the modules the enterprise will be implementing. Rate the packages as follows:

  more than 50 = 10

  between 30 and 50 =8

  between 20 and 30 = 6

  between 10 and 20 =3

  10 or less = 0

Once you have completed rating the software maturity components and they are all entered onto the Software Maturity Matrix, add all five components and place the package's total on the Total line. Determine the Software Maturity rating by calculating the average Software Maturity score. In other words divide the total by five (round to nearest whole number). Then enter the average onto the Software Maturity Rating line. Then transfer the Software Maturity rating to the Implementability Worksheet (Figure 6-9).

4. Technology Maturity

New technology means a greater risk in having a successful implementation. The less mature the technology the package uses the higher the risk of problems during implementation. There is also high risk of problems associated with a technology that is new to your company. This is true even if you want to change technology, there is an inherent additional risk and it needs to be taken into consideration. Use the Technology Implementation Rating Table (Figure 6-12) to determine the technology implementation rating. For example, all the technology used by the package is over three years old and

Technology Implementation Rating Table		
Technology Maturity	Current Company Standard	New Technology to Company
3+ years	10	8
2–3 years	7	5
1–2 years	5	3
Less than a year	1	0

Figure 6-12. Technology Implementation Rating Table

it is a new technology, to the company using the Technology Implementation Rating Table the technology implementation rating is 8. The rating should be entered into the Implementability Summary Worksheet (Figure 6-9).

5. Modifications

Cost of modification is a good indication of the amount of modification needed to meet the enterprise's requirements. The more modification needed the greater the risk of problems occurring during the implementation. Therefore inversely rank the packages based on the cost of modifications. The Modification Rating Table (Figure 6-13) can be used to determine the package modifi-

Modification Rating Table	
Modification Cost as a Percentage of Package Cost	Modification Cost
0-No Modifications	10
1–10%	8
11–20%	7
21–30%	6
31–40%	5
41–50%	4
51–60%	3
61–79%	2
80% +	0

Figure 6-13. Modification Rating Table

cation rating. Calculate the cost of the modification as a percentage of the cost of the package. For example if the cost of modifications is $12,000 and the cost of the package is $100,000 then the percentage is 12 percent ($12,000/$100,000 = 12%). From the Modification Rating Table (Figure 6-13) we determine the rating to be 7. The rating should be entered into the Implementability Summary Worksheet (Figure 6-9).

6. Third Party

If you are not using a third party to implement the package then skip to the next item. If you are using a third party, rate them in the same manner in which you are rating the vendor in the following categories:

- Vendor responsiveness (when you perform reference checks in Chapter 8)
- Vendor background
- Quality
- Implementation assistance

The rating should be entered into the Implementability Summary Worksheet (Figure 6-9).

7. Implementation Assistance

If you did not require the vendor's assistance in implementing the package and you rated Implementation Assistance a zero and proceed to the next component (quality).

Implementation assistance is divided into two parts. The first part is the type of support the vendor will supply. The second part is the quality of personnel that the vendor has that will be available to support you. The vendors score is determined by rating the type of support the vendor will supply. Then you adjust the score based on the vendor's personnel. This is done by multiplying the type of support score by the adjustment factor you determine for the quality of its personnel.

To determine the quality of the vendors' personnel, review sample resume the vendors supply for the personnel that will be assigned to you to support you. The vendor personnel adjustment factor can be determined as follows:

- Very experienced with package and your industry. Adjustment factor = 100%
- Experienced with package and your industry. Adjustment factor = 80%
- Experienced with package but not with your industry. Adjustment factor = 60%
- Not experienced with package but experienced in your industry. Adjustment factor = 60%
- Not experienced with package and your industry. Adjustment factor = 0

For example, the vendor supplies the types of support we require and its personnel are experienced with the package and our industry. The vendor would receive an 8.

Vendor Support Rating = Type of Support Rating × Quality of Personnel Adjustment Factor

$$= 10 \times 80\%$$

$$= 8$$

The rating should be entered into the Implementability Summary Worksheet (Figure 6-9).

8. Quality

Review each vendor's quality program information.

- If the vendor is ISO 9000 certified or certified against another independent standard Rating = 10.
- If it is a quality program and is not independently certified then analyze the quality program information supplied in the response to the RFP. The items that should be considered are:
- Quality program
- Quality plan
- Quality statistics used
- Quality manuals

Documentation Worksheet			
Documentation	Vendor A	Vendor B	Vendor C
Quality of the Manuals	8		
Availability of all Required Manuals	10		
Availability of Manuals Online	0		
Existence of an Index within Manuals	10		
TOTAL	28		
Documentation Rating (Total Divided by 4)	7		

Figure 6-14. Documentation Worksheet

Each should be rated from one to nine, based on the overall quality of the items listed, above nine being the highest score possible. The rating should be entered into the Implementability Summary Worksheet (Figure 6-9).

9. Documentation

Review the documentation information and the sample documentation provided by the vendor with the response to the RFP. Use the Documentation Worksheet (Figure 6-14) to enter the rating you determine using the criteria below:

■ Quality of the manuals. Rate the packages as follows:

excellent quality = 10

good quality = 8

fair quality = 4

poor quality = 0

■ Availability of all required manuals. Rate the packages as follows:

all = 10

some manuals available rate based on percentage of manuals available (i.e., 80% of manuals available rate an 8.

none = 0

- Availability of manuals online. Rate the packages as follows:

    yes = 10

    no = 0

- Existence of an index within manuals. Rate the packages as follows:

    yes = 10

    no = 0

After you rated each of the documentation components and placed it in the Documentation Worksheet (Figure 6-14) total each of the vendor's scores and place the Total row. Then divide the total by 4, which is the number of items being rated, and place the result in the Documentation Rating row. The rating should be entered into the Implementability Summary Worksheet (Figure 6-9).

10. Training

Review the training information provided in the response to the RFP. Use the Training Worksheet (Figure 6-15) to enter the ratings

Training Worksheet				
Training	Need	Vendor A	Vendor B	Vendor C
Completeness of Training Plan	10	10		
Courses Meet Enterprise's Education Need	10	8		
Size of Classes	10	10		
Vendor Will Customize Courses for Enterprise	10	0		
Course Is Hands-On	10	10		
Computer-Based Training (CBT) Available	10	10		
Audio Training Courses Available	0	-		
Video Courses Available	0	-		
Workbooks Available	10	10		
TOTAL	**70**	**58**		
Maximum Rating		70	70	70
Training Rating		**83**		

Figure 6-15. Training Worksheet

you determine. If there are training items that you do not need, do not rate that item. Using the criteria below to determine the rating of the training information and enter it onto the Training Worksheet:

- Completeness and quality of training plan. Rate the packages as follows:

  plan complete = 10

  depending on completeness of plan rate between nine and one

  no training plan = 0

- Courses meet enterprise's educational need. Rate the packages as follows:

  courses meet need = 10

  depending on how close to courses come meeting your needs Rate between nine and one

  no courses offered = 0

- Size of classes. Rate the packages as follows:

  10 or less students = 10

  11 to 15 students = 8

  16 to 20 students = 3

  21 to 25 students = 1

  more than 25 students = 0

- Vendor will customize courses for enterprise. Rate the packages as follows:

  yes = 10

  no = 0

- Courses are offered on a regular basis. Rate the packages as follows:

  yes = 10

  no = 0

- Course's schedule meets enterprise's time table. Rate the packages as follows:

  yes = 10

  no = 0

- Course is hands on. Rate the packages as follows:

  yes =10

  no and there is an advantage to having it hands on = 0

  no and there is no advantage to having it hands on = 10

- Computer-based training (CBT) available. Rate the packages as follows:

  yes =10

  no = 0

- Audio training courses available. Rate the packages as follows:

  yes =10

  no = 0

- Video courses available. Rate the packages as follows:

  yes =10

  no = 0

- Workbooks available. Rate the packages as follows:

  yes =10

  no = 0

After you rated each of the training items and placed it in the Training Worksheet (Figure 6-15), total each of the vendor's scores and place in the Total row. For each training item that you rated place a 10 in the Need column. Then total the Need column and place the results in the Total row and in the Maximum Rating row for each of the vendors. Then divide each vendor's Total by the total by the maximum rating and place the result in the Training Rating row.

For example, if we do not care about audio training courses and video courses we do not place a 10 in the Need column. Then total the seven 10 items in the column and place the results, 70, in the Total row. Then place 70 in the Maximum Rating row for Vendor A, Vendor B, and Vendor C. Total Vendor A's score

$$10 + 8 + 10 + 0 + 10 + 10 + 10 = 58$$

Then divide each Vendor A's Total by the total maximum rating

$$58/70 = 83\%$$

place the result in the Training Rating row.

The rating should be entered into the Implementability Summary Worksheet (Figure 6-9).

Calculating Implementability Fit

Now that you have rated all the packages you need to determine the packages' Implementability rating by comparing the packages' weighted score to the maximum value the packages can obtain. To calculate the Maximum Value, using the sample data shown in the Implementability Summary Worksheet (Figure 6-9), total the Company Ratings column and enter the results on the Total. Then in the next row, enter the highest rating possible. In this case that would be 10. Multiply the two numbers and place the result into the Maximum Value—Implementability line for each column Package Weighted Rating. For example, the total Company rating in Figure 6-9 is 78, and the maximum value a package can achieve for a Implementability is 10. When the two numbers are multiplied the result is 780, which is entered in Maximum Value Implementability line for each of the packages.

$$\text{Maximum Value}^1 = \text{The sum of the Company Ratings} \times 10$$
$$= (10 + 7 + 3 + 7 + 10 + 10 + 10 + 7 + 7 + 7)$$
$$= 78 \times 10$$
$$= 780$$

Enter the maximum value, in this case 780 into the row marked Maximum Value (Total Company Rating × 10) into each of the package's Weighted Percentage Fit columns.

To calculate each package's Weighted Average, you need to divide the Total Weighted Rating for that package by the Maximum Value-Implementability. Enter the result on the Percentage Fit Implementability. For example, the Implementability score for

Package A is:

$$\text{Total Percentage Fit}^{PkgA} = \text{Total Weighted Fit}^{PkgA} / \text{Maximum Value}$$
$$= 566/780$$
$$= 73\%$$

Then enter the Implementability Percentage Fit for each package from the Implementability Worksheet (Figure 6-9) onto the R^2ISC Analysis Matrix (Figure 6-7). We will continue adding the package's Percentage Fit for the other R^2ISC criteria as we proceed through this chapter.

Supportability

To achieve the overall supportability, each aspect of the package must be analyzed. Because some of the same criteria that impacts the implementability also impact the supportability. For these criteria you will use the rating that you developed in the implementability section.

1. Vendor Responsiveness

As in the implementability section, because we did not ask the vendors to rate themselves on responsiveness because we can not rely on their responses, we will rate each vendor a five. Then transfer the Vendor Responsiveness rating to the Supportability (S) Summary Worksheet (Figure 6-16).

2. Quality

Quality rating is the analysis you performed for implementability. Use the rating you developed for the Implementability rating on Figure 6-9 page 111. The rating should be entered into the Supportability Summary Worksheet (Figure 6-16).

3. Development Methodology

If this is the type of package that will not be modified then rate this a zero and proceed to the next component. If this is the type of

Supportability Summary Worksheet					
	Company Need	Package A Rating	Package A Weighted Rating	Package B Rating	Package B Weighted Rating
1. Vendor Responsiveness	10	5	50	9	90
2. Quality	10	8	80	9	90
3. Development Methodology	10	10	100	0	0
4. Modifications	7	6	42	9	63
5. Technology	7	8	56	9	63
6. Financial Stability	10	8	80	8	80
7. Warranty	7	9	63	9	63
8. Users Groups	7	10	70	0	0
9. Support Functions	10	7	70	7	70
TOTAL	78		611	85	519
Maximum Value Supportability	10		780		780
Weighted Average-Supportability			78%		67%

Figure 6-16. Supportability Summary Worksheet

package that you will be modifying, review the vendor's response to the development methodology in the Future Requirements section of the RFP. Rate the development methodology as follows:

Uses a Upper and Lower CASE tool = 10

Uses a Lower CASE tool = 8

Uses a third-generation programming language = 3

4. Modifications

This is the analysis you performed for implementability. Use the rating you developed for Supportability rating on Figure 6-9. The rating should be entered into the Supportability Summary Worksheet (Figure 6-16).

5. Technology

New technology will be harder for the enterprise to support. Therefore, if you are using new technology it will be harder to support the package than using your existing technology. (This is not to say that you should not use new technology but just bear in mind that it adds complexity. The technology rating for supportability can be one of the following:

- same technology as your current standard = 10
- technology that you are familiar with and are comfortable using = 8
- new technology with which you are not familiar = 0

The rating should be entered into the Supportability Summary Worksheet (Figure 6-16).

6. Financial Stability

Review each vendor's financial reports. If you are not comfortable reviewing a financial report you may want to have your accountant or purchasing department review the vendor's financial statement. The items that should be considered for Supportability are:

- Profitability—Look to see that the vendor is profitable and has been increasing its profits over the last three years. If a vendor is losing money consider eliminating that vendor. If you do not eliminate the vendor, rate the vendor a zero for financial stability. You can compare the profitability both on total dollars and in percentage of sales and growth trends in sales. Look to see that the vendor has been increasing its sales over the last three years. You should look for constant growth in sales.
- Chairman's message—Look to see if the chairman has a positive outlook for the future or if he sees problems in the future. The message should be upbeat. If there are problems identified in the chairman's message consider its implications on the financial health of the company.
- Notes—Review the notes in the annual report to see if there are any problems that the vendor is having or items that can have a material impact on its future
- Litigation—Review the annual report to see if there is any litigation mentioned. The litigation could be from dissatisfied

customers. If the dissatisfied customers have filed a class action suit against the vendor, investigate it thoroughly to see if the same problem could happen to you and then make decisions and ratings based on the investigation. If there are other types of litigation, again investigate the impact it may have on you and the financial stability of the vendor.

■ Current ratios—Measures a company's ability to meet short term debt (one year). It is calculated by dividing the current assets by current debt. Many professionals like companies to have a ratio of approximately two.

By comparing the financial report of the different vendors you should be able to determine if any of the vendors are having a problem and their relative financial strength. If you feel uncomfortable rating the vendors and you do not have an accounting department or purchasing department that can assist you, you can also go to Dunn & Bradstreet (D&B) for a financial rating. They offer a service that will rate a supplier. Their Internet address for this service is http://www.dnb.com1/purchase/pqualify.htm#ser.

Needless to say a vendor in bankruptcy should receive a zero.

Based on your analysis or that of D&B rate each vendor's financial stability from zero to 10 with 10 being excellent financial strength and zero meaning the company is in or heading for bankruptcy. The rating should be entered into the Supportability Summary Worksheet (Figure 6-16).

7. Warranty

Review each vendor's warranty because it will affect the support the vendor will give you on the package. The Supportability rating is based on two components: what is being covered and the length of the coverage. Use the Warranty Rating Matrix (Figure 6-17) to determine the package's warranty rating. The rating should be entered onto the Supportability Summary Worksheet (Figure 6-16).

8. Users Groups

Review each of the vendors' responses to the Users Groups. Rate them as follows:

Vendor has a national users group and a local users group, which is within 60 miles of your location = 10

Warranty Rating Matrix				
Coverage	2-Year Warranty	1-Year Warranty	6-Month Warranty	90-Day Warranty
All Items Purchased	10	8	5	2
Package and Hardware	8	6	3	1
Package Other Software	8	6	3	1
Package Only	6	4	1	0

Figure 6-17. Warranty Rating Matrix

Vendor has a national users group and a local users group, which is between 60 and 180 miles of your location = 6

Vendor has a national users group and a no local users group or one that is more than 181 miles of your location = 3

Vendor has no users groups = 0

9. Support Functions

Review each vendor's support functions to determine if they will be able to support you in the future. The items that should be considered for the Supportability are:

- Number of personnel involved in product support. Rate the packages as follows:

  30 or more = 2.5

  20 to 30 = 2

  10 to 20 = 1.5

  5 to 10 = 1

  1 to 4 = .5

  no full time resource dedicated to support = 0

- Hours of hot line. Rate the packages as follows:

  hours of coverage are the same or more than your hours of operation = 2.5

  there is one hour that you are not covered by the hot line = 1.5

  there are two hours that you are not covered by the hot line = 1 there are three or more hours that you are not covered by the hot line = 0

■ Dial-in capability of vendor. Rate the packages as follows:

yes =2.5

no = 0

■ Type of support offered. Rate the packages as follows:

offers all the types of support you require = 2.5

offers some of the support you require rate between 2.5 and 0.5 based on the percentage of support offered

offers none of the support you require = 0

The vendors should be rated by summing the four components and then entered onto the Supportability Summary Worksheet (Figure 6-16).

Calculating Supportability Fit

Now that you have rated all the packages' Supportability criteria you need to determine each of the packages' Supportability ratings by comparing the packages' weighted score to the maximum value each package can obtain. To calculate the Maximum Value, using the sample data shown in the Supportability Summary Worksheet (Figure 6-16), total the Company Ratings column and enter the results on the Total. Then in the next row, enter the highest rating possible. In this case that would be 10. Multiply the two numbers and place the result into the Maximum Value-Supportability line for each column Package Weighted Rating. For example, the total Company rating in Figure 6-16 is 78, and the maximum value a package can achieve for a Future Requirement is 10. When the two numbers are multiplied the result is 780, which is entered in the Maximum Value Supportability line for each of the packages.

$$\text{Maximum Value}^S = \text{The sum of the Company Ratings} \times 10$$
$$= (10 + 10 + 10 + 7 + 7 + 10$$
$$+ 7 + 7 + 10)$$
$$= 78 \times 10$$
$$= 780$$

Enter the maximum value, in this case 780, into the row marked Maximum Value into each of the package's Weighted Percentage Fit columns.

To calculate each package's Weighted Average, you need to divide the Total Weighted Rating for that package by the Maximum Value-Supportability. Enter the result on the Percentage Fit Supportability. For example, the Supportability score for Package A is:

$$\text{Total Percentage Fit}^{PkgA} = \text{Total Weighted Fit}^{Pkg\ A} / \text{Maximum Value}$$

$$= 611/780$$

$$= 78\%$$

Then enter the Supportability Percentage Fit for each package from the Supportability Worksheet (Figure 6-16) onto the R^2ISC Analysis Matrix (Figure 6-7). We will continue adding the package's Percentage Fit for the other R^2ISC criteria as we proceed through this chapter.

Cost

The last of the five R^2ISC criteria to be analyzed is the cost. Many companies have their own method of rating capital investments. If your company has its own method then by all means use it to develop your rating for the packages. If not use the information below to help with analysis.

To determine the package's R^2ISC costs of cost criteria rating you need to calculate the total cost of the software for three years and then compare it to your budget. The cost of software is divided into three major components, which need to be analyzed. They are:

- one-time cost
- annual operating expenses
- support services costs

The analysis is performed by reviewing the vendors' response to the RFP. More specifically you will be analyzing the following worksheets from the RFP:

Software Module Cost Worksheet (Figure 5-10, p. 85)

Hardware Cost Worksheet (Figure 5-11, p. 86)

Documentation Cost Worksheet (Figure 5-12, p. 87)

Training Cost Worksheet (Figure 5-13, p. 88)

Additional Products Cost Worksheet (Figure 5-14, p. 89)

Additional Support Services Cost Worksheet (Figure 5-15, p. 90)

Most of these worksheets have portions that will be used for each of the three major cost components. If a vendor did not include a cost for a component that the other vendors included, check with the vendor to determine if it is required but included in another part of the quote for another item, required but omitted, or not required. If it is required and omitted have the vendor update their RFP to include the cost.

One-Time Costs

The one-time costs, which are the costs of purchasing the software and its implementation, are broken down into the following:

- Software
- Modifications
- Implementation
- Hardware
- Training
- Installation
- Documentation
- Additional products

Software, Modifications, and Implementation Cost—To determine the cost of each of the vendor's software you will review their Software Module Cost Worksheet (Figure 5-10, p. 85) that was returned as part of the response to the RFP (Figure 6-18) Software Modules Cost

Software Modules Cost Worksheet

Software Modules	Software List Price	Software Discounted Price	Modifications Must Have	Modifications All	Annual Maintenance Base Package	Annual Maintenance Must Have Modifications	Annual Maintenance All Modifications
Accounts Payable	12,500	10,000	0	1,250	1,500	0	200
Accounts Receivable	12,500	10,000	0	0	1,500	0	0
General Ledger	65,000	50,000	0	0	7,500	0	0
Order Management	100,000	75,000	25,000	76,250	11,500	3,700	11,500
Inventory	70,000	50,000	0	4,500	8,000	0	600
Total	260,000	195,000	25,500	82,000	30,000	3,700	12,300
Implementation	75,000	60,000					
Grand Total Software	335,000	255,000			30,000	3,700	12,300

Figure 6-18. Software Modules Cost Worksheet—Package A

Worksheet-Package A, is vendor A's response. Take the totals of Software Discounted Price, Modifications Must Have, and Modifications All, and enter them onto the Cost Worksheet (Figure 6-19). For example, the total for Package A's Software Discounted Price is $195,500. Then take the discounted implementation cost from the Software Modules Cost Worksheet and enter it onto the Cost Worksheet. For example, the total for Package A's Discounted implementation is $50,000 and is placed in the Package A column and the Implementation Discount Price row.

Hardware, Installation, and Site Preparation Cost—To determine the cost of each of the vendor's Hardware, Installation, and Site Preparation Cost you will review their Hardware Cost Worksheet (Figure 5-11, p. 86) that was returned as part of the response to the RFP. Figure 6-20, Hardware Cost Worksheet-Package A, is vendor A's response. Take the total for Total Discounted Price and enter it onto the Cost Summary Worksheet (Figure 6-19). For example, the total for Package A's Hardware Discounted Price is $130,000. Then take the discounted installation cost from the Hardware Cost Worksheet and enter it onto the Cost Worksheet. The total for Package A's Total Discounted Price Installation is $0 and is placed in the Package A column and the Installation Discount Price row. Also take the discounted site preparation cost from the Hardware Cost Worksheet and enter it onto the Cost Worksheet.

For example, vendor B does not sell hardware, therefore it did not include the price in the RFP. After contacting Vendor B he went to a third party and received a price of $55, 000 for the hardware, 2,500 for installation, and $1,000 for site preparation. These cost were added to Vender B's on-time cost.

Training Cost—To determine the cost for training you review the Training Cost Worksheet (Figure 5-13, p. 88) that was returned as part of the response to the RFP. Figure 6-21 is the Training Cost Worksheet-Package A, vendor A's response. Take the totals cost for training from the Training Cost Worksheet and place it on the Training row for Vendor A on the Cost Worksheet (Figure 6-19).

For example, the total for Package A's training on the Training Cost Worksheet (Figure 6-19) is $46,500. This is then placed on the Cost Worksheet (Figure 6-19).

Cost Worksheet

	Cost Package A	Cost Package B	Cost Package C	Cost Package D
One-Time Cost				
Software	195,500	250,000	190,000	80,000
Modifications All	82,000	166,000	99,000	295,000
Modifications Must Have Only	25,500	86,500	42,000	120,000
Implementation	50,000	3,000	15,000	3,000
Hardware	130,000	155,000	145,000	165,000
Installation	0	2,500	12,000	
Site preparation	0	1,000	3,500	
Training	46,500	120,000	35,000	10,000
Documentation	0	2,000	800	1,200
Additional products	0		0	15,000
TOTAL – One-Time Cost	**447,500**	**620,000**	**443,300**	**394,200**
Budget	450,000	450,000	450,000	450,000
Variance from Budget	2,500	–170,000	6,700	55,800
Percentage Variance from Budget	1%	–38%	1%	12%
Rating One-Time Cost	**6**	**0**	**6**	**10**

Figure 6-19. Cost Worksheet

Cost Worksheet

	Cost Package A	Cost Package B	Cost Package C	Cost Package D
ANNUAL OPERATING EXPENSES				
Annual Maintenance Base Package	30,000	37,500	31,000	16,000
Annual Maintenance Must Have Modifications	3,700	7,000	2,400	26,000
Maintenance All Modifications	12,300	24,900	14,850	60,000
Maintenance Hardware	39,000	32,000	15,000	33,000
Maintenance Other Products	—	—	—	3,000
Total-Ongoing Cost Annual Operating Expense	**72,700**	**76,500**	**48,400**	**78,000**
Budget	70,000	70,000	70,000	70,000
Variance from Budget	−2,700	−6,500	21,600	−8,000
Percentage Variance from Budget	−4%	−9%	31%	−11%
Rating–Annual Operating Expenses	**5**	**4**	**10**	**2**
Support Services Cost				
Consulting	150/hr	200/hr	175/hr	200/hr
Programming	100/hr	125/hr	100/hr	125/hr
Telephone Support	Part of annual maintenance or 50 per call	125/hr	Part of annual Maintenance or 35 per call	100/hr

Figure 6-19. Cost Worksheet *(continued)*

Hardware Cost Worksheet—Package A

	Description	Quantity	List Price	Discounted Price	Total Discounted Price	Yearly Maintenance (unit price)	Total Maintenance
CPU							
Model	HP Model AA	1	110,000	55,000	55,000	16,500	16,500
Memory	1 gig	1					
Storage							
Size	HP Model BB 45 gig	1	10,000	5,000	5,000	1,500	1,500
Back-Up Device							
Type	N/A	0					
Terminals							
Model	HP vector PC Model BBB	25	4,000	2,000	50,000	600	15,000

Figure 6-20. Hardware Cost Worksheet—Package A

Hardware Cost Worksheet—Package A

	Description	Quantity	List Price	Discounted Price	Total Discounted Price	Yearly Maintenance (unit price)	Total Maintenance
Printers							
Model 1	HP Laser Color Jet C 20000si	4	10,000	40,000	20,000	1,500	6,000
Model 2		0					
System Software	HP-VY	1					
Uninterrupted Power Supply	Not being supplied will quote if required	0					
Shipping	Ground	–					
Total	–	–	–	–	**$130,000**	–	**39,000**
Installation	Included in above	0	0	0	0		
Site Preparation	No work required	1	0	0	0		
Grand Total	–	–	–	–	**$130,000**	–	**39,000**

Figure 6-20. Hardware Cost Worksheet–Package A *(continued)*

Training Cost Worksheet—Package A

Training Course	List Price/Student	Discount Price/Student	List Price for Private Class	Discount Price for Private Class	Number of Students for Private Class	Recommended Number of Students	Cost
Accounts Payable User Train-the-trainer	1,000	750	4,000	3,000	6	1	750
Accounts Payable User Training	500	375	2,000	1,500	12	0	0
General Accounting User Train-the-Trainer	1,000	750	4,000	3,000	6	2	1,500
Order Management User Training	500	375	2,000	1,500	12	0	0
System Overview	125	75	1,000	750	25	50	200
Using Report Writer User Training	500	375	2,000	1,500	12	0	0
Using Report Writer Train-the-Trainer	1,000	750	4,000	3,000	6	2	1,500
Systems Administrator	500	375	2,000	1,500	12	3	1,125
Security	500	375	2,000	1,500	12	2	250
Grand Total							46,500

Figure 6-21. Training Cost Worksheet—Package A

Note the Vendor B training cost on the Cost Worksheet (Figure 6-19) is $120,000, which is more than twice that of the other vendors. This is because Vendor B does not offer Train-the-trainer courses. Therefore all the training most be done by the vendor.

Documentation Cost—To determine the cost of each piece of documentation you will review their Documentation Cost Worksheet (Figure 5-12, p. 87) that was returned as part of the response to the RFP. Figure 6-22, the Documentation Cost Worksheet—Package A, is vendor A's response. Take the totals from Documentation Cost and enter them onto the Cost Worksheet (Figure 6-19). For example, the total for Package A's Documentation Cost is $0 because the vendor gives one or two copies of each manual with the software and allows copying of the manuals. If the vendor is allowing you to copy the manuals make sure it says so in the written contract.

If the vendor does not allow you to copy the manuals then make sure that you include the price of enough manuals. This can be done by comparing all the vendors' responses for the number of manuals they feel you will require.

Additional Products Cost—If the vendor requires additional products in order to efficiently run their package they should have listed it on the Additional Products Cost Worksheet (Figure 5-14, p. 89) that was returned as part of the response to the RFP. Review the completed worksheet to see if the vendor had required or suggested any additional products. If there are suggested products that are not required to run the package, determine if the other vendors included an equivalent functionality supplied by the product in their response. If the other vendors require the additional product and did not include the cost, then add the cost to the vendor's cost. The vendor may suggest a product that you already are using and for which you can use your current license for this package.

Figure 6-23, the Additional Products Cost Worksheet-Package A, is vendor A's response. Notice that the vendor gives you a choice of two databases, Wizard and Wolf. They recommend Wizard but since we already have a license for Wizard we can use it for the package without incurring any additional cost. We therefore enter a zero cost on the Additional Products line on the Cost Worksheet (Figure 6-19).

Documentation Cost Worksheet—Package A

Manual	May Be Reproduced at No Charge	Quantity Supplied at No Charge	Unit Cost	Discounted Cost	Recommended Additional Quantity	Cost
Implementation Accounts Payable	Yes	1	50	25	0	0
Accounts Payable User Manual	Yes	2	50	25	0	0
Implementation General Accounting	Yes	1	50	25	0	0
Order Management User Manual	Yes	2	50	25	0	0
Report Writer User Manual	Yes	2	50	25	0	0
Systems Administrator Manual	Yes	1	50	25	0	0
Security Manual		1	50	25	0	0
Grand Total						0

Figure 6-22. Documentation Cost Worksheet - Package A

Additional Products Cost Worksheet—Package A

Product	Description	Required/ Suggested	List Price	Discounted Price	Quantity	Total Cost	Yearly Maintenance
Wizard DB	RDBMS	Require either	45,000	30,000	1	30,000	6,000
Wolf DB	RDBMS	RDBMS-suggest Wizard	35,000	30,000	1	30,000	4,500
Grand Total Software						30,000	6,000

Figure 6-23. Additional Products Cost Worksheet—Package A

Rating One-Time Cost—Total each vendor's one-time costs and enter them on the TOTAL-One-time Cost excluding the Modifications All row on the Cost Worksheet. On the next row enter your budget for the one-time cost (do not let the vendors know your budget amount because they will try to make their quote come close to that number even if it could be much lower). Then subtract each vendor's total one-time cost from your budget and place the results on the Variance from Budget row. Then calculate the percentage the variance is from budget. This is done by dividing the Variance from Budget by the budget and place the results in the Percentage Variance from Budget Row. Based on the percentage variance determine the rating. If the variance is positive (cost is less than your budget) give the largest positive variance a rating of 10. Then rate all the other vendors who also have positive variance between 5 and 10 based on their percentage difference from the highest percentage variance. For those vendors who have a negative variance (cost is more than your budget) assign them a rating between zero and five based on how far they are from the budget. The larger the negative variance the lower the score.

Annual Operating Expenses

The annual operating expenses is the yearly cost of maintaining the software and its associated components. They are broken down into the following categories:

Annual Maintenance Base Package

Annual Maintenance Must Have Modifications

Maintenance All Modifications

Maintenance Hardware

Maintenance Additional Products

Annual Maintenance Base Package and Modifications Cost

To determine the annual cost of each of the maintaining vendor's software we will review their Software Module Cost Worksheet (Figure 5-10, p. 85) that was returned as part of the response to the RFP. Figure 6-18, Software Modules Cost Worksheet-Package A, is vendor A's response. Take the totals for Annual Maintenance Base Package, Annual Maintenance Must Have Modifications,

Modifications Must Have, and Annual Maintenance All Modifications and enter them onto the annual operating expense section of the Cost Worksheet (Figure 6-19).

For example, the total for Package A's Annual Maintenance cost for the Base Package cost is $30,000. Then take the Annual Maintenance cost for the Must Have modifications of $3,700 from the Software Modules Cost Worksheet and enter it onto the Cost Worksheet. Finally take the Annual Maintenance cost for all the modifications of $12,300 and place it in the Package A column and Maintenance All Modifications row.

Maintenance Hardware—To determine the annual hardware maintenance cost review the Hardware Cost Worksheet (Figure 5-11, p. 86) that was returned as part of the response to the RFP. Figure 6-20, Hardware Cost Worksheet—Package A, is vendor A's response. Take the total for Annual Maintenance and enter it onto the Cost Worksheet (Figure 6-19).

For example, take the total for Package A's Hardware Maintenance Cost of $39,000 on the Hardware Cost Worksheet and enter it onto the annual operating expense section of the Cost Worksheet (Figure 6-19).

Remember Vendor B who did not have a cost for the hardware when they submitted their response to the RFP. When we called to get the price for the hardware we also had to get the price for the manual maintenance of the hardware and enter it onto Vender B's Annual operating cost.

Maintenance of Additional Products

If you determined that you need the additional products that are listed in the Additional Products Cost Worksheet (Figure 5-14, p. 89) that you reviewed as part of the one-time cost, then you need to add their annual maintenance cost in this section. For those items that you need, take their total annual maintenance cost from the Additional Products Cost Worksheet and enter the total on the Maintenance Other Products line on the Cost Worksheet (Figure 6-19).

For example, on Figure 6-23, Additional Products Worksheet—Package A, in the one-time cost section we determined that we already have a license for Wizard that we can use for the package without incurring any additional cost. We therefore enter a zero cost on the Maintenance Additional Products line on the Cost Worksheet (Figure 6-19).

Rating Annual Operating Expense—Total each vendor's Annual Operating Expense and enter them on the TOTAL-Annual Operating Expense excluding the Maintenance All Modifications row on the Cost Worksheet. On the next row enter your budget for the Annual Operating Expense. Then subtract each vendor's total Annual Operating Expense cost from your budget and place the results on the Variance From Budget row. Then calculate the percentage the variance is from budget. This is done by dividing the Variance From Budget by the budget and place the results in the Percentage Variance From Budget row. Based on the percentage variance determine the rating. If the variance is positive (cost less than your budget) give the rates positive variance a rating of 10. Then rate all the other vendors who also have positive variance between five and 10 based on their percentage difference from the highest percentage variance. For those vendors who have a negative variance (cost more than the budget) assign them a rating between zero and five based on how far they are from the budget. The larger the negative variance the lower the score.

Support Services Cost

The support services are services that the vendor offers that you may want at some point in time to use. The following are a list of some of the standard support services that package vendors offer:

Consulting

Programming

Telephone support

To determine the support services cost review their Additional Support Services Cost Worksheet (Figure 5-15, p. 90) that was returned as part of the response to the RFP. Figure 6-24, Additional Support Services Cost Worksheet—Vendor A, is vendor A's response. Take each of the Support Services and enter the cost onto the Cost Worksheet (Figure 6-19).

Enter all vendor support services costs onto the Cost Worksheet

Additional Support Services Cost Worksheet—Vendor A			
	Standard Rate	Discounted Rate	Anticipated Need
Consulting	200/hr	150	120 hours
Programming	125/hr	100	0—part of modifications
Telephone Support	50 per call	50 per call	0—Part of annual maintenance
Other			

Figure 6-24. Additional Support Services Cost Worksheet—Vendor A

(Figure 6-19); save them until you start your negotiations with the winning vendor. At that point you can try to negotiate better rates.

Calculating Cost Fit

After you have completed the Cost Worksheet and entered the rating onto the Cost Summary Worksheet (Figure 6-25) you can determine each of the package's cost rating by comparing the package's weighted score to the maximum value the package can obtain. To calculate the Maximum Value, using the sample data shown in the Cost Summary Worksheet, total the Company Ratings column and enter the results on the Total line (Figure 6-25). Then, in the next row, enter the highest rating possible for a vendor for each line. In this case

Cost Summary Worksheet					
	Company Need	Package A Rating	Package A Weighted Rating	Package B Rating	Package B Weighted Rating
One-Time	7	2	14	0	0
Ongoing	10	5	50	4	40
	———	———	———	———	———
TOTAL	17	12	**64**	7	**40**
Maximum Value—Cost	10		**170**		**170**
Fit Cost	———		**38%**		**24%**

Figure 6-25. Cost Summary Worksheet

that would be 10. Multiply the two numbers and place the result into the Maximum Value—Cost line for each column Package Weighted Rating. For example, the total Company rating in Figure 6-25 is 17, and the maximum value a package can achieve for a Implementability is 10. When the two numbers are multiplied the result is 170, which is entered in the Maximum Value Cost line for each of the packages.

$$\text{Maximum Value}^{Cost} = \text{The sum of the Company Ratings} \times 10$$
$$= (7 + 10)$$
$$= 17 \times 10$$
$$= 170$$

Enter the maximum value, in this case 170 into the row marked Maximum Value (Total Company Rating × 10) into each of the package's Weighted Percentage Fit columns.

To calculate each package's Weighted Average, you need to divide the Total Weighted Rating for that package by the Maximum Value-Cost. Enter the result on the Percentage Fit Cost. For example, the Implementability score for Package A is:

$$\text{Total Percentage Fit}^{PkgA} = \text{Total Weighted Fit}^{PkgA}/\text{Maximum Value}$$
$$= 64/170$$
$$= 38\%$$

Then enter the Cost Percentage Fit for each package from the Cost Summary Worksheet (Figure 6-25) onto the R^2ISC Analysis Matrix (Figure 6-7).

Selecting the Finalists

After you have completed entering the rating onto the R^2ISC Analysis Matrix (Figure 6-7) you can determine which of the vendors will be your finalist. To make the determination we will determine which of the vendors has the best fit. To do this calculate the Weighted Percentage Fit for each package. This is done by multiplying Percentage Fit for each package by the Company Rating.

Weighted Percentage Fit
Current Requirements^{PkgA} = Company's Rating × Percentage Fit^{PkgA}

$$= 30 \times 87\%$$

$$= 26.1\%, \text{ which is rounded to } 26\%$$

Then total each package's Weighted Percentage Fit column and enter the results on the R^2ISC rating line. For example, for Package A it is:

R^2ISC Rating^{PkgA} = Total Weighted Percentage Fit^{PkgA}

$$= 26 + 16 + 14 + 13 + 6$$

$$= 74$$

The four packages with the highest R^2ISC Fit are your finalists. If the fifth-place vendor is close to the top four then include the fifth-place vendor as one of your finalists.

The next step is to narrow the finalists to the one winning vendor, this will be done in the next two chapters.

7

The Scripted Demonstration

In the previous chapter you narrowed the field of vendors to between two and four. In this chapter you will start the process of narrowing the field to one finalist.

So far in the process the vendors have been comparing the criteria to their packages. But the vendors may not always understand your requirements as they are stated in the RFP, so the information you received from vendors in the RFP may not be completely accurate. This is especially true if the requirements are unusual and go against normal procedures or regulations. For example, a utility company was looking for a fixed asset software package (this is a package that tracks a company's property and performs the depreciation that is needed for taxes and financial reporting). One of the requirements, mandated by the regulatory agency, was that annual depreciation be calculated in a manner that allowed an asset to be depreciated for more than its cost. This is contrary to all accounting and IRS rules. If you or I tried to report depreciation in this manner we could go to jail. The vendors could not believe the company really wanted this type of depreciation even though it was clearly stated in their RFP and was required by the state regulatory agency. In the vendor response to the RFP, they all rated the requirement a zero. During the demonstration the vendor was able to understand the requirement and a simple approach to meeting the requirement that took only an hour to develop. The rating for the requirement was changed from zero to three. Unfortunately, many times when the vendor "better understands" the requirement the ratings are reduced not upgraded. The cost of modifications therefore also usually increases.

The only way to really know if the package actually works as the vendor claims in their response to the RFP is to have them show you how the software meets each of your current requirements. This way you can determine for yourself how closely the package meets each of your current requirements. This is done through the use of a demonstration. Usually a salesperson will demonstrate their package pre-

147

sumably to show you how you can use the package in your business. The salesperson will try to control the demonstration by showing off what the package does best and glossing over its imperfections. If a question is asked about a feature or function that the software package does not have, the salesperson may say let's leave that for later, but unfortunately later may never come. (Or the salesperson might just pull the old "trust me.") The salesperson will point out the features that only his package has. Then they will try to convince you that you must have that feature in order to be successful. Even if there is only a minor need for it, the salesperson will point out why the feature is important to you. By the end of the demonstration if the salesperson did his job, you will be left with a warm feeling regarding the package and the demonstration. But you would not have been able to determine whether or not the package meets your requirements. If you have a demonstration with another vendor, that vendor will also show the portion of the package that highlights the features that their package performs that "no other package in the world can perform." When you ask about the features that the first package performed that their package doesn't, you are given convincing reasons why you do not need that feature. When looking back on the two demonstrations it is hard to compare them because both vendors showed different features. These vendor-controlled demonstrations are really nothing more than a glorified sales presentation. They have little value in helping you select a package. It is a contest of who is a better salesperson not which package is best for you.

Scripted Demonstration

In order to change the demonstration from a glorified sales presentation into a real tool for determining whether the package meets your current requirements and also to be able to compare the different packages on an equal basis, you must take control of the demonstration. The way to do this is to perform a scripted demonstration. In a scripted demonstration you give the vendors identical, precise directions (a script) detailing what they are to show you. Vendors are then graded on each requirement as it is demonstrated to you. In order to ensure the vendors do not try to skip over features that they do not have or use the "trust me" line they receive zero points for any feature they do not show regardless of whether or not the package could perform the operation. By making the vendors demonstrate the same functions, you can accurately determine the differences between packages.

Often the difference between a successful implementation and a failure is the number of surprises that happen during implementation. By having the vendors show you exactly how the package works drastically reduces the number of surprises. I had helped a client choose a package. I met the Chief Information Officer (CIO) about a year later and asked her how the implementation went. She told me that about six months into the implementation they had found that the package required did not work exactly the way they would have liked and the team was getting a little discouraged. Janet told them "you remember those three weeks six months ago when you sat through the scripted demonstrations and *you* picked this package because *you* felt it was the best package and it would work. At the demonstration you saw the way the package worked and *you* still picked the package. When she reminded them that they knew of the problem and they still picked the package, they went back to work and successfully implemented the package. Janet credits the successful implementation to the scripted demonstration and letting the users see the way the package would work at their company and for the users to have a say in the selection process.

The scripted demonstration is like walking through a house. Without the script you need to rely on the realtor and the written description of the house. You may have asked for a house that was light and airy and the description of the house said "beautiful house, light and airy." It sounds perfect. But, when you start walking through the house you see what they mean by light and airy. All the windows are broken and there was a big hole in the roof so the light and air are coming in from all sides. This is not exactly what you had in mind. The scripted demonstration is very much like the checklist we made up as we continued to look for a house. My wife and I then rated every house against the same checklist so we could then remember which house had what. This saved us time and some arguments.

But on a more serious note, when you actually walk through a house yourself you get a much better idea of what the house is really like, just like the scripted demonstration gives you a better assessment of the software package. On a house tour, you look at every room and determine if the house is for you or not. When you come back a second time you not only walk through every room but now you look in every corner for problems like water marks on the basement floor, which could be an indicator of flooding.

You inspect a software package much the same way. In order to know what the package really does, you need to walk through every room and look in every corner. With a software package, you see all the "rooms" by having the vendor show them to you. The scripted demonstration ensures that you see all rooms not just the ones that the salesperson wants you to see. The script changes the demonstration from a glorified sales presentation in which the vendor tells you how great their package is to a tool for selecting a package.

It is often hard to visualize how a room will look with your furniture in it. The same is true with a package. It is very important that your script for the demonstration includes the data that vendors should use during the demonstration. If you don't do this, the vendor will use their own standard data. It can be hard to visualize how a package will work in your environment if you are watching a demonstration with data for manufacturing envelopes, when you are building fire engines.

Arranging Your Requirements

Your current requirements are arranged by functional area. However, in the real world your business does not work as independent areas, it needs to work as one integrated unit. To show how the package meets your current requirements and how the business areas are integrated you need to group your requirements into a complete business flow. For example, a business flow can start when you receive a customer's order for an item, you then purchase the item, ship the item to the customer, bill the customer; the flow ends when you receive the payment. In order to review all your requirements you will need many of these cycles; we call this a scenario.

The first scenario should be for your most frequent business flow. In other words, it should include the requirements that occur most frequently in the daily operation of your business. The next scenario should be for the business flow that is the second most common. Keep developing scenarios until you have included most of your requirements. You should develop at least three scenarios that go through your entire business flow. Then you can develop mini scenarios that only go through part of the business flow that is needed to show the remaining requirements.

Scenario Worksheet

Figure 7-1 is a sample of a Scenario Worksheet. The header row of the worksheet shows the scenario number that uniquely identifies the scenario. Then there is a description where you place a high-level narration of the scenario. This allows for easy identification of what will be taking place in the detail below. The final item in the top of the worksheet is where you will put the script number that you wrote that corresponds to this scenario.

The body of the scenario should contain the following information:

- Line—unique identifier for each line of the scenario for easy referencing.
- Requirement number—cross-reference to the requirement on the Current Requirements Worksheet (see Figure 5-5).
- Requirement description—description of the current requirement as it appears in the Current Requirements Worksheet.
- Script line number—cross-reference between the scenario line item and the script line number that will demonstrate the scenario line number. You will fill this in when you write the script later in this chapter.

You will notice that line 12 on Figure 7-1, Scenario Worksheet, is requirement number 124, Ability to Automatically Perform a Three-Way Match—purchase order, receiving report, and invoice corresponds to requirements 124 on Figure 5-5, p. 69.

Scenario Worksheet

Scenario Number 3	**Description:** Receive order from new customer for items that are out of stock, place order with vendor, order more of one item and place excess in inventory, make the payment based on matching the purchase order, receiving report and invoice. The extra quantity is placed into inventory and the inventory reflects the additions. Ship items to customer and receive payment.	**Script Number 3**

Line	Requirement Number	Requirement Description	Script Line Number
1	326	Ability to enter a customer order.	2
2	359	Ability to order an item from a vendor where the total quantity goes to a customer order.	2, 8
3	362	Ability to order an item from a vendor where the part of the quantity goes to a customer order and part goes into inventory.	2, 8
4	676	Ability to create a requisition for two or more items.	3
5	688	Ability for the system to choose vendor with the cheapest price on file.	4, 5
6	703	Ability to automatically create a purchase order for the cheapest vendor.	5
7	792	Ability to print the purchase order.	6
8	943	Ability to receive the item; and create a receiving report.	7
9	956	Ability to receive an item and send directly to a customer order.	8

Figure 7-1. Scenario Worksheet

10	949	Ability to receive an item and send part directly to a customer order and part to inventory.	8
11	123	Ability to enter a vendor invoice.	18
12	124	Ability to automatically perform a three-way match—purchase order, receiving report, and invoice.	11, 14
13	949	Ability to select the payment item for payment.	13
14	128	Ability to cut checks to vendors.	14
15	1012	Ability to ship a customer's order.	15
16	453	Ability to create customer invoice.	16
17	458	Ability to enter a customer's payment.	17

Figure 7-1. Scenario Worksheet (*continued*)

The Script

The script is a set of detailed instructions that tells the vendor exactly what they are to show you at the demonstration. This means that you need to change the scenario from an "ability to" format to a "do" format (enter, show, create, etc.). Figure 7-2 is a sample script. The header row should contain the following:

- Script number—uniquely identify the script and allows for easily identification of each script to the vendors and participants of the demonstration.
- Description—a short high-level description of current requirements included in the script.
- Revision—any changes to the script. The letter is increased every time you make a change to the script. This ensures everyone is looking at the same exact script.

The body of the script should contain the following information:

- Line—unique identifier for each line of the script for easy referencing.
- Action—describes the action to be perform by the vendor.
- Requirement number—ties the script line back to the current requirement on the Current Requirements Worksheet (Figure 5-5). This can then be used to ensure that all requirements are scripted.
- Company Rating—rating your need for this script line. It should be the highest company rating of the requirements being demonstrated.
- Data—list the data item(s) needed to perform the action. You will enter this later in the chapter when you develop the data that will be used for this script.
- Expected result—the result that should occur when the line is executed.
- Business area—from which the requirement comes.

Script							Revision A
Script Number 3	Description: Receive order from new customer for items that are out of stock, place order with vendor, order more of one item and place excess in inventory, make the payment based on matching the purchase order, receiving report and invoice. The extra quantity is placed into inventory and the inventory reflects the additions. Ship items to customer and receive payment.						
Line	Action	Requirement Number	Company Rating	Data — See Data Worksheet for details — First Number is Data Ref Number	Expected Results	Business Area	Scenario No/line
1	Receive order for new customer JNC Company. Set the customer up in the system (regular customer).	279	5	1 - JNC Corporation	Customer successfully entered.	Order Management	Setup
2	Enter JNC's order into the system form JNC for: 2 Left-handed Keyboard (total quantity going to customer order) 3 Any keys.	326	5	5 - Left-Handed Keyboard 6 - Any-Keys No inventory for either item.	Order successfully entered.	Order Management	3–1, 2, 3
3	Enter a requisition for the following: 2 Left-handed Keyboard- 5 Any keys	606	5			Purchasing	3–4

Figure 7-2. Script

Script

| Script Number 3 | Description: Receive order from new customer for items that are out of stock, place order with vendor, order more of one item and place excess in inventory, make the payment based on matching the purchase order, receiving report and invoice. The extra quantity is placed into inventory and the inventory reflects the additions. Ship items to customer and receive payment. | | | | | | Revision A | |

Line	Action	Requirement Number	Company Rating	Data — See Data Worksheet for details; First Number is Data Ref Number	Expected Results	Business Area	Scenario No./line
4	Show that the system suggest the vendor to be the ABC Company over the XYZ Company and the LMNOP Company.	688	5	2,7,8,9,10 - 2ABC Company 3,,7,8,9,11 - XYZ Company 4,7,8,9,12 - LMNOP Company		Purchasing	3-5
5	Create the order to ABC Company online. Show prices. Show order details.	703	10			Purchasing	3-5, 6
5a		688	5				

Figure 7-2. Script (continued)

#	Action				Purchasing	
6	Print the order. Show details.	792	10	Order printed successfully		3–7
7	Receive the 2 Left-handed keyboard 5 any keys. Create a receiving report.	943	5		Receiving	3–7
8	Show where the system suggests the material should go.	359	5	Left-handed keyboard-all to JNC order. Any keys - 2 Into inventory. Any keys - to JNC order.	Inventory Control	3–3, 9, 10

Figure 7-2. Script (continued)

Script

Revision A

Script Number 3

Description: Receive order from new customer for items that are out of stock, place order with vendor, order more of one item and place excess in inventory, make the payment based on matching the purchase order, receiving report and invoice. The extra quantity is placed into inventory and the inventory reflects the additions. Ship items to customer and receive payment.

Line	Action	Requirement Number	Company Rating	Data — See Data Worksheet for details — First Number is Data Ref Number	Expected Results	Business Area	Scenario No./Line
8a		362	5				
9	Show that the inventory reflects the new items.	342	10		Inventory for any key is 2.	Inventory Control	
10	Review the vendor's invoice and enter it into the system.	123	10		Invoice for 2 left-handed keyboard. 5 any keys and total invoice.	Accounts Payable	3–11
11	Automatically match the receiving report, purchase order, and invoice.					Accounts Payable	3–12
12	Show that a payment is setup with the proper terms.	124	1			Accounts Payable	
13	Release the payment.	135				Accounts Payable	3–17

Figure 7-2. Script *(continued)*

14	Print check. Show that the check is produced with the correct information.	128	5	Accounts Payable	3-12, 14
15	Ship JNC's order for 2 left-handed keyboard.	1012	5	Order Management	3-15
15a	3 - Any Keys Show packing slip and all paper work.	1015	5		
16	Create the invoice for the JNC order.	453	5	Accounts Receivable	3-16

Figure 7-2. Script (continued)

Script

		Revision A		

Script Number 3

Description: Receive order from new customer for items that are out of stock, place order with vendor, order more of one item and place excess in inventory, make the payment based on matching the purchase order, receiving report and invoice. The extra quantity is placed into inventory and the inventory reflects the additions. Ship items to customer and receive payment.

Line	Action	Requirement Number	Company Rating	Data — See Data Worksheet for details — First Number is Data Ref Number	Expected Results	Business Area	Scenario No./line
17	Receive full payment for the JNC invoice. Enter it into system and match against the invoice.	458	5			Accounts Receivable	3–17
18	Show that the journal entries are produced.	22	5	General Ledger Account Numbers Inventory Cash Accounts Payable		General Accounting	
19	Post the journal entry to the general ledger.	15	5			General Accounting	

Figure 7-2. Script (continued)

■ Scenario number/line—ties the script line back to the scenario number and line number. This can then be used to ensure that all scenarios are scripted.

You should create the script using an electronic spreadsheet (i.e., Excel). This will allow you later to easily create the Demonstration Scoring Sheet, which is described later in this chapter.

Data

In order to be able to create some of the conditions in the current requirement you need specific data. For example, the requirement is to place a customer's order on hold because the customer does not have sufficient credit. The only way to demonstrate this requirement is to set the customer up with a specific credit limit and then place an order for the same customer that is over its credit limit. If you do not have the right data (order is under the credit limit) the requirement will not be demonstrated.

Use your company's actual data as part of the demonstration. This creates a comfort level and allows the participants to easily see how the package will work. For example, when you enter an order for your best customer with the items it most frequently buys it is easy for the participants to compare the current system to the system being demonstrated. If the script calls for processing a customer return use the customer that sends you the most returns. It makes a big difference in the participant's ability to visualize using the system when they have data with which they are familiar.

Once you have completed the script, add the necessary data. The Data Worksheet (Figure 7-3) details the data needed to perform the action described in the script. The Data Worksheet includes the following columns:

■ Ref. number (reference number)—unique identifier for each piece of data.

■ Data—name of data to be defined.

■ Data definition—values of the data.

Ref. Number	Data	Data Definition	Input At/Before Demonstration	Requirement Number	Script Number/ Line
		Data Worksheet			
1	JNC Company	Customer JNC Company Customer # AB12345 Address 67 Ephraim Ave. NY, NY 12345 Phone 888-555-1212 Fax 888-555-1213 Contact Ephraim Hollander	At		
2	ABC Company	Vendor ABC Company Vendor # AB12342 Address 123 Ariella Ave. NY, NY 12345 Phone 212-555-1212 Fax 212-555-1213 Contact E L Lowey	AT	1131, 1145	

Figure 7-3. Data Worksheet

3	LMNOP Company	Vendor LMNOP Company Vendor # AB1238 Address 234 Ephraim Ave. Flushing, NY 11364 Phone 718-555-1212 Fax 718-555-1213 Contact Jerry Loewy	Before	1131, 1145, 1166	
4	XYZ Company	Vendor XYZ Company Vendor # AB12345 Address 123 Ariella Ave. San Diego, CA 07051 Phone 203-555-1212 Fax 203-555-1213 Contact Sarah Ariella	Before	1131, 1145	

Figure 7-3. Data Worksheet (continued)

Data Worksheet

Ref. Number	Data	Data Definition		Input At/Before Demonstration	Requirement Number	Script Number/ Line
5	Left-Handed Keyboard	Part # Make/Buy Inventory	LH123 Buy 0	At	1	
6	Any Key	Part # Make/Buy Inventory	Key789 Buy 9	Before		
7	Vendor Base Price Left-Handed Keyboard	ABC Company LMNOP Company XYZ Company	$3.79 $4.29 $4.029	At	1202	
8	Vendor Base Price Any Key	ABC Company LMNOP Company XYZ Company	$0.49 $0.51 $0.50	Before	1202	

Figure 7-3. Data Worksheet (continued)

			At	1243	
9	Price discount from ABC Company	Discount based online total $ 1–100 101–250 250–500 501–1000 over 1001 % 0 5 10 15 20	At	1243	
10	Price discount LMNOP Company	Discount based on total order $ 1–500 500–1,000 1,001–3,500 3,501–10,000 10,001–25,000 over 25,001 % 0 5 10 15 17 20	Before	1243	
11	Price discount XYZ Company	Discount based on quantity for the line item $ 1–100 101–250 251–500 501–1000 over 1001 % 0 5 10 15 20	Before	1243	

Figure 7-3. Data Worksheet (continued)

- Input at/before demonstration—tells the vendor if they need to enter the data before coming to the demonstration or if they are expected to enter it at the demonstration.
- Requirement number—cross-reference to the data to the requirement that will be using the data on the Current Requirements Worksheet (Figure 5-5).
- Script number/line—identifies the script number(s) and script line number(s) that will use the data.

Once you have developed the data, you should place the data reference number on the Data column of the line of the script that it will be used. This allows for easy cross-referencing to the required data. For example line 1 of script 3 (Figure 7-2) calls for entering the JNC Company in the Data field column, which is the Ref. Number on the Data Worksheet. If you go to line 1 on the Data Worksheet you will see the JNC Company and the data associated.

Scoring Sheets

The final item you need to create for the demonstration is the Demonstration Scoring Sheet. It will be used by the participants to grade each line of the script as the vendor executes the script at the demonstration. It is a hybrid of the script that has room for the participants to place their score. The Demonstration Scoring Sheet (Figure 7-4) contains the following information in the header:

Script number—script being scored.
- Vendor Name—name of the vendor demonstrating the software.
- Participant—person scoring the demonstration.

The scoring sheet takes the following columns from the script:

- Line
- Action
- Data
- Business Area

Demonstration Scoring Sheet

Script # 3

Vendor Name *Robin Hood Software* Participant *Harvey Inbinder*

Line	Action	Data — See Data Worksheet for details First Number is Data Ref Number	Business Area	Score (Filled)	Comments (Out at Demonstration)
1	Receive order for new customer JNC Company. Set the customer up in the system (regular customer).	1 - JNC Corporation	Order Management	3	Required three screens to enter a vendor.
2	Enter JNC's order into the system form JNC for: 2 Left-handed Keyboard (total quantity going to customer order) 3 any keys.	5 - Left-handed keyboard 6 - Any Keys No inventory for either item.	Order Management	4	
3	Enter a requisition for the following: 2 left-handed keyboard – 5 any keys.		Purchasing	2	Need to create separate requisition for each item.
4	Show that the system suggests the vendor to be the ABC Company over the XYZ Company and the LMNOP Company	2, 7, 8, 9, 10 - 2ABC Company 3, 7, 8, 9, 11 - XYZ Company 4, 7, 8, 9, 12 - LMNOP Company	Purchasing	4	Worked nicely.

Figure 7-4. Demonstration Scoring Sheet

Demonstration Scoring Sheet

Participant *Harvey Inbinder*

Vendor Name *Robin Hood Software*

Script # 3

Line	Action	Data See Data Worksheet for details First Number is Data Ref Number	Business Area	Score (Filled	Comments Out at Demonstration)
5	Create the order to ABC Company online. Show prices. Show order details.		Purchasing	4	
6	Print the order. Show details.		Purchasing	4	
7	Receive the 2 left-handed keyboard- 5 any keys. Create a receiving report.		Receiving	4	
8	Show where the system suggests the material should go. left-handed keyboard-(all to JNC order) any keys 2 into inventory- (3 to JNC order two to inventory).		Inventory Control	4	
9	Show that the inventory reflects the new items.		Inventory Control	4	
10	Review the vendor's invoice and enter it into the system.		Accounts Payable	4	
11	Automatically match the receiving report, purchase order, and invoice.		Accounts Payable	4	

Figure 7-4. Demonstration Scoring Sheet (*continued*)

12	Show that a payment is setup with the proper terms.		Accounts Payable	4	
13	Release the payment.		Accounts Payable	4	
14	Print check. Show that the check is produced with the correct information.		Accounts Payable	4	We will need to order new checks.
15	Ship the JNC's order for 2-left-handed keyboard. 3-any keys. Show packing slip and all paper work.		Order Management	4	
16	Create the invoice for the JNC order.		Accounts Receivable	4	
17	Receive full payment for the JNC invoice. Enter it into system and match against the invoice.		Accounts Receivable	4	
18	Show that the journal entries are produced.	General Ledger Account Numbers Inventory Cash Accounts Payable	General Ledger	4	
19	Post the journal entry to the general ledger.		General Ledger	4	

Figure 7-4. Demonstration Scoring Sheet (continued)

The score sheet adds the following two columns:

- Score—where the participant places the score for the line.
- Comments—where participants place any comments they have about the line being executed. Comments will be used by the participant to remember why they gave the line its score.

It is easy to create the Demonstration Scoring Sheet if you created the script in an electronic spread sheet because all you need to do is add the additional columns in the spreadsheet.

A blank copy of the rating sheet should be sent to the vendors along with the script to reiterate how serious you are about following the script. A Demonstration Scoring Sheet should be distributed to each participant in advance of the demonstration.

Packages under $40,000

The scripted demonstration takes the vendor approximately one week or more to prepare. Because preparation is time consuming, be sure to ask for demonstrations only from those vendors about whom you are serious. If the package that is being considered costs $40,000 or more and a vendor refuses to conduct a custom demonstration, this is a good indication of the support level you can expect to receive after you purchase the package. Eliminate these vendors from the selection process.

In most cases vendors whose packages cost less than $40,000 are not able to afford a week's worth of time to prepare a demonstration. Instead of vendor-led demonstration you will have to "conduct the demonstration." This means that you or one or more of your colleagues will have to learn the package and perform and rate all the scripts as if the vendor was executing them. You should put the trial packages through the scripts you developed. The vendor should let you have the software on a trial basis for at least thirty days unconditionally. Because learning the software is time consuming, see if the vendor will perform the scripted demonstration if you compensate them. They may give you a credit for this cost if you purchase the software.

Who Should Attend the Demonstration

All members of the selection team should participate in the demonstration. You may also want to have additional personnel participate, especially those who have special insight in a specific area of the business. They can be asked to attend the portions of the demonstration in which they are expert.

Where to Hold the Demonstration

The vendor should be allowed to conduct the scripted demonstration in a location where they can best demonstrate. The location should therefore be at the vendor's discretion. This will alleviate problems such as communicating with the vendor's computer over slow phone lines, missing or incompatible hardware, problems loading programs and or databases, etc. At one demonstration I attended, the vendor agreed to demonstrate its software at the customer's location using a modem and a standard telephone line. Unfortunately for the vendor, the telephone line was very slow and after approximately two hours the line went dead. By the time the vendor lost the line the participants had already made up their mind that the package was too cumbersome.

There are three locations that vendors often choose:

■ Your location—this is the easiest location for you. But you should make sure participants do not keep getting called out of the demonstration. In order to avoid having participants constantly called out, an off-site location may be advisable. In either case, you need to provide necessary equipment, e.g., computers, phone line, the ability to load the software on to your computer, etc. It can become quite embarrassing and a waste of time if the vendor requires a modem hook up and there is no available phone line. When scheduling demonstrations, be aware that the vendor may want to come in the day before to setup. If the software can run on a computer that the vendor can bring with them without needing to hook up to a computer in their office then they should hold the demonstration at your facilities.

- Vendor's location—this means that you will have to arrange for the transportation for all participants to the vendor's site. The vendor should be able to arrange for accommodations, but it is your responsibility to cover any travel and accommodation costs. This site is often best for the vendors because they will be using their computer without having to worry about communication lines and hardware problems. They also have easy access to their support personnel in case of a problem.

- Hardware vendor's location—often the package vendor has relationships with the hardware vendor that allows them to demonstrate their package at the hardware vendor's location near you. This allows the vendor to have the hardware it requires without having to rely on phone lines. This is often good if the hardware vendor is close by and the package vendor is far away.

Timing

A vendor-controlled demonstration takes anywhere from a few hours to one day. When the demonstration is over the participants are not sure what they did and did not see of the package. The vendor could have talked about a function without actually showing it. A scripted demonstration takes a minimum of one day and often two or more to complete. After demonstration, though, you will have a good idea of whether or not the system will work for you.

At the Demonstration

The vendor should follow the scripts in order. However, sometimes the software may require that the vendor perform certain functions in a different order. When this occurs tell the vendor to let you know the line being executed. If the flow is cumbersome, lower the vendor's grade for that script line.

The participants should not be interrupted during the demonstration—it can become quite disconcerting to have members of the team walking in and out. If you are having additional personnel participate have them come and go during breaks so they don't interrupt the process. Bring copies of the script and rating forms with an explanation of what is to be accomplished and the ground rules for the demonstration for those attendees that did not bring it to the demonstration.

The demonstration should follow this agenda:

- Welcome—from an executive of your company to the vendor and attendees.
- Introduction of the attendees—each of the participants should introduce him/herself. This will allow the vendor to know whom they are addressing and you to know each of the vendor team members. Each introduction should take about one minute. Each attendee should state the following:

 Name

 Department

 How they are affected by the system

 What they are looking for from the demonstration
- The vendor personnel should also introduce themselves as follows:

 Name

 Job title

 Function at the demonstration
- Review of the way the demonstration will be scored.

The stage should then be turned over to the vendor who should follows this agenda:

- Schedule—the vendor should review the schedule for the day.
- Vendor background—the vendor should spend no more than fifteen minutes reviewing the package and company background. They should discuss the philosophy of the company and where they see the package going.
- Script—performing the actions in the script. Most of the time should be spent performing the script.

- Additional features—if there is time, the vendor can show any features that haven't been covered during the demonstration that they feel would be beneficial to you. This should only be done if the vendor has completed all the scripts.

- Thank the vendor— you or a member of the selection team should thank the vendor for the demonstration and the time they took for its preparation.

You should have lunch brought in so that you keep everyone together and do not loose the flow of the demonstration. You should also consider having breakfast in the room before the demonstration. This will get people to come earlier to socialize. Make sure to keep drinks and some light food in the back of the room during the day. Also schedule breaks every hour to hour-and-a-half.

Make sure that the vendor is demonstrating the system and not showing you pictures of screens. One time I witnessed a vendor demonstration in which the vendor had agreed to have the demonstration using a modem and a standard telephone line. This vendor had performed the scripts beforehand and took copies of the screens. At the demonstration the vendor flashed the screen shots as if they were performing the demonstration live. It worked beautifully for the vendor until someone asked a question for which the vendor had to go to another screen. At that point he told us what he was doing and that in order to answer questions he needed to access the package, which he would do later. When he dialed up the system and tried to show us the system we found it did not work exactly as shown. He had neglected to show intermediate screens that made the package cumbersome to use.

Rate the Demonstration

Each participant should rate the portion of the script which they are knowledgeable using the Demonstration Rating Sheet. The rate for each line of the script should be based on the functionality of the package, how easy it is to use, and help function available. Based on these categories, rate each line from zero to four:

0 = Cannot or does not perform the script line.

1 = Functionality is poor, need work-around, or is so complicated to use that work-around needed.

2 = Functionality is fair; do not like the functionality or ease of use but will be able to live with it.

3 = Functionality meets the script line but is not easy to use (i.e., may need to use three screens to accomplish a task that should require only one screen to accomplish and or help does not meet needs).

4 = Functionality is completely met, is easy to use, and help is adequate.

Participants should be encouraged to jot down notes about why they gave a line item the specific rating. This can be useful when there will be a review of the demonstration, so that the participant can remember why they gave the line item the specific score. Comments can include "took three screens to accomplish," "not very intuitive," etc. The comments can also include things that you would like to change in a future demonstration.

After the Demonstration

After each demonstration is completed, the participants' Demonstration Scoring Worksheet should be collected and entered onto the Demonstrator Ratings Summary Worksheet (Figure 7-5). If you developed the script and scoring sheet using an electronic spreadsheet it will be very easy for you to develop the Demonstrator Scoring Summary Worksheet. The columns in the worksheet are as follows:

Script—number of the script being rated

Line—number of the line of the script being rated

Business area—of the action being rated

Requirement Number—of the action being performed

Company Need (company need)—for the line being rated

Demonstration Scoring Summary Worksheet

Vendor Name *Robin Hood Software*

Script	Line	Requirement Number	Business Area	Company Need	Harvey	Mary	Joe	Jane	Nat	Min	Max	Dif	Avg	Wgt. Rating
					Participants Ratings									
1	1	326	Order Management	7	4	4	4	4	4	4	4	0	4	8
3	1	279	Order Management	7	3		4	3	4	3	4	1	3.5	24.5
3	2	326	Order Management	7	4		4	4	4	4	4	0	4	28
3	3	606	Purchasing	7	2	2	2	2	2	2	2	0	2	14
3	4	688	Purchasing	7	4	3	3	3	4	3	4	1	3.4	24.5
3	5	703	Purchasing	10	4	3	4	3	4	3	4	1	3.6	36
3	6	688	Purchasing	7	4	4	3	4	3	3	4	1	3.6	25.2
3	7	792	Receiving	10	4	4	4	1	3	1	4	3	3.4	34
3	8	943	Inventory Control	7	4	4	4	4	4	4	4	0	4	28
3	9	359	Inventory Control	7	4	3	3	3	3	3	4	1	3.2	22.4
3	10	362	Accounts Payable	7	4	0	4	4	0	0	4	4	2	14

Figure 7-5. Demonstration Scoring Summary Worksheet

3	11	342	Accounts Payable	10	4		4	4	4	0	4	40
3	12	123	Accounts Payable	10	4		4	4	4	0	4	40
3	13		Accounts Payable		0	0	0	0	0	0	0	0
3	14	124	Accounts Payable	3	4		4	4	4	0	4	2
3	15	135	Order Management	3	0	0	0	0	0	0	0	0
3	16	128	Accounts Receivable	7	3		3	3	4	1	3.6	25.2
3	17	148	Accounts Receivable	7	4	3	4	3	4	1	3.75	26.3
3	18	457	General Accounting	7	4		4	4	4	0	4	28
3	19	453	General Accounting	7	4		4	1	4	3	4	28
15	26	455	General Accounting	7	3	3	3	3	3	3	3	21

Figure 7-5. Demonstration Scoring Summary Worksheet (continued)

Participants' Ratings—column for each participant and their rating

Min. (minimum)—rating from a participant for the line being rated

Max. (maximum)—rating from a participant for the line being rated

Dif. (difference)—between the minimum and maximum rating of the participants as an absolute number (no minus signs)

Avg. (average)—rating of participant for the line being rated

Wgt. rating (weighted rating)—company rating times average

The day after the demonstration you should hold a debriefing meeting. Return each participant's scoring sheet on which the participant made their notes, and distribute the Demonstrator Ratings Summary Worksheet sorted by the Dif. (difference between the highest score and the lowest score of the demonstration line) column in descending order (see Figure 7-6). For any difference greater than two, discuss why. After the discussion. if a participant(s) wants to change their score, update their rating on the Demonstrator Ratings Summary Worksheet and update the average. You should limit the discussion to five minutes per line. On the first line of the Demonstration Scoring Summary Worksheet sorted by differences requirement 362, Nat had rated it a zero whereas everyone else has rated it a four. At the debriefing Nat reviewed the notes that were returned to him and realized that he had made a mistake in the rating and it should be a four. So it was changed on the rating on the Demonstrator Scoring Summary Worksheet.

Notice on the Demonstration Scoring Summary Worksheet Sorted by the Differences that Joe did not rate the Accounts Payable requirements. This was because Joe is not familiar with the area and could not properly judge the package in that area.

Updating the Current Requirements Fit

Now that you have the ratings from all the participants updated in the Demonstrator Ratings Summary Worksheet multiply the company rating column times the average column. Then sort the Demonstrator

Demonstration Scoring Summary Worksheet—Sorted by Difference

Vendor Name Robin Hood Software

Script	Line	Requirement Number	Business Area	Company Need	Harvey	Mary	Joe	Jane	Nat	Min	Max	Dif	Avg	Wgt. Rating
					Participants Ratings									
3	10	362	Accounts Payable	7	4	4	4	4	0	0	4	4	3	21
3	7	792	Receiving	10	4	4	4	1	4	1	4	3	3.4	34
3	19	453	General Accounting	7	4				4	1	4	3	4	28
3	1	279	Order Management	7	3	3	4	3	4	3	4	1	3.5	24.5
3	4	688	Purchasing	7	4	3	3	3	4	3	4	1	3.4	23.8
3	5	703	Purchasing	10	4	3	4	3	4	3	4	1	3.6	36
3	6	688	Purchasing	7	4	4	3	4	3	3	4	1	3.6	25.2
3	9	359	Inventory Control	7	4	3	3	3	3	3	4	1	3.2	22.4
3	16	128	Accounts Receivable	7	4	4		3	3	3	4	1	3.5	24.5
3	17	148	Accounts Receivable	7	4		3	4	4	3	4	1	3.75	26.25

Figure 7-6. Demonstration Scoring Summary Worksheet—Sorted by Difference

Demonstration Scoring Summary Worksheet—Sorted by Difference

Vendor Name *Robin Hood Software*

Script	Line	Requirement Number	Business Area	Company Need	Hovey	Mory	Joe	Joe C	Scott	Min	Max	Dif	Avg	Wgt. Rating
					Participants' Ratings									
3	2	326	Order Management	7	4	4	4	4	4	4	4	0	4	28
3	3	606	Purchasing	7	2	2	2	2	2	2	2	0	2	14
3	8	943	Inventory Control	7	4	4	4	4	4	4	4	0	4	28
3	11	342	Accounts Payable	10	4	4		4	4	4	4	0	4	40
3	12	123	Accounts Payable	10	4	4	4	4	4	4	4	0	4	40
3	14	124	Accounts Payable	3	4	4	4	4	4	4	4	0	4	12
3	15	135	Order Management	0						0	0	0		0
3	18	457	General Accounting	7	4				4	4	4	0	4	28

Figure 7-6. Demonstration Scoring Summary Worksheet—Sorted by Difference (*continued*)

Ratings Summary Worksheet by the Business Area (Figure 7-7). We now need to calculate the vendor's rating for each business area. (This is the updated valuation for Current Requirements Analysis Worksheet Figure 6-4, p. 99, you performed when you analyzed the RFP.)

The first step is to total the Wgt. Rating column and place the result into the row marked Total Business Area (Accounts Payable [AP]). The second step is to calculate the maximum value a package can achieve.

To do this multiply the company rating for each requirement by 100 percent for a maximum possible weighted rating for each business area. Then total all those maximum weighted ratings for the Maximum Value. Using Figure 7-7 as an example, the calculation would look like this:

$$\text{Maximum Value}^{AP} = \text{The sum of the Company Ratings} \times 4$$
$$= (10 + 7 + 7 + 7 + 7 + 3 + 3$$
$$+ 3 + \ldots\ldots + 10)$$
$$= 1{,}250 \times 4$$
$$= 5{,}000$$

Enter the sum of the Company Ratings, in this case 1,250, in the Company Rating Column in the row labeled "Total Business Area." Enter the Maximum Value for the Business Area 5,000 in the same column in the row marked "Maximum Value."

Then divide the Package's Total Weighted Rating for the business area by the Maximum Value to arrive at the Package's Percentage fit. Returning to the Demonstrator Ratings Summary Worksheet by the Business Area.

$$\text{Total Percentage Fit}^{PkgA} = \text{Total Weighted Fit}^{PkgA}/\text{Maximum Value}$$
$$= 4{,}123/5{,}000\%$$
$$= 82\%$$

Once you have calculated the packages' Percentage Fit for each Business Area, you can determine how well each package meets your

Demonstration Ratings Summary Worksheet

Vendor Name *Robin Hood Software*

Script	Line	Requirement Number	Business Area	Company Need	Participants' Ratings					Min	Max	Dif	Avg	Wgt. Rating
					Harvey	Mary	Joe	Jane	Matt					
3	12	123	Accounts Payable	10	4	4	4	4	4	4	4	0	4	40
3	14	124	Accounts Payable	7	2	2	2	2	2	2	2	0	2	14
4	8	125	Accounts Receivable	7	4	3	4	4	4	3	4	1	3.75	26.25
5	14	126	Accounts Receivable	7	3	4	4	4	4	3	4	1	3.75	26.25
5	15	127	Accounts Receivable	7	4	4	3	3	4	3	4	1	3.75	26.25
3	16	128	Accounts Receivable	7	4	4	4	3	3	3	4	1	3.5	24.5
7	23	129	Accounts Receivable	3	4	4	4	4	4	4	4	0	4	12
7	28	130	Accounts Receivable	3	4	4	4	4	4	4	4	0	4	12
5	14	250	Accounts Receivable	10	4	4	3	3	3	3	4	1	3.5	35
Total Business Area (Accounts Payable)				1,250									983	4,123
Maximum Value Business Area				1,250										5,000
Percentage Fit Business Area (Accounts Payable)														82%

Figure 7-7. Demonstration Ratings Summary Worksheet—Sorted by Business Area

current requirements based on you actually seeing the package work. You had already entered your need for each business area on the Business Area Summary Worksheet (see Figure 7-8). Now, enter your revised Percentage Fit by business area for each package to the worksheet; this can be seen in Figure 7-8. The Business Area Summary Worksheet-Vendors A, B, and C, contains the updated results for all vendors. Then multiply the Package Percentage Fit by the Company Rating to calculate the Weighted Percentage Fit. For Package A for the Accounts Payable Business Area the calculation looks like this:

$$\text{Package A Weighted Percentage Fit}^{AP} = \text{Company Need}^{AP} \times \text{Percentage Fit}^{AP}$$

$$= 5 \times 82\%$$

$$= 410\%$$

Enter this fit in the Weighted Percentage Fit column for Package A.

Business Area Summary Worksheet—Vendors A, B—Updated from Demonstration					
Business Area	Company Need	Package A Percentage Fit	Package A Weighted Percentage Fit	Package B Percentage Fit	Package B Weighted Percentage Fit
General Accounting	7	81%	567%	92%	644%
Accounts Payable	**7**	**82%**	**574%**	97%	679%
Accounts Receivable	3	99%	297%	91%	273%
Payroll	7	86%	602%	94%	658%
Order Management	10	85%	850%	98%	980%
Human Resources	3	89%	267%	95%	285%
TOTAL	**37**	**522%**	3,157%	567%	3,519%
Maximum Value (Total Company Need × 100%)			3,700%		3,700%
Percentage Fit Current Requirements			85%		95%

Figure 7-8. Business Area Summary Worksheet – Vendors A, B—Updated from Demonstration

R²ISC Worksheet—Updated from Demonstration					
High-Level Requirements	Company's Need	Package A Percentage Fit	Package A Weighted Percentage Fit	Package B Percentage Fit	Package B Weighted Percentage Fit
Current Requirements	**30**	**85%**	**26%**	95%	29%
Future Requirements	25	63%	16%	68%	17%
Implementability	20	76%	14%	65%	13%
Supportability	15	78%	12%	67%	10%
Cost	10	59%	6%	36%	4%
	───	───	───	───	───
R²ISC Rating			75%		73%

Figure 7-9. R²ISC Worksheet – Updated from Demonstration

Then enter the Current Requirements Percentage Fit for each package from the Business Area Summary Worksheet (Figure 7-8) onto the R²ISC Worksheet—Updated from Demonstration (Figure 7-9). We will continue adding the packages Percentage Fit for the other R²ISC criteria as we proceed through this chapter.

We will not calculate the revised R²ISC rating at this point because the steps described in the next chapter will be to revise the other four R²ISC criteria. It is after that point that we will calculate each package's R²ISC rating and pick the winning package.

8

Checking Out the Finalists

When you are looking to buy a new house, there are numerous things to consider. Physical structure and property aside, it's extremely important to consider the neighborhood. You can talk to neighbors and friends who live in the area. You can also ask friends and relatives if they know anyone who lives in the area who you can contact. You should do the same thing when you look for a new software package. Talk to companies that use the software you are considering and research the reputation and quality of the vendor and software program.

Just as you determine for yourself how each of the finalists meets your current requirements, you also have to determine how closely the finalists meet your implementability and supportability needs. It can be more problematic to find a problem with the vendor's credibility than to find that the package is missing a specific functionality. A function can usually be added. But there's no fixing a vendor who makes promises and doesn't keep them. You must try to determine if the vendors have any current problems that can impact the implementability of your package. At the same time you need to see if there are any indications of future problems. You need to know just as much about the vendor as you do about the package the vendor is selling.

Vendor References

Contacting companies that use the package is a good way to get information about the package and the vendor. In other words reference checking. It is possible that you will be able to use these references for information that may not be ascertained from any other source. For example, references may be able to tell you how the package works under specific conditions or within your industry. It is also interesting to contact the companies the vendor feels are the most successful with their package. Hopefully other companies' successes will help you learn how to become successful.

Many companies ask the vendor to supply them with three or four references. Keep in mind that vendors are only going to give you positive references. All vendors can supply excellent references even if it's their Uncle Joe. So they are of limited value. The starting point you should use for your reference checks is the clients the vendor supplied in response to the RFP. Choose three or four companies from the vendor's list. Try to pick one that is in a similar business to yours. Then ask the vendor for a contact that will be willing to speak with you regarding the package. You may be surprised at what you find on the list. On more than one occasion, I have found that when I asked to talk to a company on the vendor's list, the company was no longer using the software or the vendor could not give us a contact. If this happens, try to contact the Information Services (IS) department to determine why the company is no longer using the software.

Local References

In addition to the references you receive from the vendor, try to get local references on your own. They will be easy to visit and likely to be willing to be extra helpful because they are your neighbor. You can find local references by checking the help wanted section of the local newspaper for companies looking for people with experience using the software you are considering. These companies can make good references. If you cannot find a local company then ask the vendor. You should choose one of them for a site visit.

Users Groups

Users groups are another good source of information. They are an organization of users of a vendor's product that get together on a regular basis to assist each other in better utilizing the package. They also have input to the vendor on the enhancements that should be included in future releases of the software. As part of the response to the RFP the vendor should have included information on its user groups.

Users groups are some of your best references. Make sure to contact the president of the users group. Try to attend any local or national users group meetings that take place during your selection process. And request and review the minutes from the past four national users group meetings. If in those minutes the vendor indicated that it would be making specific enhancements or bringing out new modules in a specific future release, check if the release came out and if the enhancements and or modules were included.

Review the minutes of the users group meetings for consistency in the vendor's future direction. Does the vendor maintain focus or does the vendor jump from one idea to another? The user group is a good indicator of customer satisfaction with both the vendor and the package.

Interviewing References

Prepare a Reference Check Script (see Figure 8-1) to question the references to ensure that you ask well-planned questions and do not forget to ask anything important. Ask questions that do not have yes or no answers so that they give you more information about the vendor and the package. A reference check can take between fifteen minutes to a half-hour and sometimes longer. People are usually more than willing to spend the time to answer questions about a vendor. This especially true if you used the vendor to obtain the name of the person at the reference site you are calling. Organize the questions in a logical order so that you can easily log the information onto your worksheets.

The Reference Call

Before you start the reference call you should record the information that you know. This includes:

Software package for which you are checking references
Company you are calling
Telephone number of company you are calling
Name of the person you will be interviewing
Title of the person you will be interviewing

REFERENCE CHECK
SCRIPT

SOFTWARE PACKAGE: _____

COMPANY: _____ PHONE _____

NAME: _____ TITLE: _____

INTERVIEWED BY: _____ DATE: _____

Introduction
1. Introduce yourself.
2. Tell the person why you are calling.
3. Ask if this is a convenient time for them. If it's not, schedule a follow-up call.
4. Tell a little about your company.
5. Where you are in the selection process?

Company Background
6. What is the company's line of business?
7. What size is your company?
   Number of employees.
   Sales volume.
8. How many locations do you have?

Reference's Background
9. What is your position in the company?
10. What was your role in selecting the package?
11. Did you participate in implementing the package?
12. Do you currently use the package?

Use Of Package
13. What modules are you using?
14. On what platform does the package run?
15. How many locations are using the package?
16. Are there any foreign locations using the package?
17. What do they use the package for?
18. How long have you had the package?

Reasons For Selecting
19. Why did you select this package?
20. What other package did you consider?
21. Would you buy the package over again?
22. What would you change if you had to do it over again?
23. What were the benefits they received from implementing the package?
24. What advice would you give prospective users of the package?
25. Did you replace an existing system?
26. Is there any other person or company with whom you think we should speak?

Figure 8-1. Sample Interview Script

Vendor Background
27. How do you like the package?
28. What problems have there been with the package?
29. Has the vendor been responsive (hotline, consulting)?
30. How long did it take the vendor to respond to a problem?
31. How long did it take until you were up and running?
32. How reliable are the upgrades?

Implementability
33. Did the vendor assist with implementation?
34. If not, who did?
35. Would you recommend this company?
36. How did the implementation go?
37. How long did it take you to implement the package?
38. How many people were involved in the implementation?
39. How many were your company's personnel, package vendor's personnel, other personnel?
40. Was the project within budget?
41. Did the vendor remain on schedule?
42. What surprises were there in the implementation?
43. What was the hardest part of the implementation?
44. Did the vendor support implementation in a foreign country? If so, how did it go?
45. What was the hardest part of the implementation?
46. Can you recommend any particularly helpful implementation personnel?
47. Are there any implementation personnel we should avoid?
48. How would you rate the package's implementability from 1 to 10? (10 being very easy to implement.)

Modifications
49. Did you make any modifications to the package?
50. If so what type of modifications did you make?
51. How long did it take to make the modifications?
52. If you had to do it again would you make the same modifications?
53. How would you rate the vendor's modifications from 1 to 10? (10 being excellent).

Financial Background
54. Do you know anything about the vendor's financial condition?
55. Have you heard any rumors of the vendor being purchased?
56. Do the vendor's personnel seem happy?

Figure 8-1. Sample Interview Script *(continued)*

Response and Processing Time
57. How is your response time?
58. How long does your batch processing take?
59. What are your volumes?
60. What make and model(s) computer are you using?
61. What operating system and database are you using?
62. How would you rate the package's response time from 1 to 10? (10 being excellent.)

Training
63. What type of training approach did you use?
64. Did you use the vendor for training? If so, what courses did you take?
65. Would you recommend the vendor's training?
66. Did the vendor custom tailor the course(s) for you? If so would you recommend it?
67. Are there any specific courses you would recommend or not recommend?
68. Did the vendor support training in a foreign language? If so, which language and how did it go?
69. Can you recommend any particularly helpful training personnel?
70. Are there any training personnel we should avoid?
71. How would you rate the vendor's training from 1 to 10? (10 being excellent?)

Documentation
72. Have you used the vendor's manuals?
73. Did you use the hardcopy or online version?
74. If so which manuals have you used?
75. What was your opinion of the documentation?
76. Did you use the documentation in a foreign language? If so which and how are they?
77. How would you rate the vendor's documentation from 1 to 10? (10 being excellent.)

Quality
78. How would you describe the quality of the package?
79. Have you encountered any bugs in the package?
80. How was the quality of the modifications?
81. How would you describe the quality of the updates supplied?
82. How would you describe the vendor's quality?
83. How would you rate the vendor's quality from 1 to 10? (10 being excellent.)

Supportability
84. How much ongoing support does the package require? Who supports it?
85. How effective did you find the vendor's help desk?
86. How long does it take to get the answer from the help desk?
87. When was the last time you used the help desk and for what purpose?
88. How responsive is the vendor when a bug is found?
89. Do you attend the user group meetings? If so, are they helpful?
90. How responsive is the vendor to request for enhancements?

Figure 8-1. Sample Interview Script *(continued)*

Cost
91. How did you find the vendor's pricing compared to other vendors?
92. Were you able to negotiate with the vendor on price?
93. What type of discount were you able to negotiate with the vendor?
94. Has the vendor been raising its price for support?
95. What is the annual maintenance cost?

Contract Negotiations
96. What changes did you make to the vendor's contract other than price?
97. What changes would you like to make to the vendor's contract
98. What negotiation strategy did you use with the vendor?
99. How would you negotiate differently if you had it to do all over again?
100. How easy was it to negotiate the contract?
101. How long did it take to negotiate he contract?
102. In what month did you negotiate the contract?
103. With whom did you negotiate the contract?
104. Do you have any advice to us on negotiating with the vendor?
105. How would you rate the package's cost from 1 to 10? (10 being least expensive.)

Vendor Personnel
106. How satisfied were you with the vendor's personnel?
107. Can you recommend any particularly helpful personnel?
108. Are there any personnel we should avoid?
109. How would you rate the vendor's personnel from 1 to 10? (10 being excellent.)

Additional Information
110. Do you have any additional comments?
111. If you can think of any additional information that you think may be helpful to us please call me at 212-555-1212.
112. Would you mind if we call you again if we have additional questions?

Thank You
113. Thank you for the time you spent

Figure 8-1. Sample Interview Script *(continued)*

Interviewer's name

Date you are conducting the interview.

During the interview you should verify the person's title. If it changed from what you have on the form, the form should be updated.

Introduction

Start out with a brief introduction of who you are. Tell the person why you're calling even if you received their name from the vendor who has already told them you would be calling and why. Then ask if this is a convenient time. If not, schedule a follow-up call.

Tell a little about your company: the name of the company, your line of business and size. Explain where you are in the selection process.

Company Background

In order to understand how close the reference is to your company obtain background information on the company. Before you make the reference calls you should try to determine the reference's line(s) of business, size, and number of locations

This information may available from the company's web site, annual report, or if you requested the reference's name from the package vendor then the vendor can supply that information. By getting this information in advance you will not have the reference say "Oh, you mean you never heard of us." You should confirm the information with the reference.

Reference's Background

Obtain information about the person to whom you are talking so that you can understand the perspective that the reference is giving you. Ask the reference the following:

Their position in the company;

Their role in selecting the package;

Their role in implementing the package; and

If they are currently using the system.

Use of Package

It is important to understand how the reference is using the package. For example, if the package has many modules and you are buying one module and the reference that you picked is using a different module, then information about the vendor is relevant. But, the information on the package (which in this case is a different module) is less relevant. In this section ask the specific modules they are using, the platform they are running, number of locations, and how long they have the package.

Reasons for Selecting

It is always interesting to hear why the company selected the package. Did they go through an exhaustive analysis, from which you may be able to glean good information? Alternatively, did they just flip a coin? Ask why they selected the package, other systems they considered, and what they would do differently if they had it to do over again. Next, ask what system the package replaced. This would be interesting if they replaced a package that is one of your other finalists. If this is the case, understand the problems with the other package. Next, ask for any advice that they could give you and if there is any anyone else they feel would be helpful for you to contact.

Vendor Background

Unlike stock mutual funds "where past performance is no indicator of future performance," a software vendor's past performance is a good indicator of future performance. Who better to determine the past performance of the vendor than current customers? Ask references about the vendor's performance from the selection process through the present.

Implementability

If you are planning to use the vendor to assist you in the implementation of the package, then ask the references who they used and if they were satisfied with the assistance. Ask the reference whether the implementation was on time and on budget.

Most companies have some employees who are better than others. Find out from the reference which of the vendor's employees they would recommend that you try to get on your implementation and which ones to avoid.

Financial Background

The reference may have overheard comments by the vendor's employees about the company's financial condition or that it is a take-over target. Therefore, include these questions in your interview.

Modifications

Ask the reference if they made any modifications to the package. If they made modifications that you need, you may be able to purchase them from the reference company or you could try to have the vendor include them in the package because you both need the same enhancements. You should also ask the reference to rate the vendor's modification capabilities.

Response and Processing Time

The time that it takes for a computer to return control of the system is important if it takes too long. There is nothing more annoying than having to wait fifteen seconds or more for the system to respond back once you hit the Enter key. If your system will have to perform processing when the system has to be down (known as batch processing), you have to make sure that the package can perform all its processing during the timeframe that you will not need the system (i.e., evenings and weekends). If the reference is about the same size and has a similar volume as you, then you can make some comparisons about response and processing time. You will also need to know the type and model of the computer system(s) they are using.

Training

Ask the reference about the training approach they used. Did they have the vendor train a trainer and then the trainer trained the rest of the employees or did the vendor train all the employees? Also, ask about the type of training they used. Again, ask the reference about the vendor's personnel. Were there trainers who were excellent and were there trainers to stay away from? Also ask the reference to rate the vendor's training.

Documentation

As part of the reference check, ask about the quality of the documentation. Ask the reference if they used the manuals and if so which manuals. Also ask the reference to rate the vendor's documentation.

Quality

Use the reference to help determine the quality of the package and of the vendor's ability to make modifications to the package. Also ask the reference to rate the vendor's quality.

Supportability

Ask the reference about the support they have gotten from the vender for both the base package and the modifications that the vendor made. Find out about the effectiveness of the vendor's Help Desk. Also ask how helpful the users group(s) are and if the vendor is responsive to suggesting for enhancements to the package. Also ask the reference to rate the vendor's support functions.

Cost

It would be nice if the reference would tell you the price they paid for the system. But most of the time they will not divulge the price. However, you may be able to have the reference give you some idea of the price through a comparison to other packages and the type discount they were able to negotiate. Another important piece of information is whether the vendor has been raising its annual maintenance cost. If they have there is a good possibility that they will continue to do so. Therefore, it becomes important to incorporate limits to the annual maintenance fees in your contract.

Contract Negotiations

In most cases the only thing companies negotiate in the software contract is price. (In the next chapter we will discuss contract negotiations.) If they did make modifications to the contract, it is interesting to note what they were and how hard it was to gain the concessions. Also what strategy they used in the negotiations and how they would do it differently.

Vendor's Personnel

The quality of the vendor's personnel is very important to the quality of the package and its future enhancements. It is very important if you will be using the vendor to implement the package. Even though you had asked about vendor personnel in some of the questions, have another section dedicated only to the vendor's personnel. In this section ask for recommendations of which personnel to use and those to stay away from. Also ask the reference to rate the vendor's personnel.

Additional Information

The last question is to ask the reference if there is any additional information that they think would be helpful for you to know about the package, vendor, or implementing the package.

Thank You

At the conclusion of the call, thank the reference for their time and tell them how helpful they were.

Analyzing the Reference Calls

After you have completed all the reference calls for a vendor, summarize the results. Look for trends. Did all the references say the same thing or were they all different? Later in this chapter we will use this information along with the information we gather in the remainder of the chapter to update the R^2ISC Matrix.

Site Visit

Arrange to visit one or two references. You will most likely glean more information from a face-to-face meeting. Choose a company that is as similar to yours as possible so you can see how the package is used. Take one or two other people from your company with you. Make sure to buy lunch for your host and send a thank you note. If the vendor gave you the reference, they will usually want to be present during the site visit. In this case make sure you take a reference employee(s) aside when the vendor isn't around and get the real scoop.

Additional Background Investigations

Besides the reference checks you should do additional background investigations on each of the finalists.

Internet and Trade Publications

Search the Internet and recent business and trade publications for information on the vendor as well. Business publications can indicate the vendor's financial health. They may also detail any takeover rumors or management problems. Industry publications can indicate how well the package is accepted. Just remember that the vendor's publicist may have written these articles.

Research Organizations

There are organizations that constantly research vendors and software products and produce reports that can be helpful when you are reviewing the vendors' backgrounds. Some of these research organizations are:

> **Datapro**—gives a tactical insight into thousands of products from vendors worldwide. It also offers technology and product evaluations. See Appendix A for a sample report.
>
> **Computer Select**—contains industry publications verification editors who check and update it daily, with a tightly integrated search engine.
>
> **Gartner Group**—product to support product planning and purchase decisions by understanding and comparing IT products on the basis of features, functionality, vendors, technologies and user feedback. See Appendix B for a sample report.

Based on the additional information you received and the reference checks, update the vendors' background rating, if needed. Do this on both the Implementability Summary Worksheet (Figure 6-9) and the Supportability Summary Worksheet (Figure 6-16).

Financial Investigation

Review the finalists' financial stability based on the financial reports obtained as part of the response to the RFP. Liens or lawsuits against the vendor can have a major impact on its financial stability. The review of the business publications can also provide information on the vendor's financial position. You should contact the federal, state, and local courts and the county clerk in the vendor's home county to determine if there is any current or past litigation against the vendor. If you call them they either will give you the information or will instruct you to request it in writing and tell you if there is a nominal fee. Also, ask the county clerk if there are any liens against the vendor including government liens for failure to pay taxes, which can mean the vendor will be in bankruptcy or, even worse, out of business in the not too distant future.

First-Hand Reviews

The above checks were based on other people's opinions of the vendor. Now there are other items that you should review.

Training

To determine the quality of the vendor's training, audit a training course. If that is not practical then review a sample of the training material. Based on the results of the review and the reference checks, update the training rating on the Implementability Summary Worksheet (Figure 6-9) and the Supportability Summary Worksheet (Figure 6-16).

Documentation

To determine the quality of the vendor's documentation, review one user's manual and one technical manual. Based on the results of the reviews and the reference checks update the documentation rating on the Implementability Summary Worksheet (Figure 6-9) and the Supportability Summary Worksheet (Figure 6-16).

Vendor Personnel

As part of the reference call you were able to determine which of the vendor's employees you would like on your project and which you should avoid. Ask the vendor if the employees whom you identified as the ones you want will be part of your team. In order for the vendor to hold the specific employees you will probably have to give them a time frame for the decision and the start of the implementation. If they agree, make sure you have it in writing as part of the contract with heavy penalties if they are not on the project.

You should interview two or three of the vendor's personnel who are scheduled or tentatively scheduled to be assigned to your project. You are looking to determine:

- Knowledge of package
- Knowledge of the subject
- Interpersonal skills
- How they will fit into your company culture.

The interview should be between a half-hour to an hour. You can ask questions such as:

- Describe your last assignment? What were its challenges and how did you overcome them?
- What experience did you have in our industry? What do you find unique about this industry?
- What are your strengths and weaknesses?
- If you have a specific problem, ask their suggestions.

Based on the results of the interviews and the reference checks update the documentation rating on the Implementability Summary Worksheet (Figure 6-9, p. 111).

Technology

If you are going to modify the system at any point, it is important to know how well built it is. This is so that when you want to make modifications, you are not surprised at the problems presented by the way the package was developed. In order to determine this, perform a technical evaluation. This is the only part of the process that requires technical skills. If you do not have them find someone who does and have them review the architecture and program code. Based on this review update the rating on the Future Requirements Worksheet (Figure 6-8, p. 106) and technology rating on the Supportability Summary Worksheet (Figure 6-16, p. 124).

Update the quality rating on the Implementability Summary Worksheet (Figure 6-9) and the Supportability Summary Worksheet (Figure 6-16) based on the technology review and the reference calls.

Response Time

Unfortunately, you cannot determine the response time based on what you saw at the demonstration because it had only a small amount of data and users. When you add more data the response time becomes longer.

If your volumes are higher than the reference's, ask the vendor for a reference using the software on the hardware you plan to use whose volumes are larger than yours. This reference may be different from the other reference you have checked because when you specified to the vendor which references you wanted it was not based on their size. If they cannot give you such a reference, be very careful. You will need to determine for yourself that the software and hardware will give you an acceptable response time by running a stress test.

The Stress Test

Stress testing helps you determine the response time of the system by testing the system with the volumes of data you will be processing. The vendor should assist you in this test by getting a computer for you to use and by obtaining software that simulates multiple users. You need to load the system with 10 percent more data than you expect to have. Then you execute 10 percent more transactions than you anticipate processing and see the response time.

If the response time is not acceptable then you will need to change the hardware or eliminate the package.

Cost of Modification

The cost of the modifications needed to make the software meet your requirements is a good indicator of the modifications needed to meet your requirements. The more modifications needed, the more the risk to the successful implementation of the package. During the demonstration the vendor gained a better understanding of your requirements. You may have determined that the software actually met requirements that the vendor thought it did not meet, and conversely, there were requirements that the vendor thought were met by the package that you determined needed modifications.

You should ask the vendor to update the cost to meet the requirements based on the demonstration. If there is a significant change (over 10%) in the cost enter the new cost on the Cost Worksheet (Figure 6-19) and recalculate the vendor rating as you had on page 33. Then enter the results on the Cost Summary Worksheet (Figure 6-25) as you did on page 144 and update the R^2ISC matrix. You will also need to update the modification rating on the Implementability and Supportability Worksheets (Figures 6-11, p. 113 and 6-12, p. 115, respectively).

For example, the Vendor A reestimate of the cost for Modifications Must Have Only goes from $25,500 to $12,000. The difference is $12,500 and is more than 50 percent, which is more than 10 percent threshold for revising the cost rating. We therefore update the Modifications Must Have Only on the Cost Worksheet (Figure 8-2). Then calculate the revised Total-One-Time Cost, which went from $447,500 to $434,000. The next step is to calculate the Variance from Budget. This is done by subtracting the Budget from the Total-One-Time Cost (550,000 − 526,000 = 24,000). The final calculation is to determine the Percentage Variance from Budget. This is done by dividing the Percentage Variance from Budget by the budget (16,000/450,000 = 4%). Once all of the package's costs have been updated, we can update the Rating One-Time Cost. This is done in the same way we originally assigned the rating (page 203). Based on the percentage variance, determine the rating. If the variance is positive (costs less than your budget), give the largest positive variance a rating of 10. Then rate all the other vendors who also have positive variance between five and 10 based on their percentage difference from the highest percentage variance. For those vendors who have a negative variance (costs more than the budget) assign them a rating between zero and five based on how far they are from the budget. The larger the negative variance the lower the score. We therefore rerate Package A from a 6 to a 7. Then transfer the revised rating is to the Cost Summary Worksheet (Figure 8-3). Here the packages' ratings are recalculated in the same way it was done in Chapter 6.

To calculate each package's Weighted Average, you need to divide the Total Weighted Rating for that package by the Maximum

Cost Worksheet

	Cost Package A	Cost Package B	Cost Package C	Cost Package D
One-Time Cost				
Software	195,500	250,000	190,000	80,000
Modifications All	82,000	66,000	99,000	195,000
Modifications Must Have Only	12,000	35,000	12,000	110,000
Implementation	50,000	3,000	5,000	3,000
Hardware	130,000	155,000	138,000	165,000
Installation	0	2,500	2,000	0
Site preparation	0	1,000	3,500	0
Training	46,500	120,000	15,000	10,000
Documentation	0	2,000	800	1,200
Additional products	0	0	0	15,000
TOTAL–One-Time Cost (without Modifications All)	434,000	634,500	390,300	479,200
Budget	450,000	450,000	450,000	450,000
Variance from Budget	16,000	−170,000	6,700	55,800
Percentage Variance from Budget	4%	−26%	3%	19%
RATING One-Time Cost	7	0	6	10

Figure 8-2. Cost Worksheet

Cost Worksheet				
	Cost Package A	Cost Package B	Cost Package C	Cost Package D
Annual Operating Expenses				
Annual Maintenance Base Package	30,000	37,500	31,000	16,000
Annual Maintenance Must Have Modifications	3,700	7,000	2,400	26,000
Maintenance All Modifications	12,300	24,900	14,850	60,000
Maintenance Hardware	39,000	32,000	15,000	33,000
Maintenance Other Products	0	0	0	3,000
Total: Ongoing Cost	**72,700**	**76,500**	**48,400**	**78,000**
Annual Operating Expense (without Modifications All) Budget	70,000	70,001	70,002	70,003
Variance from Budget	−2,700	−6,499	21,602	−7,997
Percentage Variance from Budget	−4%	−9%	31%	−11%
Rating: Annual Operating Expenses	**5**	**4**	**10**	**2**
Support Services Cost				
Consulting	150/hr	200/hr	175/hr	200/hr
Programming	100/hr	125/hr	100/hr	125/hr
Telephone support	Part of annual maintenance or 50 per call	125/hr	Part of annual maintenance or 35 per call	100/hr
Rating Support Services	**10**	**6**	**9**	**6**

Figure 8-2. Cost Worksheet (*continued*)

Cost Summary Worksheet					
	Company Need	Package A Rating	Package A Weighted Rating	Package B Rating	Package B Weighted Rating
One-Time	7	7	49	0	0
Annual Operating Expenses	10	5	50	4	40
	——	——	——	——	——
TOTAL	**17**		**99**		**40**
Maximum Value-Cost	**10**		**170**		**170**
Fit Cost	——		**58%**		**24%**

Figure 8-3. Cost Summary Worksheet

Value-Cost. Enter the result on the Percentage Fit Cost. For example, the Cost score for Package A is:

$$\text{Total Percentage Fit}^{PkgA} = \text{Total Weighted Fit}^{PkgA}/\text{Maximum Value}$$
$$= 113/170$$
$$= 66\%$$

Then enter the Cost Percentage Fit for each package from the Cost Worksheet (Figure 8-3) onto the R^2ISC Analysis Matrix (Figure 8-4).

R^2ISC Analysis Matrix—Updated for Cost					
High-Level Requirements	Company's Need	Package A Percentage Fit	Package A Weighted Percentage Fit	Package B Percentage Fit	Package B Weighted Percentage Fit
Current Requirements	30	85%	26%	96%	29%
Future Requirements	25	69%	17%	68%	17%
Implementability	20	73%	15%	65%	13%
Supportability	15	78%	12%	67%	10%
Cost	10	**52%**	**6%**	24%	2%
	——	——	——	——	——
R^2ISC Rating			**76%**		**71%**

Figure 8-4. R^2ISC Analysis Matrix—Updated for Cost

Update Ratings

Based on the background checks and your reviews of the vendors' materials you should update the R^{2}ISC criteria ratings.

Updating the Vendor's Current Requirements Rating

There are usually no changes to the current requirements rating for the background checking because you have seen the item demonstrated with your own eyes. However, if there are any changes, go back to the Demonstrator Ratings Summary Worksheet by the Business Area (see Figure 7-7) and update the rating(s). Then transfer the rating to the Business Area Summary Worksheet (see Figure 7-8) in which you will recalculate the Current Requirements Rating. Then transfer the Current Requirements Rating onto the R^{2}ISC Worksheet. For a detailed analysis of these calculations see Chapter 7, p. 179.

Update the Vendors' Implementability Rating

Summarize the information gathered information on the Implementability Reference Analysis Worksheet (Figure 8-5). The Implementability Reference Analysis Worksheet has a row for each of the Implementability criteria and the following columns:

REF 1—summarized remarks from reference call 1.

REF 2—summarized remarks from reference call 2.

REF 3—summarized remarks from reference call 3.

Users Group—summarized remarks from reference to users group president.

Our Review—summarized of our background investigation.

Analysis—your analysis of the results of the reference calls and your analysis.

Based on the analysis you have performed, update the Implementability Worksheet.

Requirement	Ref 1	Ref 2	Ref 3	Users Group	Our Review	Analysis
			Implementability Reference Analysis Worksheet - Vendor A			
1. Vendor Responsiveness	Vendor gave more than they asked for.	Vendor was a pleasure to work with.	Wished all vendors were so easy to work with.	In most cases vendor adds the enhancements that the group requests.	N/A	All very positive.
2. Vendor Background	Not sure when company was started. Thinks there are 150 employees. Did not know the types of customer the vendor has.	Not sure when company was started. Thinks there are 143 employees. Customer base seems similar to ours.	Not sure when company was started. Not sure of number of employees. Not sure of type of customer.	Company founded eight years ago. Thinks there are 143 employees. Customer base seems similar to ours.	N/A	Same as information received from vendor.
3. Software Maturity	Package has very few bugs.	Have found no bugs in the package.	Had no problem with the package.	Members have found a few bugs in the product. Vendor fixed them quickly. New releases are relatively bug-free.	N/A	No problems with Package

Figure 8-5. Implementability Reference Analysis Worksheet—Vendor A

Implementability Reference Analysis Worksheet – Vendor A

Requirement	Ref 1	Ref 2	Ref 3	Users Group	Our Review	Analysis
4. Technology Maturity	No problem with the technology.	No problem with the technology.	No problem with the technology.	Technology is sound and has been used for over two years.	Looked solid no holes found.	Technology looks good.
5. Modifications					N/A	Revised cost for must have modification, has been reduced to $12,000.
6. Third party	Used Elsa Associates.	Used Efey Corp.	Used Ariella Associates.	No knowledge of ABC Associates.	Background check of ABC Associates; has fair references. Could not find other third party in area.	ABC Associates; has poor references. Could not find other third party in area.
7. Implementation Assistance	Used third party, see above.	Used third party, see above.	Used third party, see above.	Implementation from third party.	Vendor experienced in our area but ABC Associates is not.	Vendor experienced in our area but ABC Associates is not.

Figure 8-5. Implementability Reference Analysis Worksheet—Vendor A (continued)

8. Quality	Excellent.	Excellent.	Excellent.		Review of code very good.	All had excellent reviews of the package's quality.
9. Documentation	Documentation is fair.	Never use it.	Fair.		All documentation available. Most did not have indexes. Some were confusing at times.	All documentation available. Most did not have indexes. Some were confusing at times.
10. Training	Had some bad classes with one instructor (Mr. A).	Terrible classes with one instructor (Mr. A).	Their classes are a waste of time (used instructor Mr. A).	They had problems with getting good instructors.	Class was excellent. Instructor Mr. A still teaching most of the classes.	Looks like the class we audited had their best instructor. One instructor that teaches most of the classes is poor.

Figure 8-5. Implementability Reference Analysis Worksheet—Vendor A (*continued*)

For example, reviewing the Reference Analysis Worksheet (Figure 8-5) we can update the Implementability Worksheet (Figure 8-6) as follows:

Vendor responsiveness—all the references very positive. Rating changed to 10.

Vendor background—same as information received from vendor. Rating remains the same. Rating = 6.

Software maturity—No problems with package. Rating changed to 10.

Technology maturity—Technology is sound and has been used for over 2 years. Rating changed to a 10.

Modifications—Based on the change in cost of modification (see cost section). Rating changed to an 8.

Implementability Worksheet					
Requirement	Company Need	Package A Rating	Package A Weighted Rating	Package B Rating	Package A Weighted Rating
1. Vendor Responsiveness	10	10	100	5	50
2. Vendor Background	7	6	42	7	49
3. Software Maturity	3	10	30	8	24
4. Technology Maturity	7	9	63	7	49
5. Modifications	10	8	80	7	70
6. Third Party	10	2	20	10	100
7. Implementation Assistance	10	4	40	9	90
8. Quality	7	10	70	6	42
9. Documentation	7	3	21	2	14
10. Training	7	2	14	3	21
Total Percentage Fit	78		480		509
Maximum Package Weighted Rating	10		780		780
Vendor Implementability Rating			63%		65%

Figure 8-6. Implementability Worksheet

Third party—ABC Associates, has poor references. Could not find other third party in area. Updated rating changed to a 2.

Implementation assistance—Vendor experienced in our area but ABC Associates is not. Updated rating changed to a 4.

Quality—All had excellent reviews of the package's quality. Updated rating changed to a 10.

Documentation—All documentation available. Most did not have indexes. Some were confusing at times. Updated rating changed to a 3.

Training—Class we audited had their best instructor. One instructor who teaches most of the classes is poor. Updated rating changed to a 2.

Update the implementability rating by recalculating each packages totaling the package's Weighted Rating column and placing the results in the Total Percentage Fit line. Then divide the Total Percentage Fit the Maximum Value-Implementability, which is the same as we calculated in Chapter 6. Enter the result on the Percentage Fit Implementability. For example, the Implementability score for Package A is:

$$\text{Total Percentage Fit}^{PkgA} = \text{Total Weighted Fit}^{PkgA}/\text{Maximum Value}$$

$$= 480/780$$

$$= 63\%$$

Then enter the Implementability Percentage Fit for each package from the Implementability Worksheet onto the R^2ISC Analysis Matrix (Figure 8-7). The weighted Implementability rating is updated on the R^2ISC Analysis Matrix

Update the Vendors' Supportability Rating

Summarize the information gathered information the on the Supportability Reference Analysis Worksheet (Figure 8-8). The Supportability Reference Analysis Worksheet has row for each of the Implementability criteria and the following columns:

REF 1—summarized remarks from reference call 1.

REF 2—summarized remarks from reference call 2.

R²ISC Analysis Matrix—Updated for Implementability					
High-Level Requirements	Company's Need	Package A Percentage Fit	Package A Weighted Percentage Fit	Package B Percentage Fit	Package B Weighted Percentage Fit
Current Requirements	30	85%	26%	96%	29%
Future Requirements	25	69%	17%	68%	17%
Implementability	20	63%	13%	65%	13%
Supportability	15	64%	10%	76%	11%
Cost	10	58%	6%	24%	2%
R²ISC Rating			72%		71%

Figure 8-7. R²ISC Analysis Matrix—Updated for Implementability

REF 3—summarized remarks from reference call 3.

Users group—summarized remarks from reference to users group president.

Our review—summarized our background investigation.

Analysis—analysis of the results of the reference calls and your analysis.

Based on the analysis you have performed, update the Supportability Worksheet.

For example, reviewing the Supportability Reference Analysis Worksheet (Figure 8-8) we can update the Supportability Summary Worksheet (Figure 8-9) that was developed in Figure 6-16 as follows:

Vendor responsiveness—This is the rating we developed in the implementability section. Rating changed to 10.

Quality—This is the rating we developed in the implementability section. Rating changed to 10.

Development methodology—The package was developed in C. New modules use written in Rational Rose. Rating changed to 7 (because most of the programs are written in C they receive five points. Because they started to use Rational Rose CASE tool they receive an extra two points.)

Modifications—This is the rating we developed in the implementability section. Rating changed to 8.

	Supportability Reference Analysis Worksheet – Vendor A					
Requirement	Ref 1	Ref 2	Ref 3	Users Group	Our Review	Analysis
1. Vendor Responsiveness	Vendor gave more than they asked for.	Vendor was a pleasure to work with.	Wished all vendors were so easy to work with.	In most cases vendor adds the enhancements that the group requests.	N/A	All very positive.
2. Quality	Excellent.	Excellent.	Excellent.		Review of code very good.	All had excellent reviews of the package's quality.
3. Development Methodology	Most of the package is developed in C. New modules use Rational Rose.	Does not know.	Does not know.	Most of the package is developed in C. New modules use Rational Rose.	Most of the package is developed in C. New modules use Rational Rose.	Most of the package was developed in C. New modules use Rational Rose.
4. Modifications	Vendor does not support modifications.	Vendor does not support modifications.	Vendor does not support modifications.	Vendor does not support modifications.		Third party not reliable. But small amount of modifications we can support internally.
5. Technology	No problem with the technology.	No problem with the technology.	No problem with the technology.	Technology is sound and has been used for over two years.	Looked solid no holes found.	Technology looks good.

Figure 8-8. Supportability Reference Analysis Worksheet—Vendor A

Supportability Reference Analysis Worksheet – Vendor A

Requirement	Ref 1	Ref 2	Ref 3	Users Group	Our Review	Analysis
6. Financial Stability	Do not know.	Vendor had a problem a year and a half ago. But received venture capital moneys.	Vendor had a problem two years ago. But, worked out the problem.	Vendor had a problem a year and a half ago. They received bank financing.	Audited statements show that they may have problems in two years if sales don't increase.	Fair financials can have trouble in future. But may be taken over by JCN.
7. Warranty					Rumors of take over by JCN.	Copy of warranty reviewed as part of RFP response.
8. Users Groups	National users group very strong.	National users group. Do not attend meetings.	National users group very strong.	National users group very strong. Seventy percent of users send representatives. No local groups.	N/A	Strong national users group. No local group.
9. Support Functions	Good support. They really open an hour early and close an hour later than advertised.	Have had times when did not call back for days.	Support is very poor.	Vendor has been having problems with support which they are working on.	Time overlaps with our needs.	Support is poor.

Figure 8-8. Supportability Reference Analysis Worksheet–Vendor A (*continued*)

Supportability Summary Worksheet					
	Company Rating	Package A Rating	Package A Weighted Rating	Package B Rating	Package B Weighted Rating
1. Vendor Responsiveness	10	10	100	5	50
2. Quality	10	10	100	6	60
3. Development Methodology	10	7	70	10	100
4. Modifications	7	8	56	7	49
5. Technology	7	8	56	9	63
6. Financial Stability	10	4	40	8	80
7. Warranty	7	5	35	7	49
8. Users Groups	7	6	42	10	70
9. Support Functions	10	2	20	7	70
TOTAL	78		519		591
Maximum Value Supportability	10		780		780
Weighted Average Supportability	—	—	67%		76%

Figure 8-9. Supportability Summary Worksheet

Technology—Technology looks good; no change from original analysis. Rating stays an 8.

Financial stability—Fair financials; can have trouble in future. But may be taken over by JCN. Rating changes to a 4. Based on past problems and analysis of financial statements and possible takeover.

Warranty—Copy of warranty reviewed as part of RFP response. Rating remains a 9.

Users groups—Strong national users group. No local group. Rating updated to a 6 based on the fact there is no local users group.

Support functions—Support is poor. Rating changed to 2.

Updated the supportability rating on the Supportability Summary Worksheet (Figure 8-9) by recalculating each package totaling the package's Weighted Rating column and placing the results in the Total Percentage Fit line. Then divide the Total Percentage Fit the Maximum Value-Supportability (which is the same as we calcu-

R²ISC Analysis Matrix—Updated for Supportability					
High-Level Requirements	Company's Need	Package A Percentage Fit	Package A Weighted Percentage Fit	Package B Percentage Fit	Package B Weighted Percentage Fit
Current Requirements	30	85%	26%	96%	29%
Future Requirements	25	69%	17%	68%	17%
Implementability	20	63%	13%	65%	13%
Supportability	15	67%	10%	67%	10%
Cost	10	58%	6%	24%	2%
R²ISC Rating			72%		71%

Figure 8-10. R²ISC Analysis Matrix—Updated for Supportability

lated in Chapter 6). Enter the result on the Percentage Fit Supportability. For example, the Implementability score for Package A is:

$$\text{Total Percentage Fit}^{PkgA} = \text{Total Weighted Fit}^{PkgA}/\text{Maximum Value}$$

$$= 519/780$$

$$= 67\%$$

Then enter the Supportability Percentage Fit for each package from the Supportability Summary Worksheet onto the R²ISC Analysis Matrix (Figure 8-10). The weighted Supportability rating is updated on the R²ISC Analysis Matrix.

Selecting the Winner

Once you have updated the R²ISC Analysis Matrix, you are now ready to select the winning package. Sum the R²ISC Worksheet, and the package with the highest score is the winner.

For example, on Figure 8-11, when the total weighted R²ISC scores were added, the package with the highest score was Package C with a score of 86%. It came the closest to meeting our needs. You can also see this on the R²ISC Graph (Figure 8-12).

R²ISC Analysis Matrix

High-Level Requirements	Company's Need	Package A Percentage Fit	Package A Weighted Percentage Fit	Package B Percentage Fit	Package B Weighted Percentage Fit	Package C Percentage Fit	Package C Weighted Percentage Fit	Package D Percentage Fit	Package D Weighted Percentage Fit
Current Requirements	30	85%	26%	96%	29%	90%	27%	80%	24%
Future Requirements	25	69%	17%	68%	17%	85%	21%	95%	24%
Implementability	20	63%	13%	65%	13%	85%	17%	35%	7%
Supportability	15	67%	10%	74%	11%	80%	12%	50%	8%
Cost	10	58%	6%	24%	2%	94%	9%	44%	4%
R²ISC Rating			71%		73%		86%		66%

Figure 8-11. R²ISC Analysis Matrix

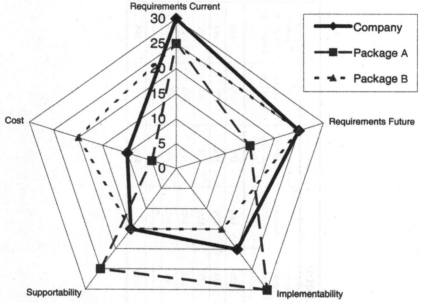

Figure 8-12. R²ISC Graph

Next Step

Contract negotiations should begin as soon as the winner has been selected. (It's advisable to keep one other vendor in the wings as backup in case you cannot agree upon a contract with the first vendor.

Now that you have selected the winner, the time-consuming part comes. That's right, negotiating the contract. This can take longer than the whole selection process.

The next chapter describes things to look out for and a negotiating strategy.

9

Contract Negotiations

The final step in the selection process is negotiating the contract. This sounds like the simplest step, but it can take as much time as the entire selection process. Many companies think that negotiating the software contract means haggling over the price. Unfortunately these companies later find out that price negotiations don't make up for the cost and aggravation of not changing some of the clauses in the contract.

When you receive the contract for a new house that you're going to buy, you review it with a fine-tooth comb and then pass it on to a real estate lawyer who does the same. You should handle a software contract just as you would a contract for a house. And keep in mind, there are actually more ways you can get hurt in a software contract than in a real estate contract.

The price of the package is determined in a number of ways including the number of users that have the right to use the software, the number of users that can use the software at the same time (simultaneous users), and size of the computer the package will run on. Determine which method is best for you and then negotiate. If you have a lot of users who will use the package only occasionally, do not use the number of users method. If you will be running a lot of other programs on the same computer that the package will be running on do not use the computer size pricing.

The vendor will present you with a standard printed contract containing lots of fine print and blank spaces for the price and the name of the modules you will be purchasing. The implication is that the only things negotiable are the price and modules. In reality, every aspect of the contact is negotiable. Do not be intimidated by the legalese and fine print.

Review each and every word in the contract. Question any point that is not in your best interest because the boilerplate contract offered by the vendor is written by the vendor's lawyers and is designed to protect only one party—the vendor.

Because each vendor has its own contract and changes it from time to time, you must diligently review every line of the contract. When reading the contract consider how each clause can be used against you. By making these changes in the software contract you can turn the document into a fair agreement for both parties. Do not expect the vendor to accept all the changes. Be prepared; negotiations can be tough.

Make sure you understand exactly what you're signing before it's too late. Consider these cautionary tales:

A company was selling off a large division including the division's computer center. When the software vendor found out about the sale, it required that a new licensee fee be paid by the buyer because a clause in the contract prevented the transfer of the software license in the event of the company's sale.

In another case, a company informed the software vendor it was moving the computer and its software to a different location. The vendor requested a new licensing fee because there was a clause in the contract stating the software was licensed to a specific machine at a specific location. The only way the contract allowed for a change in location was if the entire data center was being moved. But in this case only the single machine was being moved to a different data center. The company did not pay the new licensing fee, but it did incur legal fees and a great deal of stress in fighting the clause. All this could have been avoided if the software contract was scrutinized more carefully.

Remember that even though the vendor may have an excellent reputation and you may have been dealing with them for years, it may not be the vendor you know who winds up enforcing the contract. There has been a consolidation within the software industry. Another vendor may buy out the vendor you select or the vendor may sell the software package to another company. The lesson here is that you must always assume that every detail of the contract will be strictly enforced.

Clauses to Watch Out For

Beware of the following clauses if they appear in your contract. They should be modified before you sign on the dotted line.

Non-transferability—sounds innocent enough, but companies are finding that if they are sold, the vendor claims the software is being transferred and requires a new license fee. This type of clause should be modified to allow for transfer of the license in case of:

sale of company

sale of a division

sale of the computer (should you decide to out-source your computer operations).

The license is for a specific CPU—should you decide to upgrade or replace your computer, the vendor can legally request a new license fee. Modify this so the program can be transferred to any computer, provided the pricing is not based on the computer's size. Include a clause specifying that the cost of upgrading to a larger computer will be based on the same discount as the original purchase. If the package pricing is based on the model (size) the package is running on, then the contract should also document that the price list used for calculating any future upgrade fee is the one that was in effect when the contract was signed. If the reason for upgrading the computer is not related to this package, document in the contract that no additional fee will be charged. For example, say you've purchased accounting software and now are adding a manufacturing system. You will need a larger computer to run both systems, but the upgrade does not affect the accounting system—no more users will be on the system, and you will not be processing more transactions. Therefore, there should be no additional charge.

The license is for a specific site—Should you decide to move the computer, the vendor can (and some have) request a new license fee. Modify this so the program is licensed to your company and can be moved from site to site.

Software is for use of internal operation and for processing the company's data—This is included to prevent you from operating a service bureau that uses the software, without the software vendor receiving any additional royalties. This can also prevent you from running another of your division's data on the package. This is especially true if one of the divisions that will be running the package is not wholly owned by your company and especially if you own less than 50 percent of the division. Modify this to allow the running of any data from any company you own or with which you have an affiliation.

Nondisclosure Clause

Software vendors are very protective of their material, and rightfully so. A nondisclosure clause states that any information provided by the vendor is restricted to the licensee's authorized employees. Modify this to include consultants, contractors, or other third parties retained by the company. This type of clause can prevent you from using less expensive third party maintenance agreements or hiring an independent consultant to make modifications.

Make Sure It Is in Writing

Salespeople like to promise the world but in reality, the fine print of the contract states that all other agreements (written or verbal) such as proposals, purchase orders, etc., are superseded by the contract. Nothing but the contract carries any weight in a court of law. Hold the vendor responsible for any conditions that are in your RFP, make sure your lawyer includes the vendors response to the RFP, the purchase order, promotional material, and any other document related to the acquisition as part of the contract.

Warranty

The software vendor's warranty will state that they are only responsible for fixing defects (bugs) and to use its best efforts to fix the problems. The contract can also state that the vendor is not responsible for any losses suffered by the customer as a result of bugs in the software. Try to modify this clause so the software vendor is responsible for any damages caused by their errors, including the time you spend finding the problem and any monetary loss you suffer. This is especially important if the package you'll be implementing has never been used before. Be advised that most vendors will not go along with this change to the standard contract because the liabilities can be very high. You may just have to give in on this one.

Ownership of Modifications

Contracts are often written so that any modifications to the program become the property of the software vendor. This is ridiculous. Any changes you make or have a third party make for you should be your property. The software vendor should not be allowed to copy code that you had custom written without paying a royalty fee to you. However, in cases where the vendor makes the modifications, you should allow the vendor to have the code if they will include the modification in the next upgrade of the package. Because this will allow you to upgrade to future releases easily, have the vendor support the modification with documentation and a Help Line. If, for any reason, the modification gives you a strategic advantage over your competition, do not let the vendor use it for any other client.

Additional Copies of the Software

Some contracts limit the right to have additional copies of the software to one copy of the software as a backup if something happens to the original copy. You should have second copy for off-site storage and a third copy for disaster recovery site. If you have a test machine (where you test modifications to a program before you use them in production) you should be allowed a copy for it. Some contracts limit the use of the software to the installation site or a second site that is owned or controlled by the customer. You should be allowed to run the package on a third party's disaster recovery computer.

Some vendors specify that you may only run a second copy of the program for testing purposes, and they consider testing to mean testing the system during your implementation. Do not allow them to limit how long you can use the testing version of the program after the initial testing period especially because you need the right to test any future new releases and modifications.

Vendor Bankruptcy

Software vendors often assign your contract to a third party. This can force you to continue paying licensing fees for the software even if the vendor is out of business or goes bankrupt. Include a clause saying that if the company goes out of business or declares bankruptcy no more payments are due.

Duplication of Documentation

The contract should allow you to photocopy all of the user manuals the vendor has to offer for your software. Usually the vendor will tell you verbally that you can make as many copies as you want. In many cases they will agree to put it in writing.

Performance-Based Payment

A catch phrase with vendors today is, "I want to be your partner." Let them prove it. Let them be a partner in the success or failure of the implementation of their package. Payment for the software and implementation assistance can be based on you meeting certain criteria, e.g., cost savings you realize from the package if the implementation is on time and budget. These savings could the savings of the under portion of the implementation and the savings you realize in your business from the improved processes.

Additional Clauses to Be Added

Although the following clauses are not normally included in a contract, you should add them.

> **Limit Increases to Maintenance Fees**—Limit how much the vendor can raise the maintenance fee. Ideally the vendor should not raise its maintenance fee for three to five years and after that no more than the rate of inflation. It is not uncommon for vendors to raise their maintenance fees.

Upgrade Fees—You receive upgrades within a certain number of months after purchasing the package for free or at a reduced cost.

Source Code Escrow Account—If you are not purchasing the source code, it should be put in escrow and held by a responsible third party. In the event that the vendor goes out of business, is sold, or files for bankruptcy, the source code is given to you by the third party. You will need access to the source code to make required modifications and future enhancements.

Delivery, Acceptance, and Payment—There should be specific acceptance criteria for the system. You do not accept the software and you do not pay the vendor until he has met all of the acceptance criteria. The acceptance criteria should include both that the modification meets your functional requirements and that the response time of the system meets with the modifications.

Delivery and Acceptance of Modifications—If the vendor is going to modify the system to meet your current requirement, then there should be addition acceptance criteria including the script (which has the action to performed and the expected results) for the functionality that the modifications must successfully execute and performance measurements. If the vendor cannot meet the acceptance criteria, no payment should be made, and if there was payment made, the money should be returned.

Negotiating Strategy

Timing and quotas are key vendor motivators in negotiating a contract. The vendor has four critical dates before which it wants to have contracts signed. The most important date is the vendor's fiscal year-end. If the vendor, the sales territory, and the salesperson have not made their yearly quotas, the vendor will do almost anything to get the sale before the year-end. You can obtain the year-end date from the vendor's annual report.

The other three important dates are the end of each of the fiscal quarters. They, like the year-end, are when quotas come due. Although these sales quotas tend not to be as critical as year-end quotas, salespeople are under a great deal of pressure at this time. This is especially true for a public company that reports quarterly results.

Vendors want to maximize the revenue they receive from each contract. Knowing this fact can influence your negotiating strategy. You may give up some of the price discount that you wanted to achieve to get additional software at no charge that you can use but did not intend to purchase, and or additional services such as implantation assistance, consulting, and/or training classes. Be careful about getting no-charge software because the vendor may charge you an annual maintenance fee on the free modules

Have a predetermined outcome in mind before you begin negotiating. Remember, the vendor will become your partner and you need a vendor that will remain financially strong to be able to support the package in the future. So do not try to get the package for nothing. Make the negotiations a win-win situation.

Before you sign the contract I would also recommend having a lawyer who specializes in software contracts review the contract.

Additional Resource

For additional ideas on how to negotiate with vendors you can read: *Getting to YES Negotiating Agreement Without Giving In* by Roger Fisher, William Ury, and Bruce Patton of the Harvard Negotiation Project. Penguin Books, 1991.

10

Workshops

A workshop is a collaborative meeting of people, with a leader called a facilitator, used to quickly come to a consensus result. Workshops apply the power of many individuals, often from different areas to identify common needs and problems. In the package selection process it is used when there are more than four people are involved in the process. The purpose of the workshop will vary based on where in the process it is used.

Using Workshops in R²ISC

There are several times in the R²ISC package selection process that lends itself quite naturally to the workshop approach. These include:

R²ISC Criteria Rating Workshop

Workshop Purpose: management must agree on the rating for each of the R²ISC criteria and if the package will be used in multiple business areas agreement on the relative importance of each business area.

When more than two persons are responsible for rating the R²ISC criteria it is beneficial to have them all in the same room at the same time with the facilitator to ensure that a consensus is reached on the R²ISC criteria ratings. This is especially true if they have different points of view and different objectives. If you do not resolve differences early on, you will have problems later when you present the selected package to them for approval.

Participants: executive sponsor, steering committee, facilitator, and scribe.

Time frame: half a day to one day depending on the number and diversity of the participants.

Deliverable: R^2ISC Analysis Matrix (Figure 6-9) with company need agreed upon and if the package covers multiple business areas then Business Area Summary Worksheet (Figure 6-4) should also have the company needs completed.

Other output: Workshop Minutes

Agenda:

Introduction

Review purpose of workshop

Explain R^2ISC criteria

Discussions on impact to company

Rate R^2ISC criteria

Rating of business area (if package is for multiple business areas)

Current Requirements Workshop

Workshop Purpose: To develop and rate the detailed requirements for each of five R^2ISC criteria.

Workshops speed the process of developing requirements. It is also a good way to get consensus on the rating of each requirement. There should be separate requirements and separate workshops for each of the five R^2ISC criteria. When workshops are used to develop requirements they:

- Provide for rapid collection of requirements.
- Allow users to understand the needs of users in other departments.
- Promote user involvement and "ownership" of the resultant system.
- Lead to the development of user-driven business analysis and system definition.
- Establish early consensus between future users.

- Establish a partnership between users and IT department.
- Minimize likelihood of missing or misunderstanding requirements.

Current Requirements Workshop

Participants: selection team, business expert, project manager, additional users as required, facilitator, scribe and any other outside expert such as customer, vendors, process expert, and industry expert.

Time frame: one to three days for each functional area.

Deliverable: Current Requirements Analysis Worksheet (Figure 6-3) with company need column completed

Other output: Issues Log and Workshop Minutes

Agenda:

Introduction

Review purpose of workshop

Development of requirements

Determination of rating for each requirement

Future Requirements Workshop

Workshop Purpose: Review and rate each of the future requirements.

Participants: data processing experts, data expert, expert users (as observers), selection team, facilitator, the scribe and any other outside expert as required.

Time frame: one to three days.

Deliverable: Future Requirements Worksheet (Figure 6-10) with the names of the components and their ratings.

Other output: Issues Log and Workshop Minutes.

Agenda:

Introduction

Review purpose of workshop

Review or development of architecture and development environment

Determination of rating for each comment

Implementability Workshop

Workshop Purpose: Review and rate each of the implementability requirements.

Participants: selection team, facilitator, the scribe, and any other personnel required.

Time frame: half a day.

Deliverable: Implementability Summary Worksheet (Figure 6-11) with company ratings.

Other output: Issues Log and Workshop Minutes.

Agenda:

Introduction

Review purpose of workshop

Review of Implementability components

Determination of rating for each component

Supportability Workshop

Workshop Purpose: Review and rate each of the supportability requirements.

Participants: selection team, business experts, project manager, facilitator, the scribe, and any other personnel required.

Time frame: half a day.

Deliverable: Supportability Summary Worksheet (Figure 6-12) with company ratings.

Other output: Issues Log and Workshop Minutes.

Agenda:

Introduction

Review purpose of workshop

Review of Supportability components

Determination of rating for each component

Cost Workshop

Workshop Purpose: Review and rate each of the cost requirements.

Participants: selection team, business experts, facilitator, the scribe, and any other personnel as required.

Time frame: half a day.

Deliverable: Cost Summary Worksheet (Figure 6-14) with company ratings.

Other output: Issues Log and Workshop Minutes.

Agenda:

Introduction

Review purpose of workshop

Review of Cost components

Determination of rating for each component

Selecting the Winning Vendor

Workshop Purpose: Consensus is extremely important in selecting the package. Using a workshop ensures that everyone is heard and their opinions discussed. The purpose is to select the winning vendor and to insure that all users' give their input on the selected winning vendor.

Participants: selection team, business experts who participated in the selection process, the project manager, facilitator, scribe, and any other outside expert deemed necessary. (Only company employees should vote on the package.)

Time frame: one to two days.

Deliverable: name of winning package and completed R^2ISC Analysis Matrix (Figure 6-9).

Other output: Workshop Minutes.

Agenda:

Introduction

Review purpose of workshop

Review of each package ratings

Completion of: R^2ISC Analysis Matrix (Figure 8-4)

Approval of winning vendor

Workshop Participants

For workshop dynamics to be the most productive, the ideal makeup of the workshop is has between six and twenty-four participants with ideas and information to contribute. Of the participants approximately 75 percent should be users and 25 percent should be systems and administrative personnel (scribe, facilitator, etc.).

In addition to the users and selection team, a workshop must have business experts, a facilitator, and scribe. Their roles are as follows:

- Facilitator—This person leads the discussions, keeping them moving and focused on objectives of the workshop. The Facilitator enforces the ground rules (defined below) and ensures that all parties are treated equally, regardless of their position in the company. Before the workshop the Facilitator is responsible for the pre-workshop materials, ensuring that they are developed and distributed. The facilitator must be neutral and should not be part of the selection team.

- Business expert—These representatives of the end-user department make up most of the attendees at the Requirements Development and Rating workshop. They provide input regarding existing business practices, contribute key information about the industry when relevant, and help identify the requirements. Most importantly, the business experts should keep an ear open for ideas that have business relevance but may be overlooked while talking about systems.

- Scribe—This person takes the minutes at the workshop and collates the ideas that emerge from the workshop and prepares the workshop report. The scribe assists the Facilitator in developing the pre-workshop materials.

In addition to the facilitator and scribe there are times when the following experts can be beneficial to a package selection workshop.

- Industry expert—No company functions in a vacuum; each one is part of a larger industry that has its own processes, regulations, etc. This representative advises the group on issues that may arise pertaining to both the company and its industry. These issues can include best practices, industry trends, etc.
- Project manager—If anyone has to have the last word on the project, it's the project manager. He is responsible for completing the project on time, within budget and on target.

Workshop Preparation

Once the project manager and selection team selected the participants of the workshop, each of the participants should be formally invited to the workshop with a letter from the project sponsor. Accompanying the invitation letter there should be pre-workshop materials that include:

Agenda

Workshop's Ground Rules

Pre-Workshop Reading

- R^2ISC criteria rating workshop—(a copy of this book) R^2ISC criteria and their definitions
- Requirements and rating workshop—(a copy of this book) predefined requirements if available
- Selecting the winning vendor workshop—none

Make sure that you have all the equipment and the supplies that you will need. It becomes very frustrating when you do not have enough pens or you run out of paper. Use this checklist for equipment and supplies so you do not forget anything.

Two overhead projectors—one for the document being reviewed (i.e., current requirements) and the other for reference documents or notes

Extension cords

Transparencies of the documentation that may be required during the workshop

Blank transparencies

Overhead pens

Two flipchart stands with at least four flipcharts

Markers

Masking tape to hang flipchart sheets on walls

Computer for scribe

Computer, if needed

Data show (if information on a computer is going to be used)

Name cards

Notepads—one for each participant

Pencils

Room setup

Although you can set up your workshop room any way you like, a semicircle with tables works very well. This way all participants can see each other and are on the same level (see Figure 10-1, Room Layout for Workshops). The walls are used to hang the flip chart paper.

Ground Rules

Although spontaneous workshop discussions are important, certain rules should be established to maintain productive, positive, and fair collaborative environment. Distribute a list of the rules in advance of the meeting and tell participants the rules will be enforced through-

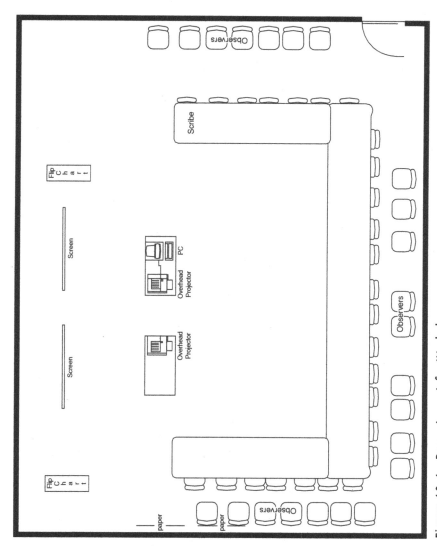

Figure 10-1. Room Layout for Workshops

out the workshop by the facilitator. Here is a list of some of the important ground rules:

- Workshop starts on time
- Punctuality counts
- Treat everyone equal
- One conversation at a time
- Respect everyone's view
- Outcome is everyone's responsibility
- Silence means consent
- Ask if you don't understand something
- If agreement can't be reached, the issue is parked on 'Open Issues List'
- No finger pointing
- No interruptions
- Shut off all cell phones
- Facilitator is neutral.

Agenda

The agenda for the workshop should be developed and sent with the invitation. When making up the agenda remember the following:

Breaks should be scheduled every hour and a half to two hours. After about two hours the level of participation decreases.

It's always a good idea to offer your participants breakfast. This usually gets them there on time.

The agenda should contain the following. For a sample agenda see Figure 10-2.

Welcome

Review objectives and output

Introduction of attendees

Review agenda and ground rules

Workshop purpose

Review Open Items list

Wrap up and thank participants

Current Requirements Workshop—Accounts Payable Agenda July 1, 2000	
8:00–8:30	Breakfast.
8:30–8:40	Welcome by John Smith - President.
8:40–8:50	Review objectives and output.
8:50–9:00	Introduction of attendees.
9:00–9:10	Review agenda and ground rules.
9:10–10:00	Develop requirements for entry of payment information.
10:00–10:15	Break.
10:00–12:00	Develop requirements for matching receiving report with?
12:00–1:00	Lunch.
1:00–2:00	Requirements for payments.
2:00–2:30	Requirements for reporting.
2:30–2:45	Break.
2:45–3:15	Requirements for reporting (continued).
3:15–4:15	Rating of requirements.
4:15–4:30	Review action list.
4:30–4:45	Wrap up.

Figure 10-2. Sample Agenda

During the Workshop

The workshop follows the agenda. When you get to the workshop purpose you get to the heart of the workshop. You review worksheets that pertain to the area being covered. If the worksheet needs additional information it should be added based on the input of the participants. If additional information is needed but not available, it is put on the Open Issues list. When the items need to be rated the participants should come to a consensus on the ratings.

- When the group reaches a consensus, the topic is closed and the discussion moves on to the next topic.
- If consensus can't be reached on a given issue, add it to an open item list and assign it to a participant who is responsible for the issues until it is resolved. There is also a resolution date assigned.

After the Workshop

After the workshop is completed the workshop report needs to be put together and the Open Issues list resolved.

Workshop Report

The workshops should have a written documentation of the open issues and results. The documents that make up the workshop Report are developed during the Workshop. They should only need some minor cleanup and or formatting. The Workshop Report should include the following:

- Open Issues list—including person assigned and due date
- Minutes of the workshop
- Results of the workshop.

All attendees should have the workshop report within one day of the completion of the workshop. If the workshop is more than one day, the results of the previous day should be available at the start of the next workshop. Solicit comments for the recipients. If there are any updates needed, make them in a timely manner and distribute them to all the participants.

Open Issues List

At the workshop the items that could not be resolved were put on an Open Issues list. The list included the person responsible for obtaining a resolution and the date that it will be resolved. Remember, just because one person is responsible for the resolution does not mean that there will not be other people needed to resolve the issue. After the demonstration someone, such the project manager, keeps a weekly status of the progress of the open issues. Once they are resolved, any worksheets that are impacted should be updated and distributed to the attendees.

11

Developing the Plan and Selecting the Team

Now that you understand the basics of R^2ISC, you can begin to use it. In order to do so you need to develop a plan and select a team of people to put that plan into action. The following section is a primer on basic project management. If you are familiar with project management you can skip this chapter. It is meant to give you an overview of the tools needed to run a successful project. If you are managing a selection process and have not managed one before, you should make sure you have at least some basic project management training.

The Plan

Developing a software selection plan is as intricate as planning to build a house. You need detailed blueprints (directions) and you must follow them . . . so walls don't go up before electrical wires are installed. (Believe it or not, this has actually happened! Or even worse, just days before a new school was to open, the builders realized they'd never built bathrooms!) Developing a plan and sticking to it is extremely important.

The size of the software system under consideration—how many people will use the system and its data, and the cost of the system—determines how formal the process needs to be and how many people need to participate. Going back to our house building analogy, when you are building a shed you can draw the plans and develop a material list on a piece of scrap paper. If you don't make too many mistakes you can get the shed built on time. Because only one carpenter is involved you do not have to worry that he will interfere with the plumber. On the other hand, when you want to build a three-bedroom house you need formal blueprints that have been approved by the city and have a detailed plan of what everyone needs to be doing. A formal plan makes sure that the right workers are on the job at the right time. You do not want the plumber to come while the foundation is drying. With the selection process, you do not want to write your script for the demonstration before you have your requirements defined.

If the project is for an ERP system that involves the entire company, you need a very detailed formal plan. On the other hand, if two or three people in only one department will use the package and its data, the plan can be informal as long as the objectives of each phase of the R^2ISC process are accomplished.

First let us define the terminology we'll be using.

Project—The selection process (or building of the house) is called the project and a project is broken down into phases.

Phase—A phase in building a house might be the construction of each floor (basement, first floor, second floor, attic, etc.). The phases in the selection process are starting the Journey, Determining Detailed R^2ISC Requirements, Narrowing the Field, Picking the Winner, Finalizing Contract, and Project Management.

Activity—Phases are further broken down into activities. Constructing each room (master bedroom, master bath, etc.) would be activities in house building. For example, the Determining Detailed R^2ISC Requirements phase is broken down into developing the requirements for each business area (i.e., general ledger, accounts payable, etc.).

Tasks—Finally, activities are broken down into tasks. Tasks would include putting up the walls in the master bedroom or installing the electrical wires in that same room. For example, the task of developing the requirements for each business area is broken down into the following tasks: identify personnel for workshop, develop invitation, invite participants, develop pre-workshop material, arrange for workshop site, conduct workshop, and complete requirements. Each task should include the time it takes to complete each task and the people who will perform the task and any other resources required. You control the overall project at the task level.

Gantt Chart—A bar chart that shows tasks and their resources over time. Figure 11-1 is part of a Gantt Chart for the selec-

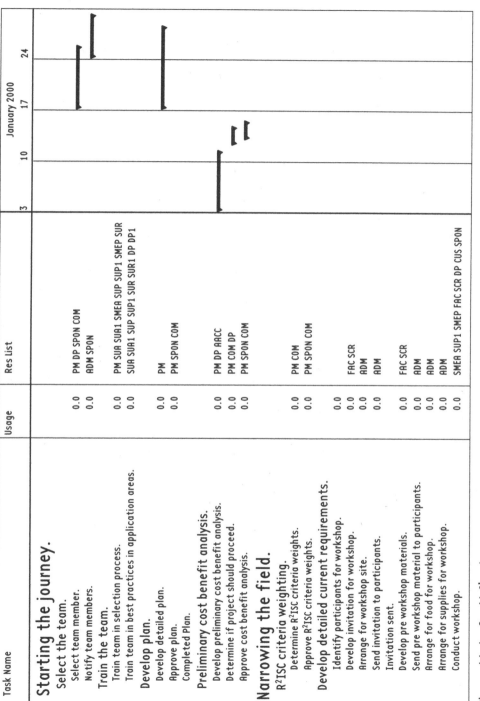

Task Name	Usage	Res List	January 2000
			3 10 17 24
Starting the journey.			
Select the team.			
Select team member.	0.0	PM DP SPON COM	
Notify team members.	0.0	ADM SPON	
Train the team.			
Train team in selection process.	0.0	PM SUR SUR1 SMEA SUP SUP1 SMEP SUR	
Train team in best practices in application areas.	0.0	SUR SUR1 SUP SUP1 SUR SUR1 DP DP1	
Develop plan.			
Develop detailed plan.	0.0	PM	
Approve plan.	0.0	PM SPON COM	
Completed Plan.			
Preliminary cost benefit analysis.			
Develop preliminary cost benefit analysis.	0.0	PM DP AACC	
Determine if project should proceed.	0.0	PM COM DP	
Approve cost benefit analysis.	0.0	PM SPON COM	
Narrowing the field.			
R²ISC criteria weighting.			
Determine R²ISC criteria weights.	0.0	PM COM	
Approve R²ISC criteria weights.	0.0	PM SPON COM	
Develop detailed current requirements.			
Identify participants for workshop.	0.0	FAC SCR	
Develop invitation for workshop.	0.0	ADM	
Arrange for workshop site.	0.0	ADM	
Send invitation to participants.	0.0	ADM	
Invitation sent.			
Develop pre workshop materials.	0.0	FAC SCR	
Send pre workshop material to participants.	0.0	ADM	
Arrange for food for workshop.	0.0	ADM	
Arrange for supplies for workshop.	0.0	ADM	
Conduct workshop.	0.0	SMEA SUP1 SMEP FAC SCR DP CUS SPON	

Figure 11-1. Gantt Chart

tion process; it lists (vertically) the phases, activities, and tasks associated with the selection process. A calendar runs horizontally across the chart so you can easily tell when activities should be completed and when milestones will be reached. The right side of the Gantt chart has a calendar on top; across from the task is a bar indicating the time frame that the activity will take place or when the milestone will be reached. The lines in some of the boxes are there to indicate the time frame in which the activity will take place.

Selection Plan

A selection plan of the phases, activities, tasks, and milestones that are need for the package selection project can be seen in Figure 11-2 Work Breakdown Structure. The plan is divided into six phases:

Starting the Journey (see Chapters 1 and 11)

Determining Detailed R^2ISC Requirements (see Chapters 2 to 4)

Narrowing the Field (see Chapters 5 and 6)

Analyzing the Finalist (see Chapters 7 and 8)

Contract Negotiations (see Chapter 9)

Project Management (see Chapter 11)

The first five phases are performed sequentially. The sixth phase, Project Management, is performed throughout the project.

The preliminary work is performed in the first phase, Starting the Journey. Here you set the foundation for the rest of the project. This phase is divided into the following four activities:

Selecting the Team—the project manager is responsible for choosing the members of the selection team that will analyze the packages.

Training the Team—the project manager ensures that the team knows what is expected of them and how to perform each task. You may need the assistance of the training department or an outside consultant.

Developing the Plan—the project manager is responsible for

Type	Name	Deliverable
Phase	**Starting the journey.**	
Activity	Select the team.	
Task	Select team member.	Team
Task	Notify team members.	
Activity	Train the team.	
Task	Train team in selection process.	
Task	Train team in best practices in application areas.	
Activity	Develop plan.	Plan
Task	Develop detailed plan.	
Task	Approve plan.	Approved plan
Milestone	Completed plan.	
Activity	Preliminary cost benefit analysis.	
Task	Develop preliminary cost benefit analysis.	
Task	Determine if project should proceed.	
Task	Approve cost benefit analysis.	Approved cost benefit Analysis
Phase	**Determining detailed R^2ISC requirements.**	
Activity	R^2ISC criteria weighting.	
Task	Determine R^2ISC criteria weights.	
Task	Approve R^2ISC criteria weights.	
Activity	Develop detailed current requirements Area 1.	
Task	Identify participants for workshop.	Workshop participants
Task	Develop invitation for workshop.	Workshop invitation
Task	Arrange for workshop site.	
Task	Send invitation to participants.	
Milestone	Invitation sent.	Invited participants
Task	Develop pre-workshop materials.	Pre-workshop material
Task	Send pre-workshop material to participants.	
Task	Arrange for food for workshop.	
Task	Arrange for supplies for workshop.	
Task	Conduct workshop.	
Task	Complete Area 1.	Requirements
Activity	Develop detailed current requirements Area 2.	
Task	Identify participants for workshop.	
Task	Develop invitation for workshop.	Workshop invitation
Task	Arrange for workshop site.	
Task	Send invitation to participants.	
Milestone	Invitation sent.	
Task	Develop pre-workshop materials.	Pre-workshop material
Task	Send pre-workshop material to participants.	
Task	Arrange for food for workshop.	
Task	Arrange for supplies for workshop.	
Task	Conduct workshop.	Requirements
Task	Complete Area 2.	
Milestone	Current functional requirements completed.	
Task	Approve functional requirements.	
Task	Incorporate into R^2ISC matrix.	

Figure 11-2. Work Breakdown Structure

Type	Name	Deliverable
Milestone	Functional requirements complete.	Current (Functional) Requirements
Activity	**Develop detailed future requirements.**	
Task	Develop technical architecture requirements.	
Task	Determine communication requirements.	
Task	Determine volume requirements.	
Task	Identify participants for future requirements workshop.	
Task	Develop invitation for workshop.	Workshop invitation
Task	Arrange for workshop site.	
Task	Send invitation to participants.	
Milestone	Invitation sent.	
Task	Prepare pre-workshop (tech rating) materials.	
Task	Send pre-workshop material to participants.	
Task	Arrange for food for workshop.	
Task	Arrange for supplies for workshop.	
Task	Technical rating workshop.	
Milestone	Technical requirements complete.	Future (Technical) Requirements
Task	Approve technical requirements.	
Task	Incorporate into R^2ISC matrix.	
Activity	**Determine detailed implementability requirements.**	
Task	Develop detailed implementability requirements.	
Task	Identify participants for workshop.	Workshop participants
Task	Develop invitation for workshop.	Workshop invitation
Task	Arrange for workshop site.	
Task	Send invitation to participants.	
Milestone	Invitation sent.	Invited participants
Task	Develop pre-workshop materials.	Pre-workshop material
Task	Send pre-workshop material to participants.	
Task	Arrange for food for workshop.	
Task	Arrange for supplies for workshop.	
Task	Conduct implementability workshop.	
Milestone	Implementability requirements completed.	Implementation Requirements
Task	Approve implementability requirements.	
Task	Incorporate into R^2ISC matrix.	
Activity	**Determine detailed supportability requirements.**	
Task	Develop detailed implementation supportability requirements.	
Task	Develop ongoing supportability requirements.	
Task	Identify participants for workshop.	Workshop participants
Task	Develop invitation for workshop.	Workshop invitation
Task	Arrange for workshop site.	
Task	Send invitation to participants.	
Milestone	Invitation sent.	Invited participants
Task	Develop pre-workshop materials.	Pre-workshop material
Task	Send pre-workshop material to participants.	
Task	Arrange for food for workshop.	
Task	Arrange for supplies for workshop.	
Task	Conduct implementability workshop.	
Milestone	Supportability requirements completed.	
Task	Incorporate into R^2ISC matrix.	
Milestone	Supportability requirements completed.	

Figure 11-2. Work Breakdown Structure (*continued*)

Type	Name	Deliverable
Activity	Determine detailed cost requirements.	
Task	Develop current cost requirements.	
Task	Develop future cost requirements.	
Task	Identify participants for workshop.	Workshop participants
Task	Develop invitation for workshop.	Workshop invitation
Task	Arrange for workshop site.	
Task	Send invitation to participants.	
Milestone	Invitation sent.	Invited participants
Task	Develop pre-workshop materials.	Pre-workshop material
Task	Send pre-workshop material to participants.	
Task	Arrange for food for workshop.	
Task	Arrange for supplies for workshop.	
Task	Conduct cost workshop.	
Milestone	Cost requirements completed.	Cost Requirements
Task	Approved cost requirements.	
Task	Incorporate into R^2ISC matrix.	
Phase	**Narrowing field.**	
Activity	Determine availability of packages.	
Activity	Develop key distinguishers.	
Task	Determine key distinguishers.	
Activity	Perform preliminary screening.	
Task	Analysis packages with software tool.	
Task	Determine vendors for consideration.	Vendors
Task	Approve vendors.	
Activity	Develop RFP.	
Task	Write RFP.	RFP
Task	Distribute RFP.	
Task	Answer vendor questions.	
Task	Bidders' conference.	
Milestone	Proposal Due Date.	
Task	Receive proposals.	
Activity	Analysis vendor responses to RFP.	
Task	Analysis proposals.	
Activity	Determine finalist.	
Task	Prepare pre-workshop material.	
Task	Conduct Finalist Selection Workshop.	
Task	Select finalist.	
Milestone	Finalist selected.	
Phase	**Pick the winner.**	
Activity	Write script.	
Task	Develop scenarios.	
Task	Write detailed script.	
Task	Develop data.	
Task	Integrate scripts and data.	Script
Task	Send scripts to finalist.	
Activity	Perform the scripted demonstration.	
Task	Arrange for scripted demonstration with finalist.	
Task	Arrange for facilities.	
Task	Conduct scripted demonstration Vendor 1.	

Figure 11-2. Work Breakdown Structure *(continued)*

Type	Name	Deliverable
Task	Review demonstration Vendor 1.	
Task	Conduct scripted demonstration Vendor 2.	
Task	Review demonstration Vendor 2.	
Task	Conduct scripted demonstration Vendor 3.	
Task	Review demonstration Vendor 3.	
Task	Conduct scripted demonstration Vendor 4.	
Task	Review demonstration Vendor 4.	
Task	Prepare scripted demonstration report.	Demonstration Report
Task	Update R^2ISC matrix.	
Activity	**Perform technical review.**	
Task	Perform complete technical review Vendor 1.	
Task	Perform complete technical review Vendor 2.	
Task	Perform complete technical review Vendor 3.	
Task	Perform complete technical review Vendor 4.	
Task	Prepare technical review report.	Technical Review Report
Task	Update R^2ISC matrix.	
Activity	**Conduct background checks.**	
Task	Obtain vendor customer list.	
Task	Select references.	References
Task	Develop reference questionnaire.	
Task	Contact references.	
Task	Contact county clerk.	
Task	Contact courts.	
Task	Select reference sites.	Reference Sites
Task	Visit reference sites.	
Task	Background report.	Background Report
Task	Update R^2ISC matrix.	
Activity	**Select winner.**	
Task	Determine winner.	Winner
Task	Preliminary approval.	
Task	Conduct full scripted demonstration with winner.	
Task	Conduct workshop.	
Task	Notify losing candidates.	
Milestone	Winner determined.	
Phase	**Finalize contract.**	
Activity	**Negotiate contract.**	
Task	Final approval of winner.	
Task	Negotiate contract.	
Activity	**Review contract.**	
Task	Financial review.	
Task	Legal review.	
Task	Approve contract.	Contract
Task	Sign contract.	Signed Contract
Milestone	Contract.	
Phase	**Project management.**	
Task	Project management.	

Figure 11-2. Work Breakdown Structure *(continued)*

developing the tasks needed to successfully select the package and assign the resources to each task.

Preliminary Cost Justification—the project manager performs a cost justification to ensure that you are not performing the process selecting a package just to find out that it is not cost justified. You may need the assistance of other team members including the accounting and finance department.

The first three activities can be performed at the same time. The final activity can only be performed after the team has been selected. Figure 11-3 is the Gantt Chart—Starting the Journey for this phase with all the task associated with this phase.

The second phase, Determining Detailed R^2ISC Requirements is where the R^2ISC weighting is performed. This phase is divided into the following six activities:

R^2ISC Weighting—the executives weigh the R^2ISC. Use a workshop to rate the criteria.

Develop Detailed Current Requirements for Each Area—the team members from the area and related areas, other employees from the area and related areas, and any experts that are hired develop the detailed requirements and rate them. Use workshops to develop the requirements.

Develop Detailed Future Requirements—technical members develop the technical requirements (data processing). The entire team at a workshop rates the requirements.

Determine Detailed Implementability Requirements—technical members develop the implementability requirements. These requirements are then rated by the whole team at a workshop.

Determine Detailed Supportability Requirements—technical members develop the supportability. These requirements are then rated by the whole team at a workshop.

Determine Detailed Cost Requirements—the appropriate team members develop the cost requirements, which are then rated by the whole team at a workshop.

Task Name	January 2000				February 2000				March 2000				
	1	2	3	4	5	6	7	8	9	10	11	12	13
Starting the journey.													
Select the team.													
Select team member.													
Notify team members.													
Train the team.													
Train team in selection process.													
Train team in best practices in application areas.													
Develop plan.													
Develop detailed plan.													
Approve plan.													
Completed plan.													
Preliminary cost benefit analysis.													
Develop preliminary cost benefit analysis.													
Determine if project should proceed.													
Approve cost benefit analysis.													

Figure 11-3. Gantt Chart—Starting the Journey

All of the activities in this phase can be performed simultaneously. Figure 11-4 is the Gantt Chart—Determining Detailed R^2ISC Requirements for this phase with all the tasks associated with this phase.

The third phase, Narrowing the Field, is where you narrow the field of software choices to three or four. This phase is divided into the following five activities:

Determine Availability of Packages—team members including the technical representatives should review literature, the Internet, and other sources to determine the packages that may meet your requirements.

Develop Key Distinguishers—team members including the technical representatives should determine the critical requirements that the package must meet.

Perform Preliminary Screening—team members including the technical representatives should eliminate packages that do not meet your key distinguishers.

Develop RFP—you write the RFP and send it to the vendors.

Analyze Vendor Responses to RFP—the team should analyze the vendors' responses. The members of the team should all take portions of the vendors' responses and compare them to different vendors.

Determine Finalists—the team determines the three or four finalist using a workshop.

These activities are of this phase are performed in sequential order. Figure 11-5 is the Gantt Chart—Narrowing the Field for this phase with all the task associated with this phase.

The fourth phase, Analyzing the Finalist, is where you pick the winner from the finalists. This phase is divided into the following five activities:

Write the Script—you and other members of the team write the script and develop the data that the vendors will use at the demonstration.

Perform the Scripted Demonstration—the vendors perform the scripted demonstration as the team rates the demonstration.

Task Name	January 2000				February 2000				March 2000				
	1	2	3	4	5	6	7	8	9	10	11	12	13

Determining detailed R²ISC requirements.

R²ISC criteria weighting.
   Determine R²ISC criteria weights.
   Approve R²ISC criteria weights.

Develop detailed current requirements Area 1.
   Identify participants for workshop.
   Develop invitation for workshop.
   Arrange for workshop site.
   Send invitation to participants.
   Invitation sent.
   Develop pre-workshop materials.
   Send pre-workshop material to participants.
   Arrange for food for workshop.
   Arrange for supplies for workshop.
   Conduct workshop.
   Complete Area 1.

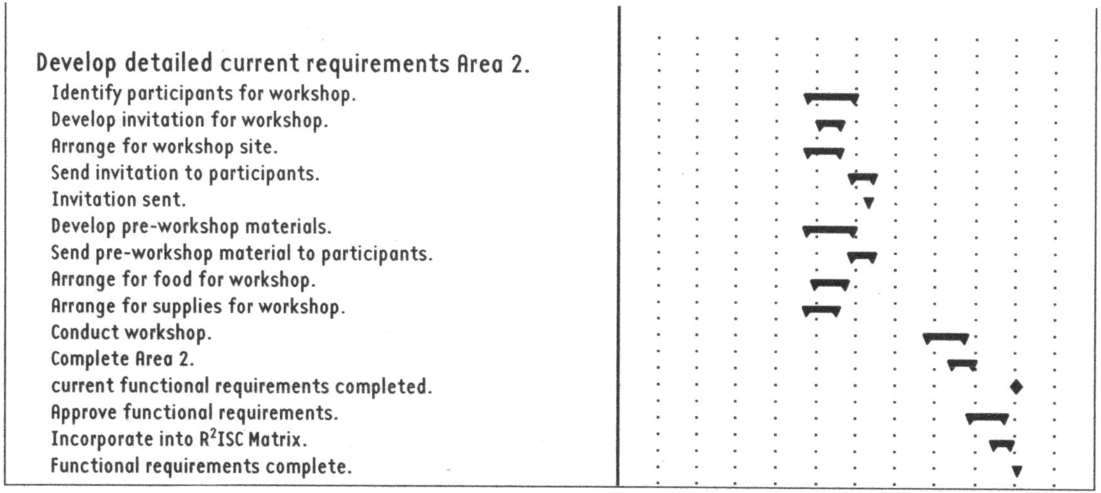

Develop detailed current requirements Area 2.
- Identify participants for workshop.
- Develop invitation for workshop.
- Arrange for workshop site.
- Send invitation to participants.
- Invitation sent.
- Develop pre-workshop materials.
- Send pre-workshop material to participants.
- Arrange for food for workshop.
- Arrange for supplies for workshop.
- Conduct workshop.
- Complete Area 2.
- current functional requirements completed.
- Approve functional requirements.
- Incorporate into R^{2}ISC Matrix.
- Functional requirements complete.

Figure 11-4. Gantt Chart—Determining Detailed R^{2}ISC Requirements

Task Name	January 2000			February 2000				March 2000			
	1 2 3 4	5	6	7	8	9	10	11	12	13	

Develop detailed future requirements.

Develop technical architecture requirements.

Determine communication requirements.

Determine volume requirements.

Identify participants for future requirements workshop.

Develop invitation for workshop.

Arrange for workshop site.

Send invitation to participants.

Invitation sent.

Prepare pre-workshop (tech rating) materials.

Send pre-workshop material to participants.

Arrange for food for workshop.

Arrange for supplies for workshop.

Technical rating workshop.

Technical requirements complete.

Approve technical requirements.

Incorporate into R²ISC Matrix.

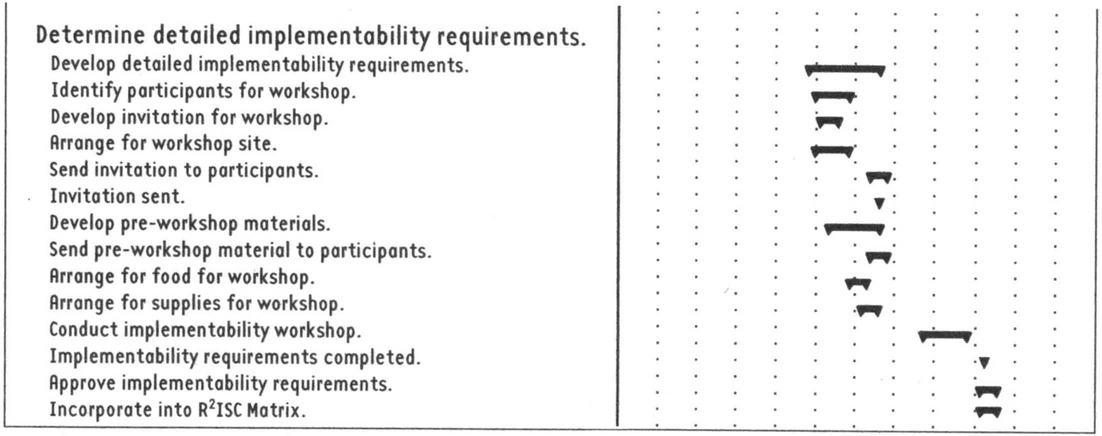

Determine detailed implementability requirements.
Develop detailed implementability requirements.
Identify participants for workshop.
Develop invitation for workshop.
Arrange for workshop site.
Send invitation to participants.
Invitation sent.
Develop pre-workshop materials.
Send pre-workshop material to participants.
Arrange for food for workshop.
Arrange for supplies for workshop.
Conduct implementability workshop.
Implementability requirements completed.
Approve implementability requirements.
Incorporate into R²ISC Matrix.

Figure 11-4. Gantt Chart—Determining Detailed R²ISC Requirements (*continued*)

Task Name		January 2000					February 2000				March 2000		
		1	2	3	4	5	6	7	8	9	10	11	12	13

Determine detailed supportability requirements.
Develop detailed implementation supportability requirements.
Develop ongoing supportability requirements.
Identify participants for workshop.
Develop invitation for workshop.
Arrange for workshop site.
Send invitation to participants.
Invitation sent.
Develop pre-workshop materials.
Send pre-workshop material to participants.
Arrange for food for workshop.
Arrange for supplies for workshop.
Conduct implementability workshop.
Supportability requirements completed.
Incorporate into R^{2}ISC Matrix.
Supportability requirements completed.

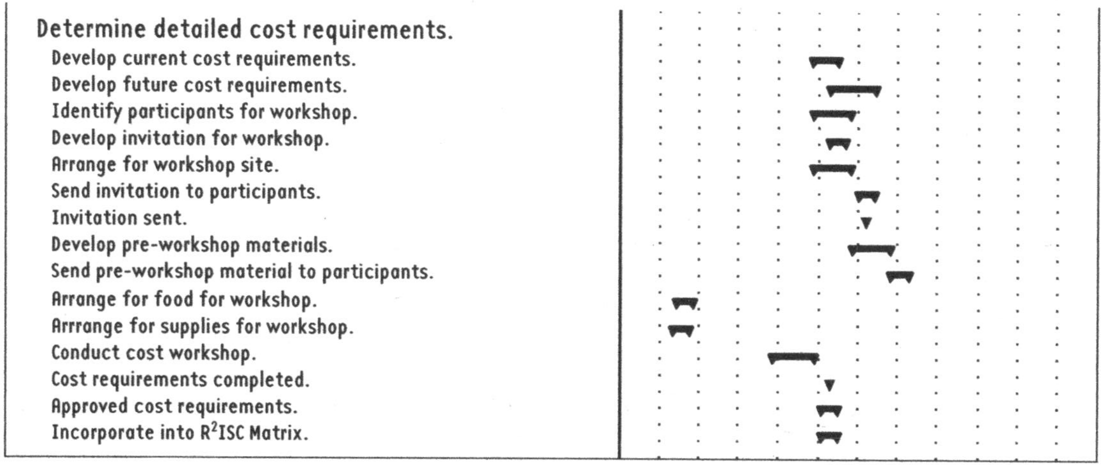

Determine detailed cost requirements.
Develop current cost requirements.
Develop future cost requirements.
Identify participants for workshop.
Develop invitation for workshop.
Arrange for workshop site.
Send invitation to participants.
Invitation sent.
Develop pre-workshop materials.
Send pre-workshop material to participants.
Arrange for food for workshop.
Arrrange for supplies for workshop.
Conduct cost workshop.
Cost requirements completed.
Approved cost requirements.
Incorporate into R²ISC Matrix.

Figure 11-4. Gantt Chart—Determining Detailed R²ISC Requirements *(continued)*

Task Name	February 2000				March 2000				April 2000			
	6	7	8	9	10	11	12	13	14	15	16	17
Narrowing the Field.												
Determine availability of packages.												
Develop key distinguishers.												
Determine key distinguishers.			━━━━━━									
Perform preliminary screening.												
Analysis packages with software tool.						━						
Determine vendors for consideration.						━━						
Approve vendors.							▂					
Develop RFP.												
Write RFP.			━━━━━━━									
Distribute RFP.							▂					
Answer vendor questions.							━━━━					
Bidders' conference.								▂				
Proposal due date.									▼			
Receive proposals.									▂			
Analysis vendor responses to RFP.												
Analysis proposals.										━━━		
Determine finalist.												
Prepare pre-workshop material.											━━	
Conduct finalist selection workshop.											▂	
Select finalist.											▼	
Finalist selected.											▼	

Figure 11-5. Gantt Chart—Narrowing the Field

Perform Technical Review—technical members of the team review and rate the package's technology.

Conduct Background Checks—team members perform background checks on the vendors, including contacting references, checking for lawsuits, and visiting key references.

Select Winner—the team selects the winner (at a workshop) using management's ratings of the R^2ISC criteria and the findings that were developed during the previous tasks.

These activities of this phase are performed in sequential order. Figure 11-6 is the Gantt Chart—Picking the Winner for this phase with all the task associated with this phase.

The fifth phase, Contract Negotiations, is often the most time-consuming. In this phase you negotiate the contract with the wining vendor. This phase is divided into the following two activities:

Negotiating the Contract—the purchasing department or contracting department and members of the team negotiate the terms, conditions, and cost of the contract with the vendor.

Reviewing the Contract—the contract is reviewed and approved by the legal and accounting/finance departments.

These activities can be performed as many times as required to obtain a successful contract. Figure 11-7 is the Gantt Chart—Finalize Contract for this phase with all the tasks associated with this phase.

Once you've completed this fifth phase you have selected the appropriate package.

The final phase, Project Management, is ongoing throughout the project.

In this phase, you, as the project manager, ensure that the project is running smoothly, report back to management on the progress, and take corrective action to ensure the project's success.

Dependencies

There are two kinds of tasks, independent and dependent. An independent task can be performed without impacting any other task. However, a dependent task has an impact on another task. For ex-

Task Name	March 2000			April 2000			May 2000			
	10 11	12 13	14	15 16 17	18	19	20 21 22			
Pick the winner.										
Write script.										
Develop scenarios.										
Write detailed script.										
Develop data.										
Integrate scripts and data.										
Send scripts to finalist.										
Perform the Scripted Demonstration.										
Arrange for scripted demonstration with finalist.										
Arrange for facilities.										
Conduct scripted demonstration Vendor 1.										
Review demonstration Vendor 1.										
Conduct scripted demonstration Vendor 2.										
Review demonstration Vendor 2.										
Conduct scripted demonstration Vendor 3.										
Review demonstration Vendor 3.										
Conduct scripted demonstration Vendor 4.										
Review demonstration Vendor 4.										
Prepare scripted demonstration report.										
Update R^2ISC matrix.										

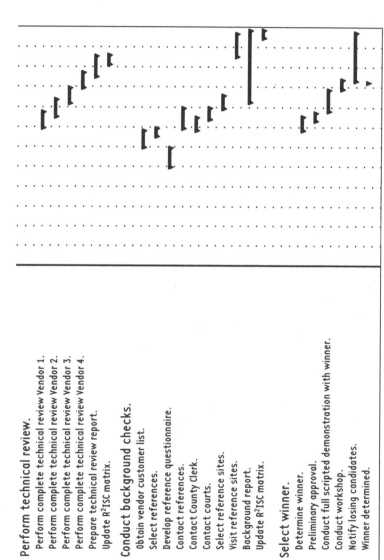

Perform technical review.
Perform complete technical review Vendor 1.
Perform complete technical review Vendor 2.
Perform complete technical review Vendor 3.
Perform complete technical review Vendor 4.
Prepare technical review report.
Update R²TSC matrix.

Conduct background checks.
Obtain vendor customer list.
Select references.
Develop reference questionnaire.
Contact references.
Contact County Clerk.
Contact courts.
Select reference sites.
Visit reference sites.
Background report.
Update R²TSC matrix.

Select winner.
Determine winner.
Preliminary approval.
Conduct full scripted demonstration with winner.
Conduct workshop.
Notify losing candidates.
Winner determined.

Figure 11-6. Gantt Chart—Picking the Winner

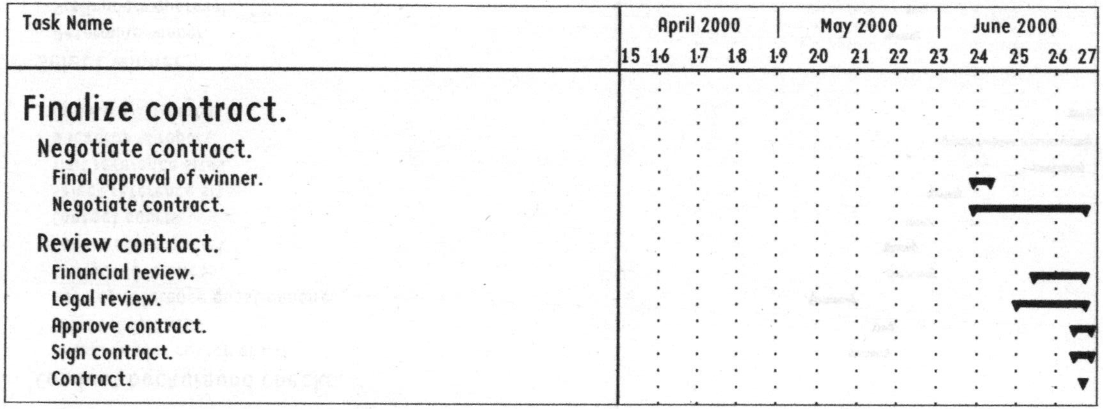

Task Name	April 2000				May 2000				June 2000			
	15 16	17 18	19	20 21	22	23	24	25	26 27			

Finalize contract.

Negotiate contract.
  Final approval of winner.
  Negotiate contract.

Review contract.
  Financial review.
  Legal review.
  Approve contract.
  Sign contract.
  Contract.

Figure 11-7. Gantt Chart—Finalize Contract

ample, you cannot put the door on a house before the house is framed. If a task is dependent, you must identify the task it impacts (its dependencies) before scheduling. (This ensures that the electrical wiring is installed before plasterboard is put on the wall.) The first task is called the predecessor and the second task the successor. The types of dependencies are:

- Finish-start—you cannot start the task (successor) till another task (predecessor) has been completed. For example, you cannot start framing the house until the foundation is completed. In the selection process, you cannot start the requirements workshop until the pre-workshop materials have been distributed.

- Finish-finish—you cannot finish a task (successor) until the other task (predecessor) has also been finished. For example, you cannot finish touching up the paint on the walls until you also finished touching up the paint on the trim. (Since the paint from the wall can get on the trim and vice versa.) In the selection process, you cannot finish the development of the script data until the scripts are completed.

- Start-start—you cannot start the task (successor) until another task (predecessor) has also been started. For example, the exterior brick face on a home cannot be put up until its block backup has been started. In the selection process, you cannot send workshop materials until you send the invitations.

Certain tasks with dependencies require a gap from the finish of the predecessor to the start of the successor. In the case of the cement foundation you may also want to wait one or two days until the cement dries. In the case of the scripted demonstration, there is a gap of one to two weeks from the completion of the scripts until the vendor can perform the demonstration because the vendor needs time to prepare their presentation.

Scheduling

When scheduling tasks you need to be sure the necessary people and other required resources (i.e., room for the demonstration) are

available. Each resource should be identified on the plan and its availability determined. When you build the schedule, be it manual or
automated, schedule personnel at no more than 80 percent of their
available time. The remaining 20 percent is for meetings, administrative functions, vacation, illness, etc. Failing to take this into account
can cause delays or burnout of personnel.

The schedule process starts either at the first day of the project
and is "forward scheduled" to the end date, or it starts at the end date
and is "backward scheduled" to determine the start date and the required resources. A Gantt Chart (Figure 11-1) pictorially depicts the
project and the interrelationship of tasks.

The Critical Path

The most critical tasks are those that, if delayed, will extend the project. These tasks are said to be "on the critical path." The time required to complete the tasks on the critical path is the minimum time
it will take to complete the project. If a task that does not lay on the
critical path takes longer than planned it will not extend the project's
length but it will increase the project's cost.

Milestones and Deliverables

The schedule should include deliverables and milestones. A deliverable is the product of a task(s). For example, the completed current
requirements list. A milestone indicates when a significant point is
reached in the process for example, when a significant task is completed (invitations sent to requirements workshop attendees), or
activity is completed (all current requirements identified and
ranked).

Managing the Project

Besides the work required for selecting the package, a certain amount
of work is required to manage the process. The project should include time for managing the whole process. List this time as a task in

a Management Phase. Allow 10 percent to 15 percent of the total project time for managing. Project management includes tracking actual progress through the plan and identifying any corrective action when needed, as well as attending meetings. Failure to allow for this time can result in the project not staying on track or even going over budget. Managing the process is comparable to a building construction manager's job. If the project is small the construction manager can help work on the building. If it is a large construction project the construction manager may not be able to help and may require one or two assistants because without them the project would not meet its schedule.

Contingencies

Even if the plan seems flawless, unexpected complications are inevitable and time must be set aside to deal with these complications. Allow 10 percent to 15 percent of the total project time for the contingency. Some estimators build a contingency into each task. I prefer to give its own phase, called "contingency." It is easier to control the variances by having the contingency in one activity because when incidents occur, the time must be reported as a problem in order to move from the contingency phase to the actual task that requires the additional time. This allows you to monitor the problem and make sure corrective action is taken. Also if the contingency is in each activity in many cases the personnel assume they have that much time to perform the task and use all the time.

Selecting the Personnel

Picking the appropriate personnel is key to the success of package selection and its implementation. You need helpful responsible people to make the process run smoothly.

You may be able to select a package with any team, but you will have problems successfully implementing the package (the real measure of success for a selection process) without the right team. You don't want to find yourself in this situation. Consider one electronics company that needed a new order management package. The president and three of his top advisors developed the requirements and evaluated the package. They picked what I would consider an excellent package. But like all or most packages it did not meet all of the users' requirements. Because there were only a few people from the company involved in the selection, any time the users found a problem with the system, no matter how minor, they blamed it on the president's package and his not understanding what they do in the trenches.

In the above example, the top executive took the blame because he was on the selection team, but that's not always the case. I dealt with a company that selected a new ERP package whose selection team was made up members from each of the functional areas and from all of the company's locations. Everything was running smoothly until the inventory control module was implemented, at which time the users began picking on any little thing saying that the "package does not work." Their complaints had very little impact on their ability to perform their jobs. When we started to investigate the situation we found out that one selection team member was not held in very high esteem by her fellow co-workers. As a matter of fact, there had been friction between her and most of her co-workers. It was only her boss who held her in high esteem. Her co-workers were taking out their resentment of her on the package.

When my wife and I were looking to buy a house, I had seen a gorgeous house that was within our price range. The owner told me that someone else was coming to look at the house so I needed to act fast. The only problem was that I was alone, I did not have my wife and kids with me. I knew that if I bought the house without their input they would all find something wrong with it. I was better off buying a house that was not as nice that my wife and kids approved of than to buy this house by myself because I would be hearing about what was wrong with the house as long as we lived there.

Without getting the "buy-in" from others within the company, a package will be referred to by the name of the person that selected it, even if it's the best package available but especially when a problem arises. People who were not involved in the selection process will always find problems and say "the package does not work." The outcome, and I have seen this happen too many times, is that they will make the software fail. Also, if the selection team gets input from others within their company, problems the team may not have seen might be entirely avoided.

Team Organization

If the package impacts you and just a couple of your colleagues, the organization of the selection team can be very informal. On the other hand, if the software will impact many people across different departments and locations, you need a very formal organization structure. The following is a description of the major players required to have a good team. Figure 11-8 is an organization chart for a package selection team.

Executive Sponsor

If you are the executive sponsor, you are the final decision maker and oversee the entire project, however, you will not work on the project on a full-time basis. You are a senior executive who works in the area the package will impact. For example, for an ERP system you are an executive vice president. You do not take an active role in the process but you must make clear (to the team and the rest of the organizations) the impact the selection of the right package will have in the company's future. You must resolve any problems that might arise within the team. Above all, you must buy into the selection process.

As the Executive Sponsor you are heavily involved in the selection process including approving the values assigned to the R^2ISC criteria. You should also give the team insight into the future direction of the company so that they can make sure the system will continue to work and will not become outdated. You should be updated at least monthly on the progress of the selection process. You will select the Steering Committee and are responsible for selecting the Project Manager.

The Steering Committee, which falls right below you in the chain of command, will present you with the final package recommendation to which you must give your final approval. It is ultimately your responsibility to authorize the purchase of the software package.

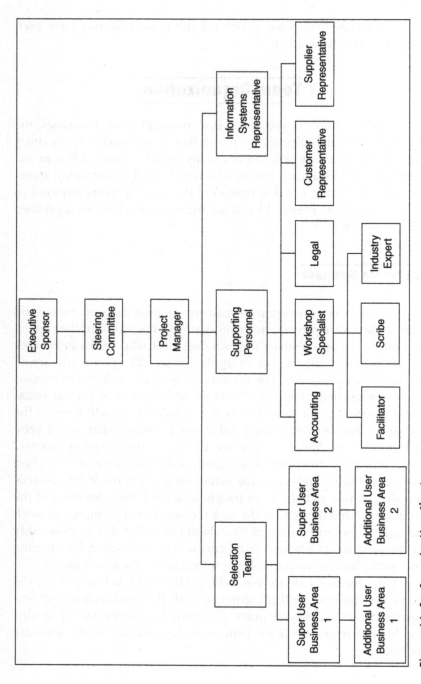

Figure 11-8. Organization Chart

Steering Committee

As the chairman of the Steering Committee you take responsibility for running and scheduling the Steering Committee meetings. The committee should meet once a week to receive updates on the project and resolve any open issues (i.e., disagreements over any important functional requirements). If the committee cannot resolve the issue or is deadlocked, the problem should be elevated to the Executive Sponsor for resolution.

If you are a member of the Steering Committee you are a senior manager from one of the areas affected by the new package. The number of areas the package covers will dictate the total number of members needed on the committee.

As a member of the committee you rate the R^2ISC criteria and the importance of each of the applications to the business. You also resolve problems the team cannot resolve. This can be because the team does not have the authority to resolve the problem or the team cannot agree on a resolution.

If you are a member of the Steering Committee you will ensure that the required resources are available to the team. For example if a person has to be freed from their current duties it is your responsibility. You are also responsible for approving the project plan and budget.

Project Manager

If you are the Project Manager you take ownership of the selection process and make sure the project stays on track. You are a middle to senior manager who works within an area affected by the package and you are highly regarded within the organization by both management and the user community. You are responsible for the day-to-day operations of the team. You are also a member of the Steering Committee.

As the Project Manager your first tasks are to choose the members of the Selection Team, and develop the plan, which is approved by the Steering Committee. It is your responsibility to monitor the actual progress of the planned budget and time schedule. If there are negative variances to the plan, you are responsible for making the appropriate changes as needed. If the project cannot be brought back on schedule or budget, it is your responsibility to recommend the appropriate changes to the Steering Committee.

Selection Team

The Selection Team performs the actual day-to-day package selection work and recommends the winning package to the Steering Committee who, in turn, will use it as the basis for its recommendation to the Executive Sponsor. The Selection Team should include representatives from the functional areas, the Information Systems department, and any pertinent Super Users.

Super Users

As a Super User you represent your functional area and if package will be used in more than one location then the Super User also represents their location. You are extremely knowledgeable about your particular functional area. Your fellow employees hold you in high regard, and you are able to "think out of the box." Your fellow employees will easily accept your decisions because they know you have the expertise of your area to know if the package will work. You are probably a member of the Selection Team or are one of the additional users that help develop the portion of the requirements you are considered an expert.

There should be a Super User from each functional area affected by the new system. For example, for an ERP system the following departments should be represented:

- Order Processing
- Inventory Control
- Engineering
- Human Resources
- Shipping
- Manufacturing
- Transportation

- Cost Accounting
- General Accounting
- Accounts Receivable
- Accounts Payable
- Treasury

If the package will be used in more than one location, each location should be represented on the team.

Keep in mind that the number of people in the team should closely resemble how many people the new software will affect.

Your primary responsibility as a Super User is to develop the current business requirements for the new system. You will also be involved in:

- developing the cost justification for both the package selection and the implementation projects.
- identifying additional users whose knowledge is needed to identify system requirements.
- developing the current business requirements and their rating(s).
- reviewing the Request for Proposal (RFP) .
- reviewing the vendors' responses to the RFP.
- reviewing the script and data to be used in the demonstration.
- attending and rating the scripted demonstration.

Information Systems

If you are the Information System (IS) representative your role on the Selection Team is to determine the technical requirements for the package. You will then analyze how well each package meets the technical requirements. (It is an added benefit if you are knowledgeable about the business function(s).) It is your responsibility to:

- Provide guidance concerning technical aspects of the package.
- Ensure the package's architecture is sound.
- Determine how easily the package can be modified to meet the enterprise's future requirements.

Although the package may satisfy the user's requirements, if it cannot be implemented because of major technical difficulties, it is of little value to the enterprise. It is therefore your responsibility to explain to the rest of the Selection Team how the package's technology impacts your Requirements Future, Implementability, Supportability, and Cost. You will explain why the package is or is not the best choice for the enterprise from a business viewpoint.

The user community should perceive you as a team player looking out for the company's best interest. The users cannot have a "them versus us" perception of you. If this occurs, you must work hard to overcome this perception and make sure you are considered part of the team, always keeping the company's best interest in mind.

Supporting Personnel

There are additional people needed by the Selection Team on an interim basis to perform only a few activities. They include:

Additional Users

The Selection Team may not possess all the expertise needed to develop the requirements or to be able to evaluate the package. So you may want to have additional users assist the team.

Additional Technical Experts

The information systems member of the team may not have all the technical expertise needed to properly evaluate the technical aspects of the package. You may therefore need the advice of specific computer technical personnel.

Customer(s)

If the new software package impacts your customers, especially if the major purpose is to better serve them, the customer(s) should become part of the team. Choosing the right customers and the right representatives is important. You should include at least one of your strategic customers. The customers should be chosen for their ability to add value to the process. They should tell you what is important to them so you can include that in your requirements and weighing the requirements. They should be leading edge companies from which you can learn something.

Supplier(s)

If the package impacts your suppliers, include them as part of the Selection Team. Remember, today suppliers are your business partners. They need information from you and they have information valuable to you. They should be chosen for their ability to add value to the process. Like your customers they should be leading edge companies whose process you'd like to mimic or at least learn from. They tell you what is important to them so that you can include that in your requirements and weighing the requirements.

Training Expert

You may want a training expert to evaluate the vendor's training material and courseware. They can also evaluate the vendor's training approach and methodology.

Consultant

Many companies use an outside consultant to assist in the process. A consultant can speed the process and prevent you from going down the wrong path. If you decide to use a consultant, the consultant should know the process well and be able to add value.

Facilitator

If you are using workshops you should have a professional facilitator. The facilitator leads the discussions, keeps the discussions moving and focused on the defined topics, enforces the ground rules, and treats all parties equally, regardless of their position in the company.

Scribe

If you are using workshops you should also have a scribe. The scribe writes down and collates the ideas that emerge from the workshop. He or she then prepares a workshop report.

Financial Expert

The Selection Team may need the expertise of a financial expert to assist in reviewing the vendors' financial reports. They can also assist you in obtaining and analyzing third-party financial information (i.e., Dun & Bradstreet). They can help you determine the vendors' financial stability.

Legal Counsel

Once the contract negotiations start, legal counsel should be brought in to review the software contract. The lawyer should be an expert on software contracts. I have seen the results of lawyers who are experts in the law but do not understand the business requirements of a software contract. These lawyers make sure that that every "i" is dotted and that all terms and conditions are fully enforceable. The only problem is that many of the terms are not in your best interest. So, you have the worst possible case, bad terms that are fully enforceable by the vendor.

Your counsel can help your background investigation and determine if there are any law suits against the vendors.

Purchasing Agent

One of your company's purchasing agents can be helpful in negotiating the contract and performing some of the vendor background checks. If your company has a purchasing agent who is familiar with software contracts, take advantage of him or her.

Additional Resources

For additional resource on project management you can read the following books:

- Dinsomore C. The *AMA Handbook of Project Management*. AMACom, New York, New York, 1993.
- Knutson J, and Bitz I. *Project Management How to Plan and Manage Successful Projects*. AMACom, New York, New York, 1991.

12

Implementation

You have already laid the foundation for a successful implementation by selecting the package using the R²ISC method. You have the proper material in the package. Now you can start the construction. You've got a good blue print; now you need the fine workmanship. But even with the finest materials problems can still arise. All the people have to come together at the right time in perfect harmony. This chapter lists some of the pitfalls to avoid during implementation.

Implementation Plan

You needed a plan during the package selection process to ensure that you stay on time. It becomes even more important in the implementation process than the selection process because you will have more people involved than were in the selection process, more people to train, and more things that have to be done in the right order. Remember there is no substitute for a good, detailed plan.

When you develop the plan, set up a lot of small successes rather than having one big success two years down the line. Many successes will keep the enthusiasm level up and help smooth out the bumps that appear in all implementations.

The vendor should supply you with an implementation plan in their RFP. Ask the vendor to update the plan for any idiosyncrasies of your specific implementation. Verify that the plan includes the following items:

- modifications
- installation of hardware
- installation of software
- implementation tailoring lab

273

- acceptance test
- training
- conversion
- roll out.

Modifications

Try to implement the package with as few modification as possible, even if means having some additional manual work or additional personnel. After you have used the package for two to three months, then reanalyze the modifications that you originally thought you needed and at that point make only the modifications that you really require. Often the modifications you thought you needed are not as important anymore or a work-around will suffice. You will probably also find things you would like to change that you hadn't considered earlier.

Implementation Tailoring Lab

An Implementation Tailoring Lab is a computer lab where the package software is installed on all the computers. This controlled environment is used to determine exactly how the package will work in your company. If any modifications can be prototyped and tested in the implementation lab. Processes are checked and documented. Do not underestimate the need for written procedures on how users are to work with the new package. Even when people have taken a course they can forget a little thing that can hold up the rest of their task. Therefore, make sure all procedures are well documented when you go live.

Rollout

When you are ready to turn the package over to the users, try to let a small group use the package (or a module) before it is rolled out to the entire company because you don't want to chance the following happening to you. I had been asked to review a cost accounting system a Fortune 50 company had been implementing. Their plan was to rollout the system in a modular form to all the divisions. As with all new implementations there were problems that had to be worked out. After the third module and hundreds of thousands of wasted dollars, the users felt the system did not work and could not be made to work. After an analysis, I determined it would be almost impossible to regain the users' trust and that the project should be cancelled. If the company had rolled out each module to one division as a test, worked out the bugs, and then rolled it to a second division as a second test, they could have avoided the cancellation.

Acceptance Test

If the vendor will be installing or modifying the package, you should have a predefined set of conditions the package must meet before you accept it. This requires testing the package and all its modifications. You should not make a final payment until the package passes this mutually agreed upon test.

Training

In order to get the most out of the package the users need to know how to use it. I have seen (too many times) where a company spends hundreds of thousands of dollars on a package and another couple of hundred thousand on implementation, but when it comes to training they try to cut the budget. This is being penny wise and dollar foolish. You will need the following types of training:

> **User**—teaches the users how to operate the package.
>
> **Operating**—teaches the technical personnel how to operate the package including how to backup and restore the system.

Data Conversion

Often the hardest thing about implementation is the conversion of the data from your old system to the new package. If there are only a few hundred records it is often best to manually clean and enter the data into the new package.

There is often data that is needed by the new package that the old system did not contain. In this case you will have to determine how to get the missing data. Here is an example of something you don't want to experience. One client I work with developed their own custom fixed asset system. One third of the time spent on the project was spent on converting the data from their old system to their new system. It had assets at different clients. Unfortunately the old system did not have a client number associated with the asset; rather, it used the client's name. As you can predict, they did not always spell the client's name the same. We had developed algorithms to try to match all the assets at a specific client. Developing the algorithms took approximately one third as much time as developing the system. So when you are planing the implementation of your new system make sure that if you have a lot of data that needs to be converted from your old system to the new package that you analyze your current data to be sure it is correct. Yes, there are many computer systems that have bad information in them. If you have bad data, allow time for data scrubbing (cleaning the data so that it is all valid data).

Offer Incentives

If the package is complex to implement and will require a dedicated team for over nine months, devise an incentive plan for the team. This is especially important if you are implementing an ERP package. Make sure the plan gives real incentives to the team—giving them a couple of dollars will not make things happen. Vendor personnel and other third-party personnel should receive incentives too. Nothing makes people react as well as money. One company I worked with created an incentive plan that worked well—they tied a financial incentive to every milestone. If even one group missed a milestone there were large reductions in the incentive to the whole team. It was amazing how well the team jelled. As soon as someone was finished with his tasks he would try and help anyone who was having a problem. If one person or group was having problems, everyone else who was finished would try to help.

You are now ready to start your journey. Just remember that the foundation you are laying by doing a good package selection will make your implementation easier and give you a better solution.

Good luck on your journey.

Appendix A

Sample Data Pro Report[1] Ross Systems Renaissance CS Financial Series

Datapro Summary

Ross Systems' Renaissance CS Financials Series is a financial management software suite of integrated accounting and financial applications designed for a client/server environment. The latest release, 4.3, is composed of six integrated applications; includes operating system support for Windows NT, HP-UX, IBM AIX, Sun Solaris, Open VMS, and other UNIX variants; and provides database support for Microsoft SQL Server, Oracle, and Rdb. Ross also offers a variety of optional features designed to enhance its core financial solutions. These features include a Project Administration Control System for project, contract, and grant management and advanced financial reporting facilities.

Author

Daniel B. Stang

Corporate Headquarters

Ross Systems, Inc.
Two Concourse Parkway
Suite 800
Atlanta, GA 30328, U.S.A.
Tel: 11-770-351-9600
Internet: http://www.rossinc.com

Overview

Ross Systems develops and markets a range of client/server business solutions in several strategic environments. Ross products encompass financial, human resources, and distribution systems, as well as manufacturing and supply chain applications. Ross Systems' Renaissance CS Financials Series is the integrated financial management applications set included in the modular Renaissance CS solution. Ross' marketing strategy includes a distinct focus on the industries using its financials offerings. SAM, Ross' Strategic Application Modeler, includes documented, proven practices for health care. The three-dimensional organizational model depicts business processes, tasks, and job descriptions and allows the user to drill down into each function directly to the transaction entry screen. For example, an Accounts Payable clerk can identify his or her role in the payment of invoices, and drill down through the model directly to the invoice payment entry screen in the Accounts Payable module.

The modules that make up Ross' financial suite include the basic General Ledger, Accounts Receivable, Accounts Payable, and Fixed Assets functions. These modules provide business-process functionality including budgetary control, allocations, commitment accounting, job costing, collection and cash management, and EDI and EFT capabilities to enhance an organization's e-commerce capabilities. All Financials functions can be completed in multiple currencies and are compliant with the Euro monetary unit. With Renaissance CS, transactions are stored in multiple currencies, eliminating the need to convert or translate at reporting time. Ross targets companies in the midtier market, with revenues of US$50 million and above. Renaissance is designed with logical, reusable components so business processes, the interface, and database engines can be distributed for maximum efficiency. The vendor's Navigational Framework allows Renaissance CS to run with a browser. Ross is also embracing Internet technologies through the development of application applets. The company supports Microsoft standards and integrates its components with Visual Basic and Visual J++. Business partnerships with BusinessObjects, FRx, Speedware, and SRC have extended the decision support capabilities of the Renaissance suite. Ross reports a customer base consisting of more than 260 health care industry clients.

Ross Systems' Renaissance CS Financials Series
Features & Functions

Operating Environment Operating Platform	Windows NT, HP-UX, IBM AIX, Sun Solaris, Open VMS, and other UNIX variants. Supports Microsoft SQL Server, Oracle, and Rdb.
Databases Included Software GEMBASE	A component-based 4GL application development environment enabling the custom design of applications.
General Ledger Description Data Entry	Provides flexible data entry, budgeting, data access, reporting functions, and setup. Flexible journals supply recurring, reversing, and automated entries. A journal template capability allows users to create journal definitions, which automatically supply account numbers and predefined or calculated transaction amounts. Calculated amounts can be based on account balances and/or mathematical formulas applied to other journal line items.
Accounting Management	Online inquiries provide current information regarding the status of all entries. An optional approval feature enables managers to verify critical entries before the entries affect the books.
Budgeting	Unlimited number of budgets can be stored simultaneously, allowing for an original budget and multiple reforecasts. Annual budget amounts can be spread evenly over budgeting period, or seasonal factors can be applied. Items such as base budget amounts, statistics, and financial results can be used as factors in determining your budget amounts.
Data Access	Online access allows users to enter, validate, correct, control, summarize, and display data. Analyzes summary and detail account balances, as well as supporting transaction detail. Detailed reference information identifies subsystem data, and express keys allow users to navigate across the entire product line. Business productivity tools communicate data throughout the organization in both text and graphical form. Generalized integration tools allow import or export of general ledger data.

Online Inquiries	Using screen snapshots, user can perform requested queries and send the results to the person who requested the information via electronic mail.
	Top-to-bottom data analysis is supported, allowing navigation through the hierarchy to identify critical performance information.
Automated Entries	Allows journal information to be loaded into the GL automatically from other systems.
	Permits review of information before it is loaded into the live journal database.
System Setup	Customized account numbers allow users to specify the length and meaning of each element of the account identifier.
	Supported size for account numbers: fifty characters, fifteen elements.
	Mass maintenance capabilities allow users to create the valid combinations of account elements.
	A financial database allows storage of any number of budgets.
	Accounting periods can be defined to correspond with the company's internal calendar.
	Adjusting periods can be set aside to allow for adjusting entries to be segregated.
Currency Control	Stores accounting information in any number of currencies.
	Reports can be generated in any currency, translating between any combination of currencies.
	Exchange-rate tables allow rate types with effective date ranges.
	Defines separate gain/loss accounts.
	European Monetary Union requirements are supported.
Reporting	Interactive screens lead users through the definition process where data is immediately validated.
	Predefined standard financial reports include journal listings, account balance, transaction reconciliation, and trial balance reports.
	A GEMBASE report writer allows users to create a report analyzing financial data by combining horizontal and vertical definitions.
	Calculations can operate on any piece of report data including variables that can be entered by the report requestor at execution time.
	Responsibility reporting allows creation of multiple reports with one definition.
	With column definition, users can show nonfinancial and financial data on the same report.

Advanced Features

Multiple-level consolidations—Elimination values can be created for each level of consolidation, yet stored separately so they do not affect the detail-level books.

Distributed processing—Data can be shared between locations and consolidated at a central site by transmitting results between computers.

Allocations—Step-down, year-to-date, inter-company, and trial allocations are provided. Allocation calculations can be based on financial results, statistics, or any other information.

Multiple-currency processing—Journal transactions can be translated upon entry, and account balances can be revalued at the end of the month. Multiple currencies can be shown on a single report adjacent to translated amounts.

Intercompany journal entries—Journal processing ensures that each legal entity stays in balance. Detailed tracking of "due to" and "due from" amounts allow users to control complex intercompany transfers.

Accounts Payable Description

Module supporting vendor management, cash management, invoice processing and matching, and payment and distribution processing. Also provides query and reporting capabilities.

Vendor Management

Shares a common vendor file with Ross Systems Purchase Order, allowing users to decide who controls the addition and maintenance of vendors.

Control can reside in either the accounts payable or purchasing departments.

Multiple addresses can be defined for each vendor.

Appropriate information associated with a vendor defaults to each invoice automatically during entry of payables.

Maintains statistics on all vendor and payable activity, detailed by type of document.

Tracks all return/amount types that the federal government requires and provides flexible 1099 generation and reporting.

Cash Management

Document aging forecasts cash requirements according to a user-defined time period.

Payment processing shows the invoices to be paid and allows user to remove invoices.

After determining the cash requirements, users can decide which invoices need to be paid and from which banks they should be paid.

Discount amounts can be calculated for each
invoice, so that a determination can be made
when and if it should be taken.

Unlimited number of currency exchange rates can
be maintained and shared by the entire Ross
product line.

Invoice Processing Optional invoice registration capabilities allow
users to enter invoice information before
payment approval and track the invoice through
the approval process.

Invoice entry information usually defaults from
the vendor file or the purchase order.

An electronic filing system records actual images
of original invoices and supporting documents.

Flexible reports and inquiries enable access to all
payables information.

Other features:

- Multicurrency processing—Users can enter
  invoices in an unlimited number of currencies
  with automatic realized and unrealized
  loss/gain calculations.
- Format codes—Users can predefine commonly
  used general ledger distribution lists that
  can be used at invoice entry.
- Budgetary control—Users can create,
  monitor, and control expenditures against
  funds and budgets.
- Electronic data interchange (EDI) support is
  also included.

Invoice Matching Tax amounts are automatically calculated and
audit reports can be included by adding a tax
code on the invoice.

Tracks VAT and GST information to the invoice line
level.

Other features include:

- Two- or three-way matching—Matches the
  invoice to the purchase order and receipts,
  or matches the invoice and purchase order
  only.
- Tolerances and suspended invoices—
  Organizations control payment of invoices
  with quantity and/or price discrepancies.
- Purchase order lookup and remarks—
  Accommodates the viewing of PO status
  information from the invoice entry screens
  and also remarks that the buyer or the
  receiving clerk entered.

Payment Distribution and Processing Distribution of accounts payable expenses to the
GL, and the associated control accounts can
occur whenever designated.

The system provides the tools needed to ensure
accounts payable and general ledger remain in
balance.

Bank reconciliation provided through integration
with Accounts Receivable and General Ledger.

Other features include:

- Payment selection—Automatically scans open
invoices, selecting those that are due for
payment.
- Manual payments—Users can allocate the
payment amount to one or more invoices.
- Payments can be printed by vendor or by
payment amount.
- Remittance advices can be printed with the
payments or as separated documents.

**Accounts Receivable
Description**

An AR module with functions that include
customer information, advanced payment
processing, collections, reporting, and inquiry.

Customer Information

Maintains statistics on customers' paying habits
and past performance.

For invoices not generated by the sales order
system, the AR module offers comprehensive
invoice and debit/credit memo entry capability.

Integration with the Ross Item Master allows
invoices to be created for stock items as well
as nonstock information.

Multiline invoices can direct individual items to
different shipping addresses.

A diary (tickler) system tracks customer contacts
and follow-up activities.

Advanced Payment Processing

Accepts single payments for multiple invoices, a
single payment for multiple customers, and
partial payments.

A cash application screen allows user to identify
the items to be paid.

Discounts or multiple payment terms can be
established. Unearned discounts can be written
off or re-invoiced after payment processing has
been completed.

Finance charges can be defined by customer or
customer category.

Collections

The system sends a memo reminder to the
customer with a planned action.

Each time a dunning letter is sent, Ross AR
automatically creates a diary entry with a
follow-up date based on severity level.

Also defines multiple dunning severity levels and
letter content according to collection
procedures.

Reporting and Inquiry	Online research of documents and payments.
	Statements can be printed for all customers or any group of customers.
	Statements can also be generated on an ad hoc basis as a collections tool for certain customers.
	Aging trial balances can be printed for different audiences; aging periods can also be defined for each report.
	Exception reporting is available to analyze a subset of customer base and commitments.
	Supports sales commission tracking and reporting.
Fixed Assets	A module providing asset control and
Description	management.
	Complies with tax rules and regulations.
Asset Tracking and Control	Information is kept on each asset including whether the asset is depreciable or nondepreciable, or eligible for energy credits.
	Transfers are allowed within an entity or organizational level or transfers to another entity or organizational level.
	Adjustments can be made to the cost basis, accumulated, and year-to-date depreciation amounts.
	Users can partially or fully retire an asset.
	Group asset tracking allows group entry of a number of identical assets into one record.
	Policy tracking provides fields to track insurance contract numbers and lease and maintenance agreements.
	Lets users customize "validation" and "common information" tables with user-defined terms.
	Extra descriptive and numeric fields are also provided.
	Charges fixed asset expenses to various expense categories, cost centers, and departments.
	Multicurrency options allow tracking assets in home currency for book and tax purposes, as well as in parent company's currency, for reporting to that company's general ledger.
	Custom reports can be generated online using the Ross FA query language capability.
Asset Management	Supports an unlimited number of books, with separate cost and depreciation methods for each.
	User-defined depreciation methods are supported, in addition to standard United States and Canadian methods.
	Monitors asset locations.

	Audit trails are automatically kept.
	A series of reports enhance budgeting and depreciation policy decision making with projection reporting.
	Ad hoc reporting allows users to create any inquiry or report needed by management.
Tax Responsibilities	Depreciation methods support includes straight-line, declining balance, sum of years digits, and accelerated depreciation methods.
	Prorated depreciation available using half-year, following month, and other conventions.
	Multinational capability provides rules for tax reporting in any country.
	Allocation control supports apportionment of epreciation across organizations that share an asset.
Project Administration Description	Designed to optimize processes and manage multiple projects.
Project Definition & Control	Allows users to build work breakdown structures of projects and is designed to reduce duplication of efforts by providing a range of project templates and capturing data in the format required by the organization.
Estimating & Budgeting	Enables users to estimate the required personnel, material, resources, subcontractors, and other variables contributing to direct project costs using either a global estimation tool, a detailed estimation tool, or a combination of both.
Planning & Resource Management	Includes an integrated planning network tool that determines the critical path for a project and manages the project's resources, identifying any anticipated bottlenecks during the execution of the project.
Tracking & Performance Management	Provides an in-depth view of the aspects of a project including tasks, costs, resource usage, involved subcontractors, and customized items.
	Supports the earned value approach (C/SCSC) and other performance measurement techniques including percentage complete and project/elements.
Accounting & Profitability	Detailed and user-defined reporting capabilities provide up-to-date information about the total costs of a given project including labor, subcontracting, equipment, and materials.
	Records all changes to the baseline plan enabling project administrators to control budgets, costs, and schedules.
Purchase Order Processing Description	Manages the procurement and delivery of required resources.

Requisitions	Multiple items can be entered on a single requisition, and may include items that are warehoused, not warehoused, or one-time purchases.
Bid Tracking	Requisitions that fall into the user-defined bid criteria go into the bid or quotation process. Releasing the bid, gathering responses, and awarding the contract follows bid creation.
Purchase Orders	Multiple methods of initiating a purchase order are supported:

Purchase Orders supported methods:

- Converting a requisition.
- Releasing against a blanket PO.
- Creating a new PO.
- Copying a prior PO, awarding a bid, or reaching a minimum order amount in inventory.

EDI	Sends outbound purchase orders to suppliers and receives invoices via Electronic Data Interchange.
Other Features/Functions Budget Control	An accounting tool to help manage expenses against budgets, at either the detail or summary account level, or both simultaneously. Allows only those transactions for which sufficient funds are available, or lets users define allowable overspending for certain accounts.
Budget Setup	Can be accomplished on a detailed account-by-account basis or on a summary-level basis, or budgets can be loaded to both detail and summary levels. Available funds are calculated based on budget amounts, commitments, and actual expenses. Available funds override gives certain individuals the ability to override a failed funds availability check. Automatic year-end rollover zeros out the available budget at year-end and rolls forward all budget balances to be used in the new year.
Centralized Currency Management	Users can define all attributes of the currencies and set up control options. Accommodates an unlimited number of rate authorities for each currency. Users can define all rate types used by the company. Creates and maintains an unlimited number of exchange rates for each multicurrency relationship. Tolerance checking is available to define the maximum allowed variance from previous exchange rate entries.

	A multicurrency transaction capability allows all transactions to be entered in local currency and translated into the base currency.
	Currency independence accommodates payments in a different currency from the transaction to which they are applied.
EMU Requirements	Additional fields allow the option of including a second "base" currency. The currency unit, the "Euro," is the standard monetary unit for the European Monetary Union. Maintaining the currencies in a second base unit allows all transactions to be kept in both currencies simultaneously, alleviating the need to convert at the time of query and reporting.
Job Costing	Assists in the management of both internal and contract jobs by collecting cost and revenue data.
	Detailed information is available on customers, locations, consultants, and subcontractors.
	A separate database allows job-related information to be managed separately from nonjob accounting data.
	Job coding structure permits job number definition by up to 10 elements and a total of 40 characters.
	Reports include standard reports; detail reports that show transactions by cost type; and summary reports that show year-to-date and job-to-date revenue, cost, margin, and percent complete.
Equipment Tracking	Reports on the profitability of equipment, and tracks repair work orders.
	Allows equipment to be tied to the appropriate asset record.
Desktop EIS	A client/server-based application that enables users to access, manipulate, and analyze decision-level information in the database.
	Information is summarized graphically. Standard and ad hoc reporting is available.

Analysis

The Renaissance CS Financials is a comprehensive suite of client/server accounting software products built on Ross' open fourth-generation language (4GL) and development environment, GEMBASE. Renaissance CS Financials' components are designed to meet the financial management requirements of today's enterprises and include basic and advanced General Ledger, Accounts Payable, Accounts Receivable, and Fixed Assets functions. Customers can also opt for Ross' PACS Project Administration and Control System: a comprehensive project management, tracking, and accounting system that allows users to build work breakdown structures; estimate and budget the resources, materials, and other requirements to complete a project; plan and manage the personnel resources needed to complete the project; and monitor the progress and costs associated with these projects. Ross also includes a Purchase Order Processing component as an option for customers that may need PO functionality but do not necessarily manage a materials management or procurement system. All Renaissance CS Financials applications utilize relational database technologies and support Microsoft SQL Server, Oracle, and Rdb.

An important component of Ross' product strategy is its fourth-generation programming language and application development environment, GEMBASE, on which all Ross CS Series applications are built. GEMBASE is available to customers who want to make changes to the applications or build applications that integrate with the CS Financials Series. The 4GL provides a centralized data definition facility and utilizes a dynamic data dictionary for data management. GEMBASE is designed particularly for midrange systems, but it can also be used to develop applications to run on PCs. It is a database-independent environment and supports legacy systems to promote an enabling migration technology supporting MS Windows, Motif, and character interfaces. Ross is also working with Microsoft to provide technological links between GEMBASE and MS products such as Visual Basic and Visual J++, thus building bridges between MS-based industry standards and the Renaissance CS Series.

Ross' approach to client/server makes the application available in either a character cell or graphical user interface display, at the user's discretion. This approach allows customers to match the desktop investment to their individual user, and to phase in graphical desktops as budgets permit and requirements change. The client/server architecture splits processing between the client and the server, distributing the processing to the system that provides the most effective performance. The server component of the Renaissance CS Series is available for Digital Equipment VAX/Open

VMS, Alpha AXP, IBM AIX, and HP-UX servers. The client component supports MS Windows and Windows NT.

Ross continuously adds international support to the overall Renaissance suite to enhance its customers' ability to do business worldwide. The series is designed for multinational organizations and includes the necessary multicurrency facilities and multilingual implementations. Functions supporting international business transactions allow for alternative forms of payments and different taxation requirements. The Renaissance Series also supports local processing requirements such as 1099s and electronic funds transfers. In addition, all Renaissance solutions now include support for the European Monetary Union's requirements and guidelines, as well as significant support for the Euro monetary unit.

The Renaissance CS Financials Series is a subset of a larger, modular enterprise software solution offered by Ross Systems. Thus, customers who invest in the Financials Series can build on their investment, adding integrated Renaissance applications as required. The overall Renaissance solution includes (in addition to financials) distribution and asset management packages delivering inventory control, sales order processing, materials management, and maintenance management applications. Ross also works with third-party vendors to provide business intelligence and decision support functionality for its Renaissance customers. The vendor sells FRx Reporting, as well as BusinessObjects for querying, Speedware for EIS, and SRC for budgeting as part of its DSSuite Decision Support Suite.

Pricing

The Renaissance CS Financials Series costs approximately US$150,000 to US$500,000, depending on modules desired and system configuration.

GSA Pricing

No.

Competitors

Ross' competitive strengths lie in the depth of its financial product offering, international functions, and understanding of the process manufacturing, health care, and public sector markets. In the client/server area, however, the vendor faces stiff competition from well-financed, large corporations as well as relatively small companies like Ross with aggressive plans to take the market by storm. Unlike some of its competitors, Ross has a broad product offering, providing functions such as currency management, budget control, and job costing. The company is also actively promoting the international functionality of the Renaissance solution. Ross has a working relationship with Microsoft and is committed to creating future technology releases using industry-standard tools. The company is comparable to vendors like Lawson and PeopleSoft operating in the "best-of-breed" health care market. Ross also competes with other enterprise solutions vendors and their products including Geac SmartEnterprise Solutions' SmartStream Financials, SAP's R/3, and Oracle's Oracle Financials. Competition is also encountered in the health care environment from "total HIS vendors" McKesson-HBO and Meditech.

Strengths

Comprehensive Financial Functionality

Ross has developed a comprehensive financial product line with its Renaissance CS Financials series. In addition to the required basics (General Ledger, Accounts Payable, Accounts Receivable, and Fixed Assets), Ross also offers a Purchase Order Processing application and the PACS system, as well as budgetary control, currency management, job costing, and a desktop executive information system. (Several competitors comparable in size provide only the traditional basics.) In addition, Ross also provides GEMBASE, its 4GL application development environment. Although many of the smaller companies with which Ross competes do not offer equivalent functionality of enabling tools, all of the larger suppliers in the market do, and Ross must compete with both groups.

Good International Capabilities

As part of its financial product offering, Ross provides good support and functionality for international companies. Renaissance CS Financials provides currency management functions and Euro support, as well as multiple currency processing capabilities, multinational processing features, and exchange rate information. The product centralizes currency management so common definitions are shared for all currency information. The currency independence feature allows payments that are made or received to be in a different currency from the transaction to which they are applied. This is critical when operating in global markets where monetary units and currency conversions become an everyday part of conducting business. Another feature is Renaissance's support for multiple numbers of exchange rates, enabling international departments to maintain daily, monthly, or spot exchange rates.

Good Array of Optional Supporting Capabilities

Ross offers a variety of optional features designed to enhance its core financial solutions and allow its customers to retain in-house functions that may have been traditionally handled by outside vendors. These include federal and state filing and reporting tasks, laser check printing, benefit access via Web (called Web-based self-service), and image scanning capability. The Web-based self-service application is a demonstration of a more modern architecture being incorporated into all Renaissance CS modules. In addition, GEMBASE's added thin-client option will allow all functions to be accessed through a browser.

Limitations

Relatively Small Company

Ross is a relatively small company compared to some of its competition. Although size does not dictate the ability to build good products, it can hinder the performance of the product's marketing and sales teams. Smaller companies may find it difficult to fund required development, spend the marketing dollars needed to promote itself, and make the research and development efforts to fund new products and technology development. Small companies in enterprise applications software markets may also find it difficult to offer the same levels of support that the larger players offer, and when the customer is running an enterprise, technical support is a significant issue.

Datapro Insight

Ross Systems develops and markets client/server-based financial, human resources, and distribution systems, as well as manufacturing and supply chain applications. The Renaissance CS Financials Series is the integrated financial management applications set included in the modular Renaissance CS solution. Composed of six core applications, including General Ledger, Accounts Payable, Accounts Receivable, Fixed Assets, Project Administration, and Purchase Order Processing, Ross' Financials Series provides the essential ingredients for an enterprise-level accounting and financial solution. In addition, all products offered by Ross, including the Financials Series, come equipped with GEMBASE, the vendor's component-based, scalable, proprietary 4GL development language. GEMBASE offers thin-client capabilities designed to promote cost-effective deployment in a WAN environment. Although, in terms of size, Ross faces stiff competition from heavyweight competitors like Oracle, PeopleSoft, SAP, and others, the company is competing nonetheless. A working relationship with Microsoft is yielding benefits that tie GEMBASE with MS Visual Basic and Visual J++. Ross is also aligning itself with key third-party vendors, providing decision-support capabilities for Renaissance. In terms of its financial performance, Ross reported a loss for the year in 1997, but rebounded in 1998, reporting $38 million in 1998 software license revenue. As long as the company continues to offer a level of customer support comparable to the heavy hitters, Ross should continue to compete strongly in its respective markets.

Notes

[1] Reprinted with the permission of the GartnerGroup

Appendix B

Sample GartnerGroup Report[1]

Strategic Analysis Report
13 January 1999
Electronic Commerce Platforms and Applications[1]
M. West, E. Purchase

Management Summary

Enterprises are gradually embracing World Wide Web-based technology and processes that change the way they conduct business. On Internet, intranet, and extranet platforms, electronic business (E-business) applications Web-enable enterprises within their intranet and beyond to protect margins, develop competitive advantages, expand their channels, and provide knowledge and access to the desktop of every employee. Meanwhile, consumers are plunging into Web commerce, particularly those in high-technology industries and other early Web adopters. In 1999, Web commerce will bifurcate into large-scale electronic retail and business-to-business (B-to-B) procurement Web sites. The smaller, entrepreneurial, and mom-and-pop shops will face continually rising barriers to entry into electronic commerce (E-commerce).

The infrastructure enabling E-commerce is also changing as independent software vendors (ISVs) offer applications for Web-based selling and enterprise procurement and as enterprise solutions vendors deploy their platforms and build alliances with ISVs—particularly enterprise resource planning (ERP) vendors. The business imperatives driving the market for E-commerce applications include: protecting profit margins, developing competitive advantage, expanding the distribution channel, and leveraging knowledge management, all of which propel E-business competition.

As enterprises attempt to expand their use of B-to-B E-commerce to outsource business processes and people and to link their systems to customers and other trading partners, today's generation of E-commerce platforms, applications, and tools will prove increasingly inadequate. Few vendors provide complete, end-to-end E-commerce applications although point products and partial solutions clutter the market (e.g., catalogs and shopping baskets, Web site management and measurement tools, transaction gateways, and payment systems).

The GartnerGroup has identified two primary segments of the B-to-B E-commerce applications market—buy-side and sell-side vendors. Buy-side vendors market applications to provide support for procurement of office supplies and maintenance, repair and operations (MRO) goods either through aggregated catalogs at the buyer's site or through interfaces to catalogs at the seller's site. Sell-side vendors provide solutions for enterprises to sell their products and services over the Internet.

Figures from GartnerGroup's Dataquest indicate that 1997 revenue for sell-side Web commerce application vendors was $16.7 million, compared to $11.8 million for buy-side vendors. The B-to-B Web commerce applications market will reach $1.27 billion by 2002 (0.7 probability). Given that these segments are small and growing, it is worth noting that sell-side vendors have demonstrated a faster path to a viable market size than have the buy-side vendors. In addition, platform, or E-commerce framework, vendors (e.g., IBM, Microsoft, Netscape Communications and Oracle) are investing in the infrastructure and alliances that will enable them to compete in the B-to-B E-commerce applications market.

This Strategic Analysis Report addresses the following Key Issues about the market for B-to-B Web commerce applications:

What are the business imperatives and market trends driving the E-commerce software market?

Which E-commerce technologies and market strategies should users pursue?

What challenges do vendors face in the E-commerce software marketplace?

Which E-commerce software vendors will dominate the market through 2003?

Notes

[1] Reprinted with the permission of the GartnerGroup

Appendix C
Request for Proposal: Elsa Company

I. Introduction

Background

This Request for Proposal (RFP) is issued by the Information Systems Department of the Elsa Company to procure a Fixed Assets software package. Elsa intends to award a contract to the vendor whose package most closely meets the requirements defined in this RFP. The vendor's ability to add value to the implementation of the system, as well as the vendor's ability to provide on-going support, are critical factors in the selection process.

Company

The Elsa Company is an independent gas distributor in California. Elsa serves 95 California towns and cities, and supplies wholesale gas to other utilities in the region. Elsa invests in cogeneration opportunities and is active in the retail sale of propane and home improvement products.

System

Elsa is currently using XYZ's General Ledger and Accounts Payable Systems and is implementing ABC Incorporated's Work Order Management System. The Work Order Management System and a Costing Module developed in-house will provide input to the Fixed Asset System. The Fixed Asset System will produce journal entries for the General Ledger. The system will include all of Elsa's plant and equipment. Below are highlights of the new Fixed Asset System.

Elsa's current technical environment consists of:

- HP 6000s
- NT local area network (LAN) linking 2,500 PCs

Information technology goals include an emphasis on applications, which are portable across different hardware vendor's platforms, and an emphasis on applications, which have a Graphical User Interface (GUI). Applications should provide an easy-to-use end user ad hoc reporting capability. Applications, which are created and maintained via CASE tools, are preferable.

II. Proposal Submission and Timing

The completed proposal is due by the close of business on April 10, 2000. All prospective proposers intending to submit a response to the

Request for Proposal (RFP) should inform the Elsa representative in writing by the close of business on April 1, 2000. Decisions not to bid will not prejudice Elsa in any way against the non-bidding company. It is requested that companies electing not to bid inform the Elsa representative as soon as possible.

Proposal Schedule

Activity	Due Date
RFP Sent	March 23, 2000
No Bid Letter	April 2, 2000
Proposal Due	April 10, 2000
Notification for Finalist	April 24, 2000
System Demonstration	Week of May 11, 2000
Begin implantation	May 23, 2000

Elsa reserves the right to change the schedule to include a best and final offer. All response material will be expected by specific dates. No response or additional material will be accepted after the specified dates.

Ten (10) copies of each proposal must be submitted to:

Mr. Ephraim Ariella
Elsa Company
300 Main Street
Anywhere, NY 11111

Proposals submitted after close of business on the due date on the schedule shown may not be considered. Mail or other delivery service delays will not be cause for a change in this policy.

Company Representative

For the duration of the proposal cycle, and until final contract signing, the company representative will be:

Mr. Ephraim Ariella
Elsa Company
300 Main Street
Anywhere, New York 11111
Telephone: (900) 555-1212

All communication and correspondence should be addressed to the above.

III. Terms and Conditions of Proposal

The terms Elsa and Elsa Corporation are to be viewed as synonymous for the purpose of this RFP. The prospective respondent(s) refer(s) to companies that agree to submit proposals, or have received a copy of the RFP. The respondent(s) refers to companies that submit proposals. Qualifying respondents refer(s) to the three or four respondents who are selected for demonstrations. The selected respondent refers to the company which it is anticipated will be awarded the contract.

The respondents are required to submit a signed statement that they understand and will accept the terms and conditions presented in Section V (Standard Requirements) of the RFP. The respondent must identify any terms or conditions with which it is unable to comply.

Application Source Code

The selected respondent will provide all application source code and documentation to Elsa as a condition of the contract. All work performed by the selected respondent, for customization performed on standard product offerings, will become the property of Elsa, and cannot be offered for resale by the selected respondent, unless otherwise agreed to by Elsa. Elsa reserves the right to use and modify any and all application source code at its discretion. Elsa will not offer the software for sale, but will use it in the conduct of its own business as prescribed by the software agreement.

RFP Costs

Costs incurred by the respondents in preparation of the response to this RFP are the sole responsibility of the respondents.

Proposal Ownership

The proposal will become the property of Elsa upon submission by the respondent to the Elsa representative. All received proposals will be held in strict confidence, and will not be made available to competitors.

RFP Amendment

Elsa reserves the right to amend the RFP at any time prior to final vendor selection.

Rights Reserved

Elsa reserves the right to reject any and all responses received as a result of this request. Subsequent RFPs, if any, will be at the sole discretion of Elsa. This RFP and the responses to this RFP may, at Elsa's option, become part of an executed contract.

RFP Issuance

Elsa assumes no contractual obligations nor are any intended by:

- Issuing an RFP
- Receiving, accepting, and evaluating the vendor proposals
- Making a preliminary vendor selection

Notification

All respondents participating in this RFP process will be notified of acceptance or rejection. Elsa reserves the right not to disclose reasons for rejection.

Confidentiality

Elsa requires that recipients of this RFP maintain the contents of this RFP in the same confidence as their own confidential information and refrain from any public disclosure whatsoever. Elsa will maintain all responses in confidence, exercising reasonable care to limit access to those who have a need to know.

Publicity

Publicity or news releases pertaining to this RFP, responses to this RFP, or discussions of any kind related to the RFP or response documents, may not be released without prior written approval of Elsa.

Accuracy

The RFP furnished by Elsa is not guaranteed to be free of errors, omissions, or deficiencies. In the event such errors, omissions, or deficiencies are discovered by the respondent, the respondent shall promptly notify Elsa in writing within 48 hours after discovery. Notwithstanding the existence of error, omissions, or deficiencies in the bid document, the respondent hereby warrants that all items to be supplied under any resultant contract shall meet the performance requirements of this RFP.

Review Rights

Documents submitted may be reviewed and evaluated by any persons at the discretion of Elsa, including the independent consulting firm of LMNOQ Consulting.

Validity

All proposal pricing is to be valid for a period of 180 days from the proposal due date. Proposals are to be signed by a duly constituted corporate official, legally capable of binding the respondent.

Favored Customer

By submitting a response to this RFP respondents certifies that the prices quoted on the products are no higher than those ordinarily granted to its most favored customers in reasonably comparable situations.

Respondent Responsibility

Unless otherwise stated, the selected respondent will be responsible for all aspects of providing the system proposed, including hardware, software, customization, installation, training, maintenance, and support.

Respondent Relationship with Subcontractor

If any aspects of supplying the proposed system are not accomplished directly by respondent personnel, they must be subcontracted by the respondent. In that case, the respondent must establish or maintain a relationship with a subcontractor. The subcontractor will then come under the "one umbrella of responsibility" provided by the respondent. The respondent will be solely responsible for subcontractors' actions, and must cause its subcontractors to fully perform all required obligations.

All subcontractor and respondent personnel disputes and jurisdictional conflicts related to this project will be settled by the respondent, so as not to adversely affect the service supplied to Elsa.

Respondent Selection

Elsa reserves the right to accept or reject any or all responses. Additionally, Elsa reserves the right to cancel the RFP at any time prior to contract award.

Contract Inclusions

Elsa considers a proposal an offer to develop a contract based on all the commitments in the proposal. The RFP will take precedence over the proposal unless otherwise stipulated.

Latest Version

The respondents proposed off-the-shelf software must be a release or version that is currently in production and marketed. The respondents are required to inform Elsa of any planned releases of new versions of the proposed software being brought to market within six months of proposal submission.

Software and Hardware Warranties

The respondents shall warrant that it has the right to license and/or sell to Elsa any software or hardware necessary to the operation of the system defined in the RFP.

The respondents shall warrant that the software does not violate or infringe upon any patent, copyright, trade secret or other property right of any person, and the contractor will hold Elsa harmless and indemnify Elsa.

IV. Proposal Format

The RFP has been structured to assure complete response in a standard format, and provide for a fair and informative evaluation of the alternative solutions. To support this process Elsa requires respondents to:

- Be clear and concise.
- Use the forms and tables provided.
- Avoid making unsubstantiated claims.
- Follow the prescribed proposal format.

Provide information only on products that are stable or publicly available when responding to this RFP. Do not include any proprietary information that is not available to the public.

The ability of the respondents to provide clear, concise, well organized, and informative proposals will be judged favorably.

Quality of Proposal

Proposals should be prepared simply and economically, providing a straightforward, concise description of the capabilities to satisfy the requirements of this request. Emphasis should be placed on a workable proposal, delivery dates and pricing.

Executive Summary

Overview of the respondent's response and systems integration approach to meeting the requirements of this RFP. Also include an overview of your company and its philosophy and financial condition.

Hardware Proposal

The respondent must document in detail the source, manufacturer, and configuration of each hardware component listed in the proposal. In addition, the proposer must describe how this hardware will integrate with equipment that will be in place at Elsa during the implementation.

Alternative hardware platforms may be offered as part of a total solution. Each alternative hardware option must be identified and itemized separately in the Cost Worksheets.

Software Proposal

The respondent must document in detail each software component listed in the response to this RFP. In addition, the respondent must describe how this software will integrate with other software that will already be in place at Elsa during the implementation.

Installation and Implementation

The respondent is expected to describe in detail its implementation plan, including the use of all subcontractors proposed. A conversion plan should be presented.

Testing

The respondent must describe a detailed testing approach and plan.

Training

The respondent's training program must describe the location and type of training proposed, including training materials and follow-on support. Also include a course schedule for this year.

Documentation

Respondents must submit a separately bound set of system and user documentation for all software and hardware components, as well as repair and recovery procedures.

Maintenance (Hardware and Software)

Respondents must describe the maintenance program and the level and manner of response it will provide when problems or questions arise. Different levels of support may be proposed, including a description of the cost and scope of support offered by each level.

Current Requirements Checklists

Respondents must complete the Features Lists provided in this RFP and included them in the response. Instructions for completing the Features List are provided in Section VII, *Current Requirements Checklist.*

Completed Costing Worksheet

The respondent must provide completed cost proposals for hardware, software, and services using the cost worksheets included in this RFP as a guide. The cost for system modifications, if any, must be itemized and cross-referenced to the Features Lists. Instructions for completing the costing worksheet are provided in Section VIII

Qualifications

Respondent must answer general questions regarding the software, Section IX, and their company, Section X.

Financial Stability

Respondents must include a financial statement and other documentation that demonstrates the stability of the systems integrator, and the hardware and software vendors. Instructions for completing the respondent financial stability qualifications are provided in Section XI.

Warranties

Respondents must include copies of warranties for software and hardware recommended.

Sample Contracts

Respondents must include in their response a set of sample contracts for hardware, software, and services.

Certificates of Representation

Respondents must document that they are authorized to represent and resell the software and hardware in their proposal.

Implementation Plan

The respondents must describe their implementation approach. The plan must cover every site and result in the complete implementation of the package as required in this RFP. Elsa requires a controlled, phased conversion to the new package.

Oral Presentation

Respondents may be required to make an oral presentation at their own expense. The intent of this presentation will be to provide an opportunity to clarify the proposal and to ensure thorough and mutual understanding. Elsa will schedule the time and location for this presentation.

V. Respondent Evaluation

Elsa will evaluate all respondents according to several criteria which will include, but are not limited to the following:

> **Understanding of the Requirements**—The respondent must demonstrate an understanding of Elsa's objectives with regard to its project.

Overall Capability of the Respondent—The overall capability of the respondent will be reviewed to determine its capacity to complete a project of this type. The evaluation will include a review of the technical personnel to be assigned to the project and the project implementation plan proposed.

Functional Capability—The capabilities of the system proposed as measured against the functional requirements will be evaluated.

Ability to Demonstrate Expertise—The number and type of references that are similar in scope to this project will be evaluated. Site visits may be used to judge the level of expertise of the proposer and end-user satisfaction with the technical capabilities and services provided to them.

Ability to Offer New Technologies—Respondents will be evaluated on the basis of their ability to provide the latest hardware and software technologies, and innovative approaches to meeting Elsa's operational requirements. While Elsa's review will focus on the respondents' ability to meet Elsa's functional requirements, respondents are encouraged to offer new approaches. Information on the flexibility and adaptability of the systems proposed should be included.

Ability to Provide Hardware and Software Support—The respondent must demonstrate its ability to provide Elsa with prompt maintenance and repair service on all hardware proposed, in addition to telephone support when problems arise.

Applications Software Support Capabilities will also be Evaluated—Proposals should indicate the levels of staff and support that are available to modify, tailor, and maintain the system.

Compliance with the Terms and Conditions of the RFP—Proposers must demonstrate their ability to meet the terms and conditions of the RFP and contract documents.

Cost—The cost of the proposal will be reviewed after Elsa has first studied the technical responses.

Qualifying Respondents Identified

Elsa will evaluate the proposals and references and determine the best three or four proposals. The qualifying respondents will be notified as will the respondents eliminated.

VI. Standard Requirements

The following is a list of requirements that must be met by all vendors.

Regulatory Compliance—Equipment delivered to Elsa or used to supply services or goods to Elsa must comply with all provisions of the following:

- National Electrical Code (latest edition)
- State and Local Electrical Codes
- Occupational Safety and Health Act (OSHA)
- Applicable Environmental and Pollution Control Regulations
- National Electrical Manufacturers Association
- Standards for Electrical Motors, Controls and Enclosures
- National, State, County and Municipal Structural, Safety and Building Codes
- Federal Regulations, i.e., FCC, FAA, DOT, etc.
- Electronic Industry Association (EIA) Standards.

Vendor Responsibility—It is the responsibility of the vendor to ensure the quality and integrity of the system, verifying specifications, safety devices, code requirements, location and field dimension, etc. to make sure that the system is supported.

Vendor Liability—The vendor will ensure that no goods delivered/installed will cause failure or damage to a Elsa site. Any damage will be repaired to Elsa's satisfaction, at the vendor's expense.

Installation Tests—An installed system will be tested and as-certained that it is capable of operating satisfactorily in compliance with the following:

- Specified functions and features
- Operations performance and capacity
- Data communications interfaces
- Associated technical requirements.

Right to Monitor—Elsa reserves the right to have its representative monitor the project and perform an audit prior to system acceptance to assure compliance with system specifications and installation contracts.

Final Acceptance Test—The vendor is required to test all functions and capabilities of the system prior to turning it over to Elsa for acceptance.

Acceptance Test Procedure—Acceptance will include passage of a detailed acceptance test procedure. Failure of any part of the test will be considered failure of the entire test. The test will be repeated after corrective work has been done and until satisfactory results are obtained, within the guidelines of the acceptance criteria.

Right to Maintenance—Elsa reserves the right to have its maintenance and/or system support personnel available during debug to observe and learn the maintenance and troubleshooting of the system.

Installation Hours—Elsa and the vendor will jointly agree upon all installation hours. Installation will occur during those times of day when activities are the least disruptive to ongoing operations.

Warranty Correct/Replace—The vendor is required to correct and replace any defect covered by warranty and effect off-line recovery from any subcontractors and/or suppliers. Elsa will not enter into warranty negotiations with subcontractors and/or suppliers.

Warranty Start Date—The warranty(s) is to start no sooner than 90 days following final acceptance.

Warranty Coverage—The warranty is required to cover a period of no less than 12 months' duration.

Hold Harmless—The vendor must hold Elsa harmless and against any and all cost, royalties, damages, and/or expenses of any nature or kind whatsoever, which may occur as the result of the performance of any services which infringe on any patent or copyright.

Agreements/Insurance—Hold harmless agreements, and applicable liability insurance will be required as part of contract finalization for the selected vendor. Evidence of all required insurance as well as executed agreement will be required prior to the commencement of work.

Weekly Reports—Vendor may be required to submit written weekly status reports, including a comparison of actual work against planned schedules.

Schedule Slippage—If actual work is behind the planned schedule, and if this will cause a slip in the completion date, steps necessary to bring the project back on schedule must be outlined and implemented at the vendor's expense.

Waiver of Liens—At the time of the final invoice, the vendor will be required to submit to Elsa waivers of liens from all suppliers and/or subcontractors. Waivers may be required periodically during the project as specific non-recurring phases are completed, and payment is made.

Data Rights—Elsa will retain all rights, title and ownership of all source code, object code, designs and design documents, flowcharts, and specifications related to development, if any, funded by Elsa.

Elsa Derivative Rights—Elsa will retain all rights, title and ownership of all source code, object code, design and design documents, flowcharts and specifications Elsa develops for this project.

Elsa will retain all rights, title and ownership of all source code, object code, designs and design documents, flowcharts and specifications derived from Elsa's developments for this project.

Liquidated Damages—Elsa requires liquidated damages for failure to perform in accordance with requirements and schedules. Size and scope of liquidated damages to be negotiated and mutually accepted by the parties.

VII. Current Requirements Checklist

The Current Requirements Checklist lists Elsa's requirements for the package. It also rates Elsa's need for the requirement as follows:

M Must have in order to run business.

S Should have to run business.

L Like to have.

X No need.

The respondent should complete the columns marked Package Rating as follows:

4 System meets requirements.

3 System can be modified to meet requirement with 8 man hours of programming.

2 System can be modified to meet requirement with 40 man hours of programming.

1 System can be modified to meet requirement with 120 man hours of programming.

0 System would require more than 120 man hours of programming to meet this requirement.

The column headed "cost" should be used to place the cost of modifying the software, if it does not do so, to meet Elsa's "Must Haves" and meet (2) requirements. If the package does not meet the requirements marked 3 (Must Have) or 2 (Need to Have), please put the cost of modifying the package in the column headed "cost."

Report Writer

#	Requirement	Elsa Need	Cost	Package Rating
1	Ability for the report writer to store predefined report formats.			
2	Ability for the report writer to define a combination of titles and/or columnar captions.			
3	Ability for the report writer to define different data line formats within the same report.			
4	Ability for the report writer to determine the number of individual print lines per page.			
5	Ability for the report writer to make separate calculations horizontally between columns.			
6	Ability for the report writer to permit each calculation to contain multiple factors, including user-defined constraints.			
7	Ability for the report writer to specify the spacing between columns.			
8	Ability for the report writer to draw an unlimited number of separate levels of subtotals within the body of the report.			
9	Ability for the report writer to permit total lines to be formatted differently than data lines.			
10	Ability for the report writer to designate the specific fields that comprise the sort key (minimum of 5 sort fields).			
11	Ability for the report writer to produce reports in report distribution sequence, rather than in report number sequence.			
12	Ability to permit graphing of report data.			
13	Ability to use all arithmetic functions.			
14	Ability to perform statistical functions.			
15	Ability to run a report by company or combination of companies.			
16	Ability to choose at run time which company, date range, etc.			
17	Ability to perform 4 major math functions (add, subtract, multiply, and divide).			

Reports

Insert the type of reports that the new software package needs to be able to produce.

Security

#	Requirement	Elsa Need	Cost	Package Rating
1	Ability to provide user defined authorization tables for add, change, delete and view functions.			
2	Ability for users to define comprehensive and flexible security to restrict access to specific screens.			
3	Ability for users to define comprehensive and flexible security controls which restrict access to specific fields.			
4	Ability to provide user defined security for specific files.			
5	Ability to secure access to the system utilizing passwords and user identification numbers as assigned byMIS staff.			
6	Ability to define security by individual.			
7	Ability to copy security profiles.			
8	Ability to restrict users from accessing specified programs or modules.			
9	Ability to define security by department.			

General System

#	Requirement	Elsa Need	Cost	Package Rating
1	Ability to export data to external programs (ex.—Excel, SAS).			
2	Ability to import data from external programs.			

3 Software specifically designed for
process manufacturers.

4 Turnkey system available.

5 Multicolored screens supported.

6 System includes online tutorial.

7 Online transactions batch controlled.

8 System is menu-driven with ability to
override with command keys.

9 Report spooler for unattended printing.

10 Back-up and restore utility.

11 Graphical User Interface (GUI).

12 Ability to set appropriate fields to
default values.

13 Ability to maintain a complete audit trail.

14 Ability to provide user-defined purge
criteria for audit trail records.

15 Ability to provide user-defined edits
such as:
—range test
—alpha/numeric check
—required/optional field
—table validation
—date validation

16 System provides screen help online.

17 Ability to interface with other system
files for field validation

18 System provides field help online

19 Ability to modify screens to fit needs
for data collection and input efficiency

Vendor

#	Requirement	Elsa Need	Cost	Package Rating
1	Vendor supplies training on the system.			
2	Vendor will modify code.			
3	Vendor will support its modified code.			
4	Vendor support available in California area.			

5 Over ten installations.
6 Vendor supplies 800 telephone
   support.
7 Vendor support which is available
   between 7:00 a.m. and 8:00 p.m. EST.
8 Vendor will provide source code.
9 Vendor in business more than 5 years.
10 Guaranteed response time for
   service/support with a two to four
   hour maximum for critical problems.
11 Vendor has installed package within
   utility industry.
12 Vendor provides user forum
   for enhancements.
13 Vendor will update system for all
   changes in tax code before effective date.

Hardware

#	Hardware	Elsa Need	Package Rating
1	HP 6000		
2	IBM RS6000		
3	IBM AS400		

Volumes

Field Name	Number Records	Yearly Growth Percentage
Customers	120,000	5%
Fixed Assets	123,000	7%
Locations	90	3%

VIII. Cost

All proposals will be evaluated on their technical merits before a cost evaluation is made. This section provides guidance on preparing cost worksheets that must accompany the technical response to the RFP.

Complete cost itemizations, and subtotals and totals for each category, must be provided for all hardware, software, and ancillary services, including but not limited to:

1. **Hardware**—Costs must be itemized for all equipment proposed. Optional equipment, such as additional terminals, scanners, bar code printers, and the like, should be identified as such and unit costs provided. A clear distinction must be made between required and optional equipment being proposed.

2. **Software**—Software costs must be provided separately for package software and any modifications that may be required. All modifications noted in Section VII of the Current Requirements Checklist must be itemized on the features list and total costs provided under software costs.

3. **Installation**—This must include ALL installation costs, through final implementation and acceptance of the system.

4. **Conversion**—Costs for converting historical data must be estimated. Sufficient information should be provided to enable Elsa to determine the number of years of historical detail data to convert based on the conversion costs.

5. **Documentation**—The cost of documentation not included in the hardware and software costs, and the cost of additional copies of manuals, must be itemized.

Additional costs for custom manuals, as necessary must also be clearly identified.

6. **Training**—Start-up training costs should be identified by type of training required, the target audience, and whether the training is on-site or off-site.

7. **Annual Operating Expense**—The estimated total annual operating costs of the system, including not only hardware and software maintenance, but also training that may be required with expected upgrade and any other costs, must be provided.

8. **Additional Support Services**—The costs for additional support services, including hourly rates and estimated expenses, must be provided.

Cost Worksheet

1. Software Modules

Software	List Price	Discounted Price	Modifications	Yearly Maintenance Base Package	Yearly Maintenance Modifications
Module 1					
Module 2					
Subtotal					
Installation & Test					
Grand Total Software					

2. Training

Training	Cost	Discount
Training Course		
Course 1		
Course 2		
Documentation		
User		
System		
Other		
User Training Guides		
Guide 1		
Guide 2		
Other		
Grand Total		

3. Conversion

Rate	Hours	Discount
Conversion		

4. Rates for Consulting

Rate	Discount
Management Consulting	
Programming	
Training	
Telephone Support	
Other	

5. Hardware

Software	Description	Quantity	List Price	Discounted Price	Total Price	Yearly Maintenance	Total Maintenance
CPU							
Model							
Memory							
Storage							
Size							
Back-Up Device							
Type							
Terminals							
Model							
Printers							
Model 1							
Model 2							

5. Hardware (continued)

Software	Description	Quantity	List Price	Discounted Price	Total Price	Yearly Maintenance	Total Maintenance
System Software							
Shipping							
Subtotal							
Site Preparation							
Uninterrupted Power Supply							
Installation							
Grand Total							

IX. Software Information

1. What programming language(s) is (are) used?

2. How much main memory does each module require?

3. Describe the available *user* documentation included in the base package price.

4. Describe the available *data processing* documentation included in the base package price.

5. Will the vendor correct, without charge, any bugs that are discovered after installation of the application has been completed? For the life of the system?

6. Will errors in the system that are discovered and corrected at another user's site also be corrected for Elsa? Will you advise Elsa if bugs are found?

7. Will the vendor supply the improved version of the applications if and when developed?

8. What criteria are used to determine full acceptance of the system (one month of full operation, system level test, etc.)?

9. Does the purchaser gain ownership of the source code?

10. Is the software based on a relational data base or 4GL? Specify:

11. Control of input accuracy: The system must provide sufficient control totals (internal and external) within each application and system wide to verify the arithmetic accuracy and correct posting of accounting data. Which applications would have these controls?

12. Audit trails—Does the system provide sufficient documentation of events to trace the flow of transactions from source document to printed final reports, and from final summaries back to the original source?

13. Training and Implementation—Include a suggested implementation schedule for these major phases of implementation: user training; software delivery and implementation including file loading, and user testing of all application; and parallel testing.

14. Please list courses scheduled for this year.

15. Who developed the software?

16. Who owns the software?

X. General Vendor Qualifications

1. How many Fixed Asset systems similar to the system being proposed to Elsa have you implemented to date?

2. Provide references for three utility clients that have implemented your system. Include company name, address, and person to contact with title and phone number. Each reference should have an environment similar to that of Elsa. Also indicate the hardware and software systems that the company is using.

     (1)

     (2)

     (3)

3. How many of the systems similar to the one proposed to Elsa have been implemented in the California Metropolitan area?

4. What is your guaranteed response time for service and support?

5. How much on-site training and support is provided under your contract?

6. Describe all training courses (cost, location, duration, frequency, description).

7. Do you lease, rent, and/or sell hardware and/or software?

8. How many programs are there in the Fixed Asset System?

9. What statistics are required to develop a model to determine the machine processing time of a normal cycle, i.e., file size, transactions processed, generation of standard reports?

10. Does a *user group* exist? If yes, describe including frequency and location of meetings, years in existence, membership fees, number of active members, name and phone number of person in charge of the group. Include the minutes from the last users' group meeting.

11. How many employees of the respondent are capable of making the modifications recommended in the proposal?

12. How many employees of the respondent are capable of training Elsa?

13. How many employees are permanently assigned to the response line?

14. How many employees of the respondent are capable of assisting Elsa during implementation?

15. Does the respondent use non–permanent employees in the roles identified in questions 11–14?

16. Please provide resumes of personnel who will be assigned to Elsa in the roles identified in questions 11–14.

XI. Vendor Financial Stability

1. Please include an audited financial report.

2. Is the respondent owned by another company? If so, please provide its name, address, and audited financial report.

3. Please list two financial references including your lending bank.

4. Are there any IRS liens against the respondent or its parent company?

5. Are there any post due notes on loans?

6. Are there any judgments against the respondent?

7. Is the respondent or its parent company in bankruptcy procedure?

8. Is the respondent or its parent company in the process of or contemplating filing for bankruptcy?

9. List any litigation the respondent or its parent company is involved in?

10. How many employees are employed by the respondent?

Appendix D
Gantt Chart

Task Name	January 2000		February 2000		March 2000		
	1 2 3 4 5	6 7 8 9	10 11 12 13				

Starting the journey.

Select the team.
  Select team member.
  Notify team members.

Train the team.
  Train team in selection process.
  Train team in best practices in application areas.

Develop plan.
  Develop detailed plan.
  Approve plan.
  Completed Plan.

Preliminary cost benefit analysis.
  Develop preliminary cost benefit analysis.
  Determine if project should proceed.
  Approve cost benefit analysis.

Determining detailed R²ISC requirements.

R²ISC criteria weighting.
Determine R²ISC criteria weights.
Approve R²ISC criteria weights.
Develop detailed current requirements Area 1.
Identify participants for workshop.
Develop invitation for workshop.
Arrange for workshop site.
Send invitation to participants.
Invitation sent.
Develop pre-workshop materials.
Send pre-workshop material to participants.
Arrange for food for workshop.
Arrange for supplies for workshop.
Conduct workshop.
Complete Area 1.

Figure AppD-1

Task Name	January 2000				February 2000				March 2000			
	1	2	3	4	5	6	7	8	9	10	11	12	13
Develop detailed current requirements Area 2.												
Identify participants for workshop.												
Develop invitation for workshop.												
Arrange for workshop site.												
Send invitation to participants.												
Invitation sent.												
Develop pre-workshop materials.												
Send pre-workshop material to participants.												
Arrange for food for workshop.												
Arrange for supplies for workshop.												
Conduct workshop.												
Complete Area 2.												
Current functional requirements completed.												
Approve functional requirements.												
Incorporate into R^2ISC matrix.												
Functional requirements complete.												

Develop detailed future requirements.
Develop technical architecture requirements.
Determine communication requirements.
Determine volume requirements.
Identify participants for future requirements workshop.
Develop invitation for workshop.
Arrange for workshop site.
Send invitation to participants.
Invitation sent.
Prepare pre-workshop (tech rating) materials.
Send pre-workshop material to participants.
Arrange for food for workshop.
Arrange for supplies for workshop.
Technical rating workshop.
Technical requirements complete.
Approve technical requirements.
Incorporate into R²ISC matrix.

Determine detailed implementability requirements.
Develop detailed implementability requirements.
Identify participants for workshop.
Develop invitation for workshop.

Figure AppD-2

Task Name	January 2000				February 2000				March 2000			
	1	2	3	4	5	6	7	8	9	10	11	12	13
Arrange for workshop site.													
Send invitation to participants.													
Invitation sent.													
Develop pre-workshop materials.													
Send pre-workshop material to participants.													
Arrange for food for workshop.													
Arrange for supplies for workshop.													
Conduct implementability workshop.													
Implementability requirements completed.													
Approve implementability requirements.													
Incorporate into R²ISC matrix.													
Determine detailed supportability requirements.													
Develop detailed implementation supportability requirements.													
Develop ongoing supportability requirements.													
Identify participants for workshop.													
Develop invitation for workshop.													
Arrange for workshop site.													
Send invitation to participants.													

Invitation sent.
Develop pre-workshop materials.
Send pre-workshop material to participants.
Arrange for food for workshop.
Arrange for supplies for workshop.
Conduct implementability workshop.
Supportability requirements completed.
Incorporate into R^2ISC matrix.
Supportability requirements completed.

Determine detailed cost requirements.

Develop current cost requirements.
Develop future cost requirements.
Identify participants for workshop.
Develop invitation for workshop.
Arrange for workshop site.
Send invitation to participants.
Invitation sent.
Develop pre-workshop materials.
Send pre-workshop material to participants.

Figure AppD-3

Task Name	February 2000		March 2000		April 2000	
	5 6 7 8	9 10 11 12	13 14 15 16 17			
Arrange for food for workshop.						
Arrrange for supplies for workshop.						
Conduct cost workshop.						
Cost requirements completed.						
Approved cost requirements.						
Incorporate into R²ISC matrix.						
Narrowing the field.						
Determine availability of packages.						
Develop key distinguishers.						
Determine key distinguishers.						
Perform preliminary screening.						
Analysis packages with software tool.						
Determine vendors for consideration.						
Approve vendors.						

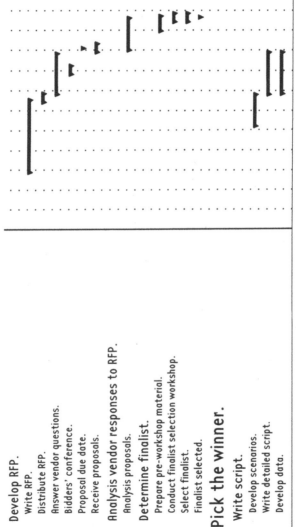

Develop RFP.
Write RFP.
Distribute RFP.
Answer vendor questions.
Bidders' conference.
Proposal due date.
Receive proposals.
Analysis vendor responses to RFP.
Analysis proposals.
Determine finalist.
Prepare pre-workshop material.
Conduct finalist selection workshop.
Select finalist.
Finalist selected.
Pick the winner.
Write script.
Develop scenarios.
Write detailed script.
Develop data.

Figure AppD-4

Task Name	March 2000			April 2000			May 2000			
	10 11 12 13	14	15 16 17	18	19 20 21 22					
Integrate scripts and data.										
Send scripts to finalist.										
Perform the scripted demonstration.										
Arrange for scripted demonstration with finalist.										
Arrange for facilities.										
Conduct scripted demonstration Vendor 1.										
Review demonstration Vendor 1.										
Conduct scripted demonstration Vendor 2.										
Review demonstration Vendor 2.										
Conduct scripted demonstration Vendor 3.										
Review demonstration Vendor 3.										
Conduct scripted demonstration Vendor 4.										
Review demonstration Vendor 4.										
Prepare scripted demonstration Report.										
Update R^2ISC matrix.										

Figure AppD-5

Task Name	April 2000			May 2000			June 2000		
	15 16 17 18	19	20 21 22	23 24	25 26 27

Select winner.
Determine winner.
Preliminary approval.
Conduct full scripted demonstration with winner.
Conduct workshop.
Notify losing candidates.
Winner determined.

Finalize contract.
Negotiate contract.
Final Approval of winner.
Negotiate contract.

Review contract.
Financial review.
Legal review.
Approve contract.
Sign contract.
Contract.

Project management.
Project management.

Figure AppD-6

‖ Index

www.ingramcontent.com/pod-product-compliance
Ingram Content Group UK Ltd.
Pitfield, Milton Keynes, MK11 3LW, UK
UKHW020136190625
459827UK00001BA/206